The Business of Gamification

At the turn of the century, the term "gamification" was introduced as a concept to understand the process of using game mechanics in "nongame" contexts. The impact of gamification was soon evident to business practices, where it had impact both on marketing and more broadly, on the organizations themselves. As the number of individuals playing video games grows, there seems to be an acceptance of game mechanics elsewhere. Its effectiveness is highly dependent on both technical possibilities and cultural acceptance, two factors present today.

The aim of *The Business of Gamification* is to critically analyze the practical and theoretical consequences of gamification. Practically, how has gamification been applied in businesses to this point, and what are the future scenarios? Theoretically, what are the contributions of gamification to existing academic knowledge? How does this change our understanding of how business are performing and its consequences for organizations, consumers, and society in general?

This edited volume contains new, and stringent, perspectives on how gamification is contextualized in business settings, both in theory as well as in practice. This book will provide a wealth of research for individuals seriously interested in the industry at the academic level. As a result, this book will serve as a reference in curricula associated with video game development for years to come.

Mikolaj Dymek is an associate professor in the Department of Media and Communication Science at Mid Sweden University, Sweden.

Peter Zackariasson is an associate professor in marketing in the School of Business, Economics and Law at the University of Gothenburg, Sweden.

Routledge Advances in Management and Business Studies

For a full list of titles in this series, please visit www.routledge.com/series/SE0305

57 **Decision Making Groups and Teams**
An Information Exchange Perspective
Steven D. Silver

58 **Research Methods for Human Resource Management**
Edited by Karin Sanders, Julie A. Cogin, and Hugh T.J. Bainbridge

59 **Cross-Border Mergers and Acquisitions**
UK Dimensions
Moshfique Uddin and Agyenim Boateng

60 **Monitoring Business Performance**
Models, Methods, and Tools
Per Lind

61 **Managerial Flow**
Veronica Vecchi, Ben Farr-Wharton, Rodney Farr-Wharton, and Manuela Brusoni

62 **Management, Society, and the Informal Economy**
Edited by Paul C. Godfrey

63 **Foresight in Organizations**
Methods and tools
Edited by Patrick van der Duin

64 **The Philosophy of Management Research**
Eric W.K. Tsang

65 **The Business of Gamification**
A Critical Analysis
Edited by Mikolaj Dymek and Peter Zackariasson

The Business of Gamification
A Critical Analysis

Edited by Mikolaj Dymek
and Peter Zackariasson

NEW YORK AND LONDON

First published 2016
by Routledge
711 Third Avenue, New York, NY 10017

and by Routledge
2 Park Square, Milton Park, Abingdon, Oxon OX14 4RN

First issued in paperback 2018

*Routledge is an imprint of the Taylor & Francis Group,
an informa business*

© 2017 Taylor & Francis

The right of the editor to be identified as the author of the editorial
material, and of the authors for their individual chapters, has been
asserted in accordance with sections 77 and 78 of the Copyright,
Designs and Patents Act 1988.

All rights reserved. No part of this book may be reprinted or
reproduced or utilised in any form or by any electronic, mechanical,
or other means, now known or hereafter invented, including
photocopying and recording, or in any information storage or
retrieval system, without permission in writing from the publishers.

Trademark notice: Product or corporate names may be trademarks
or registered trademarks, and are used only for identification and
explanation without intent to infringe.

Library of Congress Cataloging-in-Publication Data
Names: Dymek, Mikolaj, editor. | Zackariasson, Peter, 1972– editor.
Title: The business of gamification : a critical analysis / edited by
    Mikolaj Dymek and Peter Zackariasson.
Description: 1 Edition. | New York : Routledge, 2016. | Series:
    Routledge advances in management and business studies ; 65 |
    Includes bibliographical references and index.
Identifiers: LCCN 2016021318 | ISBN 9781138824164 (hardback :
    alk. paper) | ISBN 9781315740867 (ebook)
Subjects: LCSH: Video games industry. | Video games—Marketing. |
    Business enterprises—Technological innovations.
Classification: LCC HD9993.E452 B875 2016 | DDC 338.4/77948—dc23
LC record available at https://lccn.loc.gov/2016021318

ISBN 13: 978-1-138-34014-5 (pbk)
ISBN 13: 978-1-138-82416-4 (hbk)

Typeset in Sabon
by Apex CoVantage, LLC

vi *Contents*

6 Inside the Gamification Case of a Mobile Phone Marketing Campaign: The Amalgamation of Game Studies with Marketing Communications? 99
MIKOLAJ DYMEK

7 Samsung Nation: A Gamified Experience 122
TRACY HARWOOD AND TONY GARRY

8 Play a Game, Save the Planet! Gamification as a Way to Promote Green Consumption 144
CHRISTIAN FUENTES

PART III
Conceptual Perspectives 161

9 Gamification for Sustainability: Beyond the Ludo-Aesthetical Approach 163
PER FORS AND THOMAS TARO LENNERFORS

10 Designing for the Play Instinct: Gamification, Collective Voodoo and Mumbo Jumbo 182
STEPHEN WEBLEY AND KAREN CHAM

11 Total Gamification and the Limits of Our Imagination 208
PER H. HEDBERG AND MATTIAS SVAHN

12 Old Things—New Names 219
PETER ZACKARIASSON

Index 227

Contents

About the Editors	vii
About the Contributors	viii
Introduction	xi

PART I
Internal Organizational Perspectives

1

1 Role-Playing Games at Work: About Management,
Gamification and Effectiveness
EMMANUELLE SAVIGNAC

3

2 Feeding the RedCritter: The Gamification of Project
Management Software
RAUL FERRER CONILL

21

3 Gamification as Ideological Praxis: On Play, Games and
the Modding of Management
ALF REHN

40

PART II
External Organizational Perspectives

57

4 Game of Gamification: Marketing, Consumer Resistance
and Digital Play
LENA OLAISON AND SAARA L. TAALAS

59

5 Win, Earn, Gain: Gamification in the History of Retailing
FRANCK COCHOY AND JOHAN HAGBERG

81

Editors

Mikolaj Dymek, previously of Royal Institute of Technology where he presented his PhD thesis on the global video game industry, Uppsala University during his post-doctoral research project, and currently associate professor at Mid Sweden University, does research at the intersection of marketing communications, public relations, digital media and game studies. He has also been active for several years as a marketing analyst as part of a three-year participative research programme at a consumer communication agency, but currently also as an independent consultant. He has (with Peter Zackariasson) a book on the marketing of video games due in 2016 through Routledge.

Peter Zackariasson is an associate professor in marketing at the University of Gothenburg, School of Business, Economics and Law. Since 2001 he has studied the cultural industries, their production and consumption. The result of this research has been published in international journals and books.

Contributors

Karen Cham is an expert in digital transformation design, a digital first, design lead, user-centred method for engineering transformation of complex human-centred systems such as multiplatform global marketing campaigns; organizational infrastructures; markets and economies; virtual worlds and simulations. Her first website was 1994, touchscreen and game 1995 and machine intelligence project 1996. She won EU recognition for the micro-business model in 1997 and devised Sprint0 at EHS in 1998. Clients include PlayStation, Diesel, ITV, Which? and Top Shop. Her research has always concerned the "semantic gap" in the user experience, current R&D is in nudge mechanics, neuro-navigation and neuro-transformation.

Franck Cochoy is professor of sociology at the University of Toulouse Jean Jaurès and a member of CERTOP-CNRS, France. He works in the field of economic sociology and focuses on the human and technical mediations that frame the relationship between supply and demand. He has conducted several projects in such areas as the role of marketing, packaging, self-service and so on. He recently published *The Limits of Performativity: Politics of the Modern Economy* with Liz McFall and Martin Giraudeau (eds.) (Routledge, 2014), *On the Origins of Self-Service* (Routledge, 2015) and *On Curiosity, the Art of Market Seduction* (Mattering Press, 2016).

Raul Ferrer Conill is a PhD candidate in media and communication at Karlstad University, Sweden, and holds an MA in global media studies and an MSc in project management. His current research focuses on the gamification of digital journalism. Raul has presented his work at leading international conferences like ICA, ECREA and Persuasive Technologies and has been published in journals such as *Journalism Studies* and *Computer Supported Cooperative Work* (CSCW). Other research interests cover native advertising, motivation and technology. Raul has 14 years of experience as a web designer and developer.

Per Fors is a doctoral student at the division of Industrial Engineering and Management at Uppsala University. Per is mainly interested in issues in

Contributors ix

the crossroads between sustainable development and the ICT industry, such as Green IT, ICT4S, gamification for sustainability and more.

Christian Fuentes is a researcher at the Centre for Retail Research at Lund University and at the Centre for Consumer Science, University of Gothenburg. He undertakes research in the fields of mobile shopping, e-tailing, green marketing, green consumption, practice theory, actor-network theory and consumer culture. He is currently involved in several research projects exploring how digital devices enable and shape consumption and marketing practices. Dr. Christian Fuentes can be contacted at: christian.fuentes@ism.lu.se.

Tony Garry's research interests include services marketing, relationship and network marketing and consumption communities and tribes within both offline and online contexts. His research outputs have been published in journals such as the *Journal of Marketing Management*, *Journal of Services Marketing*, *Journal of Consumer Behaviour* and the *Journal of Business and Industrial Marketing*. He has also coauthored a book on relationship marketing.

Johan Hagberg, PhD, is associate professor in marketing at the School of Business, Economics and Law, University of Gothenburg. He received his doctorate in 2008 with a thesis on retail change, where he studied the emergence of e-commerce in Swedish retailing. From 2011 to 2015 he was director of the Centre for Retailing at the University of Gothenburg. His current research investigates consumer logistics and the digitalization of retailing and consumption. His publications include articles in *Industrial Marketing Management*, *Journal of Marketing Management*, *Urban Studies*, *Marketing Theory*, *Journal of Historical Research in Marketing* and *Consumption Markets & Culture*.

Tracy Harwood researches in the areas of consumer behaviour/usability, technology/usability in emerging contexts (marketing, retail), virtual/online commerce, e-communities/tribes, marketing, machinima/digital arts and e-commerce interface. She manages the university's Usability Lab and is a National Teacher Fellow.

Per H. Hedberg has a PhD in experimental psychology from Columbia University and PhD in business administration from Stockholm School of Economics. He is an assistant professor in psychology at Södertörn University, a research fellow at the section for media psychology at Stockholm School of Economics, and the academic director of Stockholm School of Economics, Russia.

Thomas Taro Lennerfors (PhD, Docent) is an associate professor at Uppsala University, Sweden, and a visiting researcher at Meiji University, Japan. His work concerns ethics, business and technology. Apart from four

x *Contributors*

monographs, and some book chapters, he has published for example in *Culture and Organization, Futures, Business and Society, Harvard Business Review* and *Business History Review*.

Lena Olaison, PhD, is assistant professor, Department at Management, Politics and Philosophy, Copenhagen Business School, Denmark, and research fellow, Life at Home and Sustainable Production Research Initiative, Linnaeus University, Sweden. She is a member of the editorial collective of *ephemera: theory and politics in organizations*.

Alf Rehn plays the university like Super Mario Bros., trying to collect power-ups but mostly swatting away goombas. He can be found at www.alfrehn.com.

Emmanuelle Savignac is a French anthropologist and graduate of the Ecole des hautes études en sciences sociales (EHESS) member of CERLIS. For 15 years she has been studying new work and management practices in several contexts. She analyzed in particular fun management practices in multimedia and video games new companies at the end of the 1990s. Her research is now dedicated to the gamification of work questions and the uses of games by management.

Mattias Svahn is a research fellow at the Stockholm School of Economics Institute of Economic Research, where he researches digital media consumer psychology with a focus on gamification design, ambient media and guerilla media. He has about ten years in game design research, with a focus on pervasive games. He is currently working on a book on the near future of gamification on request of The Swedish Retail and Wholesale Development Council. He is also a visiting professor at the Stockholm School of Economics in Riga, teaching digital media consumer behaviour and market research methodologies. See www.svahn.se

Saara L. Taalas is professor in business studies and head of Life@home and Sustainable Production research initiative in Linnaeus University, Sweden. Her research interests focus on the creative content, systemic entrepreneurship and roles of active audiences in value creation. Her work has been published in journals such as *Entrepreneurship and Regional Development, Management and Organizational History, Philosophy of Management* and *International Journal of Management Concepts and Philosophy*.

Stephen J. Webley my research has several interlinked spheres: games and war studies, cultural theory, and psychoanalysis. My current research focuses on Lacanian readings of philosophy and cultural theory for culture and organisation studies and games studies. Reading Clausewitzian war studies through the lens of psychoanalysis is key to my work, as it allows for the correct situating of Clausewitz as post-Kantian and post-Hegelian philosopher and places the marxisante critique of ideology as essential to understanding the role of entertainment and commerce in late-modern society. Along with war and game studies, I specialize in consultancy for game and simulation design and interactive narratology.

Introduction

"Work Hard, Play Hard"

This edited volume on the business of gamification aims to provide insightful research perspectives on gamification in business contexts from academic, qualitative and critical points of departure. Gamification is according to its (probably) most popular definition the application of game mechanisms and/or elements in non-game contexts (Deterding et al. 2011). Whereas this is indeed a theoretical starting point, the genesis of the volume is quite the opposite—gamification as a practice has been most warmly welcomed by the world of business and management, whose enthusiasm regarding the notion has spread to all corners of societies. Gamification is here sometimes viewed as a truly revolutionising concept that might change the way employees perceive work (as such) and as a direct consequence, might transform corporations and business in general. This purported transformation is driven by the sudden assent of playfulness as a domesticated concept in the diligent world of industrious work and business. It's as if the unofficial mantra of the corporate world's hardworking elites—"work hard, play hard"—can by means of gamification suddenly merge as one into a playful and even more productive reality. In Western society a popular, and partially convincing, narrative is propagating that corporate life (or any other organisational life for that matter) is finally and gradually relaxing its rigour and "kicking its feet back"—and that gamification constitutes a major leap forward in this direction. Organisational hierarchies are dismantled in order to become "flat" and "democratic", job titles are simplified or informalised (e.g., "Chief Happiness Officer", Buffer 2016), corporate core values are entertainingly rewritten, for instance, "create fun and a little weirdness" (Zappos 2016) or "Don't take ourselves too seriously. Have Fun." (AWeber 2016), casual Fridays (the almost institutionalised requirement in contemporary office environments to "dress down" on Fridays to celebrate the approaching weekend), telecommuting that allows working from environments considered leisure or playful (beach house, coffee bar, pub, etc.), office spaces becoming open and flexible and flaunting mandatory "play corners" including "quirky" and "playful" furniture and video game consoles, and

xii *Introduction*

many other signals reinforcing the narrative of the rise of the relaxed work life in organisations. Gamification thus introduces the *coup de grâce* for the old and obstinate organisations of yore, by expunging outdated hierarchies and pointlessly excessive strictness, and instead installs play and games as a profitable and productive core dimension of the contemporary work life.

This description, of course, many academics would claim, has limited foundation in business reality, or in research into contemporary business, management, games, digital media or any other related field of gamification (e.g., Bogost (2011a) declares that gamification in business is "Viagra for engagement dysfunction", or (2011b) "chocolate-covered broccoli"), or the nascent field itself. Frequently, critical observers point out that in many business implementations, gamification, as a notion, becomes the latest business/management/process/strategy panacea catch phrase target solution to aim at all the various dysfunctionalities that characterise contemporary business-life. However, is this a reflection of the failure of gamification as a business strategy, or does it merely reflect the failure of the business world to organise *anything*, including gamification, in a meaningful way (cf. with Alvessson's (2008) discussion about "garbage can" and "circus" metaphors of management)? Gamification in business contexts has received enough zealously triumphant and hackneyed evangelism to last many decades and has already confused its many sprawling meanings to the point of ridicule. There is an opaque jungle of obfuscating and unreliable arguments revolving around the gamification notion, and it is challenging to unravel its layers of meanings as this radically affects the conceptualisation of the phenomenon.

Despite this criticised hyperbole from empirical fronts, solid and stringent academic interest in gamification in business is growing in academia globally, and we need to take heed of this impetus. There is a tangible demand to critically examine the intersection of gamification and business. But first some background.

Why This Volume?

How did this volume come about? The editors, Mikolaj Dymek and Peter Zackariasson, both have backgrounds as avid gamers but also as having written dissertations on fairly similar topics—the business and industry of video games. Peter has a business and administration perspective (Zackariasson 2007) and Mikolaj an industrial economy/management perspective (Dymek 2010) on this fascinating and burgeoning digital cultural industry. As we continued our research journeys, Peter evolved into the cultural, creative and marketing aspects of digital culture. Mikolaj's research expanded into marketing communications and particularly digital media aspects of consumer PR, as part of a three-year participatory research project at a high-profile "communication agency" in Stockholm, Sweden, funded by the Bank of Sweden Tercentenary Foundation. In 2011 it was here Mikolaj started his research into gamification—but also working part-time as a consultant on commercial gamification projects in marketing communications campaigns. Part of this experience is later presented as a chapter in this volume. It was one year after the exceptionally popular presentations at the prominent TED Conferences by gamificiation gurus such as Tom Chatfield (2010), Jane McGonigal (2010), and Gabe Zichermann (2011), and about the same time as Deterding, Khaled, and Nacke (2011) presented their highly cited definition of gamification at the MindTrek: Envisioning future media environments conference in Tampere, Finland. As an "expert" on gamification, his project at the agency rode the wave of explosive popularity that the concept experienced during a number of years in all areas of business, not only in the marketing communications industry.

Since then the concept has led a double life of sorts—on one hand experienced an explosive rise to fame, hyperbole and unrealistic expectations in the hands of the IT, marketing communications, strategy consultancy and other industries, and on the other hand gained a somewhat delayed and initially slightly skeptical, but with time increasingly intrigued, show of academic interest. From an industry point of view, the gamification trend might be just that—a trend, and already passé if judging by the slightly uncouth indicator of Google Trends charts indicating a peak in 2014 on the web for gamification searches (although possibly making a comeback in 2016?). This, however, doesn't necessarily mean that real interest is fading—for instance "video games" peaked in 2012, and searches for "marketing" or "business" have been in steady decline since 2004, probably not reflecting real-world interest in these concepts. This does, however, illustrate the nature of industry trends, where trends assume, in media and public discourses, the form of short-lived fads of intense hyperbole that quickly disappear, leaving the rest of the world to continue the arduous task of sorting out all the (conflicting) meanings of these management/industry trends. "Globalisation" or "outsourcing" might not be the hottest trending topics of strategy consultancies for several decades because it has been long ago digested by the world of management gurus—but the world is still in the thick of dealing with the consequences of these strategies. Similarly, it could be argued that gamification might have passed as a trend—e.g., one of the world's leading IT management consultancies Gartner in (2011) officially predicted a $70+ billion USD market (Gartner 2011) for gamification business, while as soon as the next year it gave gamification the kiss of death by predicting that 80 percent of all gamification applications within business will fail (Gartner 2012). The rest of the world might still very much be dealing with gamification-like strategies for years to come. In other words, gamification as a trendy label of industry/management strategy might soon pass, but the principle of applying game mechanisms in non-game contexts—which seems to be the most cited definition of gamification—will probably continue within industry and business worlds. This is supported by the empirical cases presented in this

xiv   *Introduction*

volume, and the numerous applications of gamification observed in practically all major areas of societies in the Western world.

As a research discipline this field is very young—hence the need for this volume—but also sometimes skeptical due to its untested nature. Trends and fads within the fast-paced IT worlds are particularly leerily approached by academia since occasionally what seems like the beginning of a major transformation turns out to be a short-lived fad—and sometimes even slightly awkward one. While the immense popularity of the virtual world of "Second Life" 10 years ago was heralded as the beginning of a three-dimensional Internet and the arrival of a consummate cyberspace, and occasionally researched with similarly revolutionary claims—as an online world it was a failure, and as a research field it turned out to be not much different from the significantly older field of virtual communities (e.g., Rheingold 1995). Despite this risk there is clearly an interest in the gamification concept from academic research. Several doctoral theses have already been published, and some interesting research books and volumes are being published, when omitting the plethora of business-oriented books with heavily applied and normative perspectives from the borderlands of corporate and academic research. This volume attempts to distinguish itself by focusing on qualitative academic research on gamification in business settings going beyond applied perspectives centred around business objectives, such as resource optimisation and best practice implications. Most of the notable gamification research currently seems to stem from media technology, user interface/experience design and service marketing.

Gamification—Can We Define It?

So what is this gamification all about, and can we define it? We can certainly conclude that the definition of Deterding, Khaled, and Nacke from 2011 that defines gamification as the "use of game design elements in non-game contexts" is by far the most popular theoretical conceptualisation in this volume (cited by every chapter directly or indirectly), but probably also within the nascent gamification field as well as many academic databases such as Google Scholar and similar.

There is really limited theoretical insight from entering yet another inquiry into the definition of the gamification notion, since there is a multitude of approaches within industry/practice, corporate research as well as academic research. Simply put, there is no, and will probably never be, any final word on what gamification "is". There is, however, a vivid need of conceptual clarification within this growing field of scientific inquiry. This is due to the apparent novelty and formative nature of this concept.

If we take a look at the definitions of gamification in this volume, the oft-cited Deterding et al. (2011) constitutes a common starting point. Nevertheless, the definition relies on placing X (i.e., games) in non-X contexts, or basically expanding the boundaries of X—which begets the obvious questions of:

- What is X?
- What and why non-X contexts?
- What does X-ing really mean, and what are the consequences for non-X?
- To put it simply—what and where are the boundaries of X?

What is X (i.e., games)? This is the core of the gamification discussion and relates to perspectives and polemics within new media, game studies, design studies, behavioural studies, economics (e.g., decision theory), game theory, to mention a few, and in the context of this volume also management, business and organisation studies. Gamification is a nascent field and needs perspectives from more established and adjacent perspectives. The big question is who "owns" the interpretation of gamification—game studies, human-computer interaction or some other field? Fors and Lennerfors (chapter 9) bring in established perspective from game studies, such as narratology and ludology, to explain the core of gamification—as does Cochoy and Hagberg (chapter 5) and Dymek (chapter 6). Savignac's analysis (chapter 1) of gamification is based on Gilles Brougère's theoretical perspectives at the intersection of games studies and pedagogy. Webley and Cham (chapter 10) posit philosopher Johan Huizinga as the originator of any thorough understanding of gamification.

What is more important is perhaps—where does gamification come from as a concept? The chapters of Savignac or Webley and Cham claim that the initial conceptualisations are those of design studies, and more specifically human-computer interaction, user interface design and user experience design—that is, something that deals with the user-interactions with (predominantly) digital interfaces. This is very much in line with contemporary notions of what the "core" of gamification constitutes—gamifying user-experiences (off/online) by use of digital media. Cochoy and Hagberg, Olaison and Taalas (chapter 4), Dymek and others have countered some of these claims by highlighting how gamification has been employed in marketing in non-digital forms for decades (e.g., as Frequent Flyer Programmes), and in the case of retailing (Cochoy and Hagberg) since the turn of the 20th century, for the exact same reasons as lauded today, such as increased awareness, sales and consumer activation by gameplay participation.

The external boundaries of games/gamification in terms of "non-game like" contexts and manifestations are also in need of explorations. Savignac investigates role-playing games as gamified processes of organisational learning, Ferrer Conill (chapter 2) describes the use of gamification in virtual project management, Rehn in management processes (chapter 3), Fuentes (chapter 8) in sustainable consumption vis-à-vis an educational smartphone app, Olaison and Taalas about the game of hacking marketing campaigns

xvi *Introduction*

in social media, Dymek in a geo-location based marketing communications campaign for a mobile phone launch, Harwood and Garry (chapter 7) about the gamification of a web-based brand community or Webley and Cham's gamification as part of service experiences.

The *-ication* suffix of gamification indicates a process, a transformation and activity. Fors and Lennerfors focus extensively on the longevity of this activity—the need to consider a long-term perspective of consumer/user transformation by means of gamification, whereas Rehn claims gamification is a process focused on standardising à la "McDonaldisation". Olaison and Taalas compare gamification to digital rhetorics and how games can be used to break rules, instead of merely following them, Fors and Lennerfors expand Kierkegaard's existential philosophy to consider gamification as mainly an aesthetical mode of existence but possibly also an ethical mode, which also resonates with Cochoy and Hagberg's hypothesis of gamification as a process of game addiction, but not with Ferrer Conill's elaboration of gamification as a clash between logics of managerial control and playful work.

What are the outer boundaries of gamification? Hedberg and Svan (chapter 11) propose that there are practically no limits to how far games and gamification can expand into society, and they outline a post-human society of total gamification. Fors and Lennerfors foresee the need for a long-term gamification that omits short-term rewards and focuses on long-term ethical behavioural change vis-à-vis sustainability.

As illustrated, this volume provides rewarding insights on how the notion of gamification within business contexts can be explored and definitions advanced. Various critical dimensions are creating a foundation for development and further research.

Book Structure

This book's chapters are structured according to three parts, which are based on groups of similar perspectives on the organisation (i.e., the business/company implementing gamification), but also conceptual texts about notion as such. The three groups are: internal organisational, external organisational and conceptual perspectives on gamification.

Internal Organisational Perspectives

The first perspective is exploring the use of gamification in contexts of the internal dimensions of the organisation/business, such as enterprise education, projects and management. In mainstream discourses uses of gamification are frequently discussed in examples of highly visible and mediatised applications with direct consumer access (i.e., external applications). Gamification's purported ability to generate fun, engagement and community is, however, as useful inside as it is outside of the organisation. Numerous cases of internal business applications of gamification exist, but they are not always made for public insight. Consequently, there is essential need to explore these dimensions as well.

Chapter 1, Emmanuelle Savignac's "Role-Playing Games at Work: About Management, Gamification and Effectiveness" analyses the use of role playing as part of business training sessions where employees play "business theatre". Savignac theoretically expands the notion of gamification by including business theatre role playing as gameful elements in non-game contexts, by emphasising Goffmanian frames and, based on the game definition of Gilles Brougère, the game mechanism elements of play, roles and fiction. Savignac concludes by discussing the link between gamification and the outcomes of business theatre sessions.

Chapter 2, Raul Ferrer Conill's "Feeding the Red Critter: The Gamification of Project Management Software" focuses on the introduction of game mechanisms in project management software—the quintessential case of internal business gamification, due to the "projectification" of business and the rising popularity of virtual project organisations by means of digital project management tools. In the conclusions Ferrer Conill juxtaposes the celebratory perspective on gamification—as something that generates employee engagement and motivation—with a perspective where gamification in this setting becomes a tool of management, control and exploitation.

Chapter 3, Alf Rehn's "Gamification as Ideological Praxis—On Play, Games and the Modding of Management" investigates the ideological contexts of gamification in business and management. It does so by relying on Ritzger's McDonaldisation theory, whose basic assumption is that the business logic of McDonald's (efficiency, calculability, predictability and control) has become the mantra of contemporary market economy, and conquers ever more markets, industries and fields of society. Gamification in management might disguise these exploitative undercurrents by becoming a tool of hidden control, but Rehn's text ends by asking if gamification might not instead expose the hollowness of management since it has been turned into a game.

External Organisational Perspectives

Representing the biggest chapter group, these five texts explore how gamification is employed by organisations to manage and communicate with external dimensions of the organisational context. Prominent external business functions are for instance marketing, various types of communications, sales, retailing, public relations, lobbying, but also distribution, logistics, supply networks, stakeholder/community management and several others. This book part consists of the popular theme (with three chapters) of business cases from marketing communications, one additional chapter with a consumer-centric digital/marketing communications analysis and finally one text based on a rewarding historical study of gamification in retailing.

xviii *Introduction*

Gamification in external organisational settings receives more attention in mainstream media discourses since consumers have direct access to these, which makes them more popular—but also more scrutinised.

Chapter 4, Lena Olaison and Saara L. Taalas's "Game of Gamification—Marketing, Consumer Resistance and Digital Play" analyses four cases (Waitrose, Norwegian Air Shuttle, ECB and Nutella) of consumer resistance in game-based marketing communications campaign. In these campaigns consumers instead of following the rules of the game subverted them by creating their own alternative games that questioned and ridiculed the intention of the brands. This is based on Olaison and Taalas's assumption that games are not only a "rule-following activity" but also a process of alternative play that can manipulate and evade the rules themselves. The authors conclude that these disruptions are a form of consumer activism, and that this type of gamification is a culture-producing activity that creates a playground that is not controlled or owned by the brand.

Chapter 5, Franck Cochoy and Johan Hagberg's "Win, Earn, Gain: Gamification in the History of Retailing" chapter takes the multiple meanings of the French word *gagner* (win, earn, gain) as the departure point for a historical analysis of gamification in retailing stretching from the retailer competitions and loyalty schemes of the 1920s to the current generation of retailing smartphone apps that combine play with retail strategies. Based on Schüll's theory of "addiction by design" and a historical review, the authors illustrate how games in retailing have been rationalised as something that provides a feeling of contest victory, or something that introduces elements of earning, and finally something that focuses on gaining. Gamification in retailing thus evolves from basic contests of winning or earning, to something that emphasises gaining (e.g., play and enjoyment).

Chapter 6, Mikolaj Dymek's "Inside the Gamification Case of a Mobile Phone Marketing Campaign—The Amalgamation of Game Studies with Marketing Communications?" examines a gamified marketing campaign for the high-profile launch of a new mobile phone model. The empirical data is based on parts of a three-year participative study performed at a prominent communications agency. The chapter analyses the gamification dimensions with several frameworks from game studies and combines those with a marketing communications perspective in order to explore avenues of future research. A pivotal conclusion is that a pertinent research issue is constituted by the role of games in marketing—obfuscating diversion of sales driving strategies, or the introduction of a new (playful) mode of interactive marketing communications?

Chapter 7, Tracy Harwood and Tony Garry's "Samsung Nation: A Gamified Experience" explores the use of gamification in the brand community platform of consumer electronics brand Samsung. Using participative observation, this analysis focuses on issues of pre-formed customer loyalty, intrinsic/extrinsic rewards and value cocreation. With frameworks from gamification research and marketing theory, the authors investigate whether this implementation of game mechanics can reinforce brand community and drive engagement towards the brand. Harwood and Garry conclude by emphasising game design shortcomings, but also the lack of corporate engagement with customers. The authors finalise their argument by asking a pivotal question: does gamification in this case reinforce high-quality consumer behaviour, or does the flawed game design even corrupt and bastardise the brand community?

Chapter 8, Christian Fuentes's "Play a Game, Save the Planet!—Gamification as a Way to Promote Green Consumption" studies gamification of green consumption practices, and is based on a critical approach to gamification studies by means of a digital ethnography of a smartphone app ("The Green Guide" app) that promotes sustainable consumption. This app was released by Sweden's most influential environmental nonprofit organization, and through its innovative communication format, it aims to reach environmentally conscious consumers. The analysis indicates that the gamification app enables and encourages a series of potentially "gameful" green consumer actions and connects these to the production of green experiences, green identities and green status, but by doing so it also reproduces several of the contemporary consumers culture practices associated with unsustainable consumption.

Conceptual Perspectives

The final part of this book is centred around the examination of gamification in business from conceptual points of view. These four chapters discuss what gamification in business might mean as concept and what its limitations are. In terms of the previous two perspectives, internal or external organisational, this perspective sometimes includes both and prefers to centre on certain dimensions of the gamification logic. All of these chapters as a point of departure include some type of business gamification implementation (e.g., sustainability, user experience design, business consultancies), but the analysis is applicable on any business setting—and in many cases any general discussion regarding gamification as such, beyond the scope of business perspectives.

Chapter 9, Per Fors and Thomas Taro Lennerfors's "Gamification for Sustainability: Beyond the Ludo-Aesthetical Approach" investigates gamification for sustainability. The study's point of departure is the need for evolved gamification strategies in the field of sustainable lifestyles. The authors focus their analysis on a core dimension of gamification—the ability to change behaviour, and particularly with a long-term perspective. Existing approaches of gamification for sustainability are criticised as being centred on visualisation and information, resulting in a need within gamification applications for the promotion of sustainability that draws on a wider palette of affects. The authors propose a combination of existential philosophy, mainly Søren Kierkegaard's work, combined with game studies producing a gamification categorisation based on aesthetical and ethical modes of existence, fused with narratological and ludological game perspectives. As a final remark the authors ask, in line with their own use of existential philosophy, whether the analysis of gamification should not be positioned within certain fields of philosophy, which have observed the issue of games for centuries, or whether gamification should be investigated separately.

Chapter 10, Stephen Webley and Karen Cham's "Designing for The Play Instinct; Gamification, Collective Voodoo and Mumbo Jumbo", begins by stating that gamification is a "humpty dumpty term" of limited conceptual meaning. The chapter uses design studies, user experience design, game studies, game philosophy, gamification and business perspectives to conclude that gamification for business growth does not need to be complicated, evangelical or mystified. Furthermore, to use the human instinct to play for corporate or social ideology is not necessarily coercive nor dubious, but it is also not necessarily a magic bullet for change. In other words, the authors are claiming that we need to refocus our attention to the ideological context of gamification in corporate settings and not limit our analysis to the user experience design dimensions. The text does so by tracing the origins of gamification in user interface and experience design, through a business case of Brazilian call centres, and an analytical plunge into game philosophy via game studies. They finalise their analysis by proposing a new type of feedback loop that incorporates user, customer and shareholder experience in a framework for the analysis of gamification of business.

Chapter 11, Per H. Hedberg and Mattias Svahn's "Total Gamification and the Limits of Our Imagination", imagines a world where every aspect of society has been gamified and we start living in a world of total gamification. The authors draw on game philosopher Huizinga's notion of "magic circle" to outline how in the age of gamification this boundary between the temporary game world and the ordinary world is expanding and will soon lose its meaning as games turn into a Goffmanian "total institution". This total institution is not, however, one of oppression and coercive structures—but a human-designed ecology where participation is fuzzy and notions of voluntariness become irrelevant. This total gamification creates an enjoyable post-humanity best described as human ant-society beyond Tönnies's sociological community notions of Gemeinschaft and Gesellschaft. Is there any way to stop this development, the authors ask, and point to societal issues of sacredness as a possible venue of exploration?

In Chapter 12, the concluding chapter, Peter Zackariasson's "Old Things—New Names", the role of gamification is debated. The chapters critically take a stand for the concept as building on previous knowledge, offering a convincing framing. It comes from an understanding that gamification indeed is bullshit, but in the capitalistic ideology it has been put to work—and proven most successful at it! Although as gamification is making its move into academia as a theory, Peter argues for the importance of scientific rigour and resistance.

Mikolaj Dymek and Peter Zackariasson

References

Alvesson, Mats. 2008. "The Future of Critical Management Studies." In *The SAGE Handbook of New Approaches in Management and Organization*, edited by Daved Barry and Hans Hansen, 13–26. London: SAGE Publications.

AWeber. 2016. "About AWeber." http://www.aweber.com/about.htm.

Bogost, Ian. 2011a. "Gamification Is Bullshit." *The Atlantic*. http://www.theatlantic.com/technology/archive/2011/08/gamification-is-bullshit/243338/.

———. 2011b. "Persuasive Games: Exploitationware." *Gamasutra*. http://www.gamasutra.com/view/feature/6366/persuasive_games_exploitationware.php.

Buffer. 2016. "The Buffer Team." https://bufferapp.com/about/team.

Chatfield, Tom. 2010. "7 Ways Games Reward the Brain." *TEDGlobal*. https://www.ted.com/talks/tom_chatfield_7_ways_games_reward_the_brain.

Deterding, Sebastian, Miguel Sicart, Lennart Nacke, Kenton O'Hara, and Dan Dixon. 2011. "Gamification—Using Game-Design Elements in Non-Gaming Contexts." *CHI EA '11 Proceedings of the 2011 Annual Conference Extended Abstracts on Human Factors in Computing Systems*, Vancouver, Canada.

Dymek, Mikolaj. 2010. "Industrial Phantasmagoria—Subcultural Interactive Cinema Meets Mass-Cultural Media of Simulation." PhD diss., Royal Institute of Technology, Department of Industrial Economics and Organization. Stockholm, Sweden.

Gartner. 2011. "Gartner Says Spending on Gaming to Exceed $74 Billion in 2011." *Gartner Inc*. http://www.gartner.com/it/page.jsp?id=1737414.

———. 2012. "Gartner Says by 2014, 80 Percent of Current Gamified Applications Will Fail to Meet Business Objectives Primarily Due to Poor Design." http://www.gartner.com/newsroom/id/2251015.

McGonigal, Jane. 2010. "Gaming Can Make a Better World." *TED Conference*. https://www.ted.com/talks/jane_mcgonigal_gaming_can_make_a_better_world.

Rheingold, Howard. 1995. *Virtual Community: Finding Connection in a Computerised World*. New ed. London: Minerva.

Zackariasson, Peter. 2007. "World Builders: A Study on the Development of a Massively Multiplayer Online Role-Playing Game." PhD diss., Umeå School of Business, Umeå, Sweden.

Zappos. 2016. "About Zappos Culture." http://www.zappos.com/d/about-zappos-culture.

Zichermann, Gabe. 2011. "How Games Make Kids Smarter." *TEDxKids@Brussels*. https://www.ted.com/talks/gabe_zichermann_how_games_make_kids_smarter.

Part I
Internal Organizational Perspectives

1 Role-Playing Games at Work

About Management, Gamification and Effectiveness

Emmanuelle Savignac

> Games make us happy because they are hard work that we choose for ourselves, and it turns out that almost nothing makes us happier than good, hard work.
>
> *Jane Mc Gonigal*

Introduction

The aim of this article is to study management games using simulation, specifically role-playing games (RPGs) for managers. I have deliberately chosen to analyze these games in terms of enterprise gamification—that is to say considering that a game structure (i.e., role-playing games) is brought from games to be adapted to the context of work and its organization. This choice will lead us to debate in what way and how a role-playing game may integrate the concept of gamification. It will also lead us to question the concept of game, considering like Mollick and Werbach (2014, 440) that "given the confluence of approaches in enterprise settings" it would be quite artificial to separate games and gamification (understood as gameful elements or game-like mechanisms).

Studying several cases of role-playing games for managers, my chapter will analyze two structural aspects attached to role-playing games: the question of roles and the question of fiction. This will lead us in turn to consider in the last part of this chapter what these gameful elements produce, by analyzing the functions that underlie the structure of role playing.

Gamification as a Transmedial Question

Initial research about gamification considered it in its relation to the digital media industry (Raessens 2006; McGonigal 2011). In that sense, gamification was initially thought of as part of design studies and more specifically, studies examining human-computer interactions. When applied to the business or marketing sectors, this meaning of gamification may seem to be of little value, hence the criticism it has been subjected to for being a mere "pointification" device (Robertson 2010) with levels, badges and feedback processes, instead of an engaging user experience. Ian Bogost argues that the "-ification" ending in "gamification" suggests the notion of automatism and accordingly, creates a "typical points-and-badges client" (Bogost 2014, 71). Gamification "tames games, making them safe and predictable" (Bogost 2014, 67).

Analyzing gamification and the transmedial nature of games, Deterding et al. define gamification as "the use of game design elements in non-game contexts", specifying that "the term should not be limited to digital technology" (Deterding, Deterding, Dixon, Khaled and Nacke 2011).

This definition, somewhat broader than the previous one, led researchers and actors of gamification (such as consultants, experts, designers . . .) to discuss the notion and its perimeter.

At the last Gamification World Congress,[1] the question of the limits of the concept was discussed.[2] Part of the discussion focused on the exclusivity (or not) of the link between gamification and digital solutions. Most speakers agreed that gamification was not "confined to digital solutions" (Sylvester Arnab[3]).* "[I]t can be both digital or no tech at all, it is about creating game-like experiences" (An Coppens, founder of Gamification Nation).* The definition focuses on two aspects: on the one hand, gamification would be a question of "design", namely a "toolset" to design non-gaming products or activities, and on the other hand, gamification systematically refers to "game mechanisms", "game dynamics", "game attributes" or "game thinking". Therefore, games in all their dimensions would be the material to the design. As such, the definition of gamification moves from a strict acceptation of its inclusion in digital forms only (like videogames) to the possibility that gamification occurs in a wide variety of forms, which may sometimes be hybrid ones. In fact, we may observe that the definition of gamification in the field of design or management seems to be more dependent on its aims than the shapes or the mediums it may take, as it has "to build strong relationships and involvement, and to increase motivation, commitment and user engagement levels; all these in B2B/B2E and B2C sectors" (Carlos Martin, consultant),* involves "design for fun, design for motivation" (Thijs de Vries, designer),* concerns "the strategic use of games and game elements to create value for stakeholders" (Marigo Raftopoulos, strategy advisor and designer),* and is meant "'[T]o drive game-like player behavior' such as engagement, interaction, competition, collaboration, awareness, learning, and/or just about any behavior you want to drive" (Michael Wu, chief scientist at Lithium technologies).* The use of game is oriented, in gamification processes, towards productive goals. We may notice that it contrasts with the autotelic dimension of play and fun.

From that point of view, many actors in this business sector and field of research separate gamification from "fun games" as being "purely for entertainment". In that conception, we still find the separation between play and game. Gamification strictly belongs to the game aspects, and its achievements do not refer to fun aspects even if fun may be considered (or not, according to the plurality of points of view on this topic) as part of game mechanisms.[4] Finally, we may observe that gamification is not defined as a whole or separate object but as a structure, or as a process of selecting game principles with the aim of applying them to non-game activities, contexts and objects: "Gamification does not involve creating games, it is about using the things that make games engaging in non-game settings" (Andrzej Marczewski, Gamification expert).*

Returning to the Game Theory: What about the Elements Constitutive of "Game"?

The centrality of the reference to game as structure (thought, attributes, mechanisms . . .) brings us back to the whole game theory that developed at the beginning of the 20th century. In these theories, the complexity of the concept of game has often been underlined. In games, following Caillois (1967) and his distinction between *ludus* and *paidia*, Henriot (1989) but also Bateson (1977), we find above all the structure that is central to the meaning of *gamification*. Several authors, beginning with Huinzinga (1938), have tried to determine the specifics of games. From his perspective, a game expresses the free will of a person, has a pleasurable aim, allows us to escape from our daily routine, is delimited in time and space, has rules, is uncertain as to its outcome and is autotelic (i.e., has no other aim than itself), so that in playing games the individual is conscious that he or she is in a make-believe world. In the wake of Huizinga, many authors have tried to expand his description of the characteristics of games. One of them, French academic Gilles Brougère (2005), puts forward five characteristics, allowing us to define what a game would be like. A game, according to him:

- is a second-degree activity (with reference to Bateson and his concept of metacommunication)—a game has a double aspect, at once seeming to be real and being a game;
- is characterized by decision-making. Brougère goes beyond the idea, shared by Huizinga, Caillois and many others, that a game is free. For him, decision, rather than being a factor entering the game, operates in relation to action. "Playing is deciding", and this definition meets the theory of games (Von Neumann and Morgenstern 1944);
- follows rules, whatever the game. These rules are the result of an agreement between the players, regardless of the prescribed rules of the game;
- is frivolous and "built to minimize its consequences" (Brougère 2005, 56);
- is uncertain as to its outcome because it has to be understood as a dynamic process rather than a state or a result. Uncertainty is one of its components.

Brougère concludes that these elements are not the same for all games but that we may find them in every game at different levels.

Inferring from these characteristics a general definition of what a game may be like, I am led to interrogate the meaning of gamification in "non-game contexts" such as workplaces.

Game Mechanisms Element Number 1: The Play Frame

Relying on the typology established by Roger Caillois (1967), I notice that competition games (*agon*) and simulation games (*mimicry*) are used much more in workplaces than games of chance (*alea*) or vertigo-inducing games (*ilinx*). If competition games often prevail in the case of commercial teams, simulations games are used both in a business and management context.

For the past three years, I have been studying role-playing games in several workplaces (a communication agency, an international hotel group, an organizational consulting agency, a public research center, etc.). These games have training purposes (they are used for management tasks such as recruitment, changes, the prevention of psychosocial risks, etc.), teambuilding purposes and sometimes, as in the case of what is called *reversal days,* may have an organizational communication purpose.

Method used:
My corpus is made up of several role-playing games. It includes data directly gathered from:

- direct observations and participating observations of four training sessions (in a consulting agency), of business theatre[5] sessions (in a public research center, in a hospital, in three business theatre companies at meetings for their customers) and two reversal days (in a communication agency and a hotel group).
- 16 interviews of business theatre trainers and actor trainers and on 28 interviews of senior executives, managers and CEOs using role-playing games for their team management.

Secondhand data are also derived from:

- Whole rushes of films about role-playing games used for recruitment and another one for teambuilding (16 hours of films); 10 hours of rushes of films recording training sessions, and a 75' film of a reversal day.
- A documentary about recruiting games (RPG)[6] and parts of a documentary about neomanagement shot in a service company (using RPGs).[7]
- six episodes of the French TV series *Vis ma vie—mon patron à ma place* and six episodes of the French adaptation of the *Undercover boss* TV series. In these TV shows, a CEO is led to play the role of his or her employees.

When observing a role-playing game, we may find the essence of game in the "act as if" or the "act not for real". These are the social games played by children and animals that were studied first by ethologists, psychologists, and education sciences researchers. (Groos 1898; Winicott 1975)

Indeed, the practice of social games is common to men and animals (such as a certain number of mammals but also corvids, for example). In particular, we share simulation games with them when we act "not for real" (when playing as if we were fighting, for example). The "acting not for real" characteristic is conveyed through a paraphernalia of signs (what ethologists name "game physiognomy"), which creates a commentary on the action that is taking place. Bateson (1972) invites us to consider game, not as a substance but as a shape that structures an activity. That shape will allow us to distinguish a real fight from a "not for real" fight. This shape of the game, when it occurs, creates a discourse on the activity it incorporates.

This is what Bateson calls the "metacommunicational" dimension, which is specific to games: each individual game conveys a discourse whose object is "the relation between counterparts" (Bateson 1972, 248). Bateson says that when both animals and humans play, they are actually sending their game partners a message meaning: "this is play". This message is non-verbal in the case of animals. For human beings, it may be either a verbal one ("Let's play!", "Let's pretend I am a knight and you are a dragon") or a nonverbal one (for instance when I pretend I am a colleague suffering from a burnout). It may also occur within the context or in relation to game accessories. Not being able to understand this metacommunicational dimension, that is to say this second degree specific to games, is a symptom of schizophrenia, according to Bateson (1972).

Bateson, following his thoughts about the game as a shape, coined a brilliant concept: the concept of "play frame" (it is this concept of frame that Erving Goffman would later develop in his own theory). Bateson says that in the play frame we find play actions that do not mean what they would mean outside this frame: "The playful nip denotes the bite, but it does not denote what would be denoted by the bite" (Bateson 1972, 250).

Bateson understands the frame as a set of messages. It is the frame that conveys the message on the situation, as Bateson nicely puts it: "The frame tells the viewer that he is not to use the same sort of thinking in interpreting the picture that he might use in interpreting the wallpaper outside the frame" (Bateson 1972, 258). One must be careful to properly understand the message underlying this metacommunication. Otherwise, people will mistake the wrong fight for a real one, and the conditions of communication will become just impossible.

In order to explain the relations between game and reality, Bateson uses a metaphor: the difference between the map and the territory. This leads us to wonder what is kept from the territory in the map and what has been left out. In a simulation game of recruitment for example, what is kept and what is excluded from the representation? What are the "transformation rules" from one frame to another, allowing us to use his expression? With the map, we have a process of symbolization in as much as it is a metaphor of the territory. This would be the case—being a metaphor—for each kind of game and especially simulation and role-playing games.

Simulation and role-playing games, as a metaphor (Bateson 1972; Henriot 1989), are a fiction (Caillois 1967; Piette 1997; Hamayon 2012)—albeit a fiction built with reference to reality. Games may be understood as situated between two frames: a fictional one and a frame of reference. There is a space between these two frames that leads us to analyze what the transformations between the two are and what the rules for this transformation are. In simulation games, I may observe a double action: a simulation (through role-playing) and also a reference to a model. Another double action lies in the fact that, as players, even if we play against other people, we play together. We'll see how this question of the relationship between players is particularly central when the game is played in workplaces.

Game Mechanisms Element Number 2: Role-Playing

Goffman uses this concept of frame to construct his own "frame analysis" (1974). This theory is congruent with his previous theories about the roles we act in several social environments (as a repertoire of roles that we are able to mobilize). Other roles may be part of the frame: it is one of the framing elements that will give its definition to the situation. Roles, as predictable constructs, participate in the discourse that comments on the situation (metacommunication). It allows us to interpret/understand the situation we are faced with. On the other hand, the frame will influence the role. It is the frame that indicates the modalities needed for the actions in the situation experienced. In the play frame, I may for instance react in ways that normally would not be mine in the situation I am simulating (the "real" situation the game refers to). I may also emphasize emotions that I would usually tone down. I may act in a fictional way, for instance by setting ("not for real") traps for other players. In circumstances other than games, I would not set them these traps for fear they might "lose face" (in Goffman's sense of that word), something I might wish to avoid. Furthermore, the others' readiness to play or not will influence my desire and abilities for originality.

But in some way, I play insofar as I have the possibility to investigate and put to the test the margins the game provides. In this sense, games become a space between the reference to reality that I simulate and the fiction that I play. Researchers like Brougère or Henriot specify that although games are fictional, they are not fictitious (since they really take place). Be it a CEO playing the role of one of his accountants during a role-reversal day, or a manager who plays the role of one of his staff members who has to be convinced of the necessity of a change, it is not fictitious, although what is played is a fiction.

What does it mean performing a role-playing game in the workplace? What is the significance of this action in relation to the "real" world of work?

Belgian sociologist Jacques Coenen-Huther, in a paper dedicated to the question of social roles (2005), returns to two "historical" meanings of the concept of role: the first is inherited from Ralph Linton and relates to the aspect of status (1936). The other one appeared at about the same time (1934) in the work of sociologist and social psychologist George Herbert Mead. Mead, one of the fathers of symbolic interactionism, understands roles as an interface between an individual and his social environment.

If I look into the definition of role in its relation to status, the former, says Linton, consists in the implementation of the rights and the duties that are the constituent part of the status (Linton 1936). In my own field, one of the business theatre companies is named "A role to play". In particular, it offers training sessions to managers. One of the services offered is named "Managing, a role to repeat". When I carried out semi-structured interviews with trainers, the same reference to what managerial behaviors should be like or not would always recur.

We may find in these examples the notion of the role that we have to play—in a somewhat strict sense of the concept—as we embody a status. This approach to the issue is thus equivalent to the demand to be (a manager) (i.e., to fulfill his/her own role). In my field, this representation of the role leads to training sessions where the propositions of a manager in a specific situation are tested, strained, questioned, accepted, or refused. Through the performance of an actor-trainer and an actor, the representation of what a business and what work relations consist in highlights hypotheses regarding people's behavior in the context of a specific situation (a conflict, a negotiation, a recruitment process, etc.). The roles played by the actor-trainer and the short briefing given to the trainees, restricts and consequently, regulates, the range of possibilities of actions.

The participants in the training session have to debate this performance. Sometimes they are invited to make their own propositions by suggesting new behaviors, new modes of interaction or verbal formulations in the scene they have just been watching. What is played again and reevaluated from the initial staging may be done by individuals and will be discussed in the group. It can also be done collectively. In that case, the group gives their instructions to the actor for playing the scene again. "The group finally says: you can't do it like that" (an actor trainer). If they are invited to play a situation again, the participants are sometimes invited to keep elements previously defined as being "good" ones and all listed on the flip-board by the trainer during the debriefings.

There are, in those two modalities, a collective work of discussion, then the establishment of a consensus about what could be "a proper way of doing it" by people who are sharing the same status. This status can be linked to the "profession" (such as medical staff in a hospital for instance) or hierarchical functions (as in the case of management, for example).

We may find here the idea of "profession" as the result of an historical process shaped by social organisations (Dubar and Tripier 1998) and, accordingly, instructions for professional identity. We may also find here the initial sense of "profession"—that is to say "the action to profess aloud its own opinions or beliefs" (Dubar and Tripier 1998, 4), as in a profession of faith. In fact, the work on roles performed during the sessions of business theatre companies allows one to put into words professional practices. In the training sessions I have observed, this practice is verbalized and acted out (because it is played). The action is meant to be seen—literally it gives rise to a performance—and evidences the Goffmanian metaphor of the repertoire of roles that anyone has to control and perform in their social life. The parts performed by the participants in the training sessions are performed in order to be discussed and reworked. Trainers say that "It allows to reframe, or rather to frame", "It helps them understand what is the flexibility that people have in the workplace" even if they add that "They already know all that". What is paradoxically worked on is something already known, pre-existing. Playing a role is therefore a matter of rehearsing one's professional discourse, behavior and body posture (the nonverbal language, the codes related to the expression of emotions, etc.).

Game Mechanisms Element 3: Creating a Fiction

First Function of the Fiction: Exploring and Overcoming Uncertainty

During business theatre sessions, the training starts with a short skit, which is obviously a caricature of a case history. The trainer collects information from his customer (a CEO, a HR executive . . .) and from the two or three individuals who have been identified by the customer as points of contact: "We're going to play a story built from elements that we gather in a very short time sequence. It is this body of events which creates a caricature" (a trainer).

From the trainer's point of view, this reduction, akin to a caricature, has two functions:

- it allows one to distance oneself : "We may talk about something with distance, by using this scenario (. . .) It allows us to avoid approaching topics too frontally".
- it helps one accept the reality through the mediation of a fiction: "If you tell them: 'I'm going to play something real', they'll say, 'But it's wrong!' If you tell them that it's a caricature, they'll say that it seems to be real".

I see a paradox in the fact that access to reality needs fiction. To initiate the skit, many trainers will indicate that it is fiction. As in a fiction, its reception will consist in accepting it as reflecting reality.

The same ambiguous link between fiction and reality may be seen in the fact that trainers often say that "it is necessary to break codes". For example, actors and trainers know that "the actors express emotions which are not the same as those a colleague would express" (a trainer). This gap (kept to a minimum) creates the possibility of distancing oneself and allows for the consideration of the codes. Business theatre professionals have to depict the workplace in a real enough way (by collecting anecdotes, minor verbal or dress codes . . .). At the same time, they have to depict it in a way just flawed enough so as to leave room for the participants in the training session to (critically) comment on the scene. The fictional dimension in a role-playing game, because of the thin distance with reality, allows people to verbalize the norms. Here, we find once more the difference between the map and the territory. This collective action of commentary and criticism is created by the participants' interiorization of the constraint. Each person is drawn out "to formalize the behaviors that don't work and how to think differently" (an actor trainer). This formalization is not prescribed by anybody: "My job is to say to them: you decide" (a trainer).

Actors-trainers will often test the participants' ability to react to the unforeseen. What is fictional here is no longer the fictional frame but the reference to reality. What happens is not a simulation but situations "that they'll never see" (an actor trainer). One of the aims of the training session for managers is "to stop being in the usual control of what commonly happens in an office" (an actor trainer). Here, the trainee is tested in his or her ability to adapt to the unexpected—that is to say to adapt to any kind of interaction that they might encounter. The importance of status is still maintained. The debriefing is the time when all the participants will debate to decide if the trainee has stuck to his role (his status) or not, despite the vicissitudes of the interaction performed. This risk of loss of control fully participates in the game as uncertainty and is structurally part of it. Consequently, I may see a double relationship between the unforeseen and work, and between uncertainty and game, through:

- On the one hand, dealing with uncertainty: professional situations are made of unforeseen events. Training managers, in order to get out of a routine, will prepare the participants to this uncertainty. A trainer told us that "they [the managers] have to work with fluency, flexibility, agility". His job, he says, is "to make them accept any kind of situation". We find here the understanding of the game shared by ethologists, pedagogues and theoreticians of games. In this conception, the game would prepare to life by increasing human abilities to overcome obstacles and difficulties.
- On the other hand, and more specifically, there is a little risk of losing face that creates intensity in the game. Trainers consciously break the ritual codes of interaction in workplaces and in so doing, do not follow the social rule of predictability (Goffman 1959). Because some actions are unpredictable, the smoothness of the interaction is threatened and

the trainee is led to save face by reasserting his behavior in the situation. There is here a double issue for the participant:

- As a player he has to comply with the instructions given at the beginning of the training sessions. These instructions may be meant to bring a subordinate back into the frame, to convince him or her of taking charge of an issue, etc. He or she may lose the game if he or she does not overcome the obstacles that the trainer has created. There are losers and winners.
- Simultaneously, there is another issue: he or she has to save face in front of a group of colleagues (8 to 12) who are generally his or her peers but also his or her potential competitors in the company. These colleagues are present during the game and are invited to comment on it. They will evaluate the player's performance but also the performance of a professional in the situation played. Has he or she succeeded? Has he or she been able to convince, to impose, to pilot or to reframe? As Goffman puts it in *Encounters*: "games give the players an opportunity to exhibit attributes valued in the wider social world, such as dexterity, strength, knowledge, intelligence, courage and self-control" (Goffman 1961, 68). In the cases under study, I believe that the capacity to manage a team involves the capacity of controlling the game and being successful.

Second Function of the Fiction: Telling a Tale about Experience, Work Relationships and Hierarchies

A distinct relationship with fiction occurs with role-reversal days or when a CEO takes the place of the members of his staff for a TV show. The game consists in reversing roles and places for one or a few days. This game is based on the "job rotation" method, which is used to widen employees' skills and to train people to several workstations. In the games studied, rotations can be between professions (that may have antagonistic relations) but also between hierarchical places. For example, many managers from a hotel group headquarters will do all the jobs within a hotel for a day. As another example, a few executives from big companies will experience the jobs of their less-qualified employees. In hierarchical reversals, "unskilled jobs" are tested and the manager has the opportunity to understand their value for the company. Reversal days are inscribed in gratitude rituals. Everyone is celebrated as a professional. The place of each one is thus shown and restored to the employee whose place has been taken during this day: "I could never do what he/she does" (even cleaning the toilets) is often heard during these reversal days when employees or bosses take one another's places. There is a clear aim of teambuilding through the upgrading of less-valued jobs.

Cross-comprehension is one of the arguments used to explain the reversal day applied to professions. In the case of hierarchical reversals, the "field" is the argument: "to experience the field". The message conveyed to the employees is about proximity but also humility, just because the highest can do what the lowest does. And he or she does it without shame but with sincerity and a genuine interest. What we may note is that this kind of reversal always occurs from top to bottom: a manager can do the cleaning, but the cleaner cannot do the management.[8]

Reversal days pose an external communication challenge: press relations are increased for this event, and in the case of the hotel, the guests are told in advance about the event. In the case of TV reality shows, what is broadcast is the image of managers, ready to leave behind their material benefits to face "reality", exposing themselves to the most merciless and physically demanding jobs in their companies.

Role-reversal days are strictly limited in time, just as training days using role-playing games or business theatre are. For one day, people "act as if" the hotel's director was the maid. The play frame is strongly distinct from the reference to reality frame. Only the roles are kept, to be performed. In the companies I have studied, the role-reversal day is a day when people dress up in costumes. Managers wear maids' uniforms, and enjoy that a lot. The one-day substitute for the CEO leaves his piercing at home, shaves his cheeks, and wears a nice shirt. The guest adviser woman playing for one day the role of a graphic designer young colleague wears sneakers, and her son asks her if she is on holiday. The function of costumes may be to make colleagues laugh as when, for example, one dresses as a hostess with a dress and high-heeled shoes. Whereas it is allowed to laugh about female colleagues, it will be more difficult to do so about subordinates. The costumes, in this case, show the main attributes of the profession. Role playing becomes here a signifying system, involving gestures and tasks supposed to be characteristic of the job. These signs may be overplayed and allow one to perceive which role is endorsed. The stereotypes of the profession are mobilized so as to indicate the places but also the game situation (or game physiognomy).

One may notice that the game of taking another colleague's place does not give rise to the possibility of fully experiencing the other's activity. The CEO of a day—the only case I met of a bottom-up reversal—can see that he has very little possibility of taking initiatives or making decisions; the salesperson who takes the place (for one day) of the programmer will not be allowed to use the code (or even the computer) but will be invited to read "Computing for dummies" all morning long. On the contrary, when the places are taken by the hierarchical staff in a top-down logic, initiatives and actions are often taken even if they modify the subordinate's work. When the managers play at being members of their staff, they will actively do the job, not for themselves but "in the place" of the person usually occupying the position. For example, it will allow the CEO of a communication agency and one of his managers to modify the accountant's scoreboards: "She, she's an accountant, we are practitioners, so we are able to have a practical thought" (the CEO). Without any mediation, workstations may be controlled and adjusted. As a matter of fact, the role-reversal day strengthens the hierarchical line even though its stated purpose is to turn hierarchical relationships upside down. The question of the direction taken by the reversal, almost exclusively top-down, raises two issues:

- Who has the right to play the role of whom (or not)? What I see is that it is possible to play the role of a peer (manager to manager) or a subordinate.
- Who is easily replaceable (or not), and whose work can be learnt or adjusted to in a few hours?

For the managers taking their subordinates' roles, they expect to learn from the game; they wish the game will allow them to know their subordinates' work, by "experiencing it". Thinking that a manager is able to understand what work is like by experiencing it is accepted by all and seen as a very valuable way of thinking. This argument will be repeated by all the managers and CEOs playing this game. Playing the other's role would allow to build up an accurate overview of his/her work. This knowledge would, literally, be constructed in the employee's place, in the absence of the "real" worker. Taking the other's place would replace the mediation by the worker of what his work difficulties, characteristics and specificities are. We may see there is a difference of level in the various kinds of role-reversal days. Some are introduced by a "real worker" who explains his job to his boss or his colleague, and some are organized in the absence of the workers. In the case of the French version of the TV reality show *Undercover Boss*, for example, the mediation and its possibility are denied: for the bosses performing in this TV show, it appears clearly impossible for them to think that their employees could tell them the truth without cheating or playing down "reality".

We may, however, consider that the temporality of the game induces a bias in the notion of experience. No experience of work can be achieved in a few hours. The time allowed for the experience cannot provide any information about the effects of repetitiveness, routine, attrition, strain or speed. This is reinforced by the fact that managers can often choose their workstations, and when they have to do something, the task is either undersized or the staff of players is much more important for the job than the staff of workers: "They needed much more people to do the job, much more than the usual staff. We were far from the productivity standards" (HR manager of a hotel group).

The objective of proximity also raises questions if we consider that, in TV reality shows, it is, for many people of the staff, the first time they meet their boss. Proximity does not seem to refer to a "real proximity" but to a proximity in the game where the highest one goes down to the same level as the lowest one. In TV shows, the people CEOs replace are not middle managers for example, but collaborators at the bottom on the hierarchy scale. It is the play frame that creates this proximity.

Despite the ambiguity of "taking somebody's place" that I have highlighted before, the recognition of the value of each individual's work is another way of understanding this question of proximity. All the managers and CEOs playing the game will emphasize the value of their staff's work. In the hotel group I studied, jobs thought to be difficult and merciless, such as the maid's, will gain pride of place. The organizers of the day think that if managers of the head office spend one day cleaning the hotel's rooms, it is as a sign of respect for unqualified jobs.

The head of human resources of the hotel group will say: "It's really giving back dignity to the small jobs that are essential for our activity. It's placing the basic jobs at the center of our business project".

Unlike role-playing games in training sessions, close to simulation games, role-reversal games are much more flexible in their reference to "reality". Their aim is not being trained for an activity, just because this activity is not the player's.[9] Here, the question of the other's place is central: playing the other's role is supposed to allow for better understanding, recognition and proximity. But we may see that it is also a substitution process that creates the opportunity to think from the other's vantage point instead of thinking with him or her.

The Functions of the Role-Playing Game Mechanisms

As Jean-Marie Schaeffer does, I wish to ponder on what impact fiction—as part of the gamification process—may have on reality: what does it alter in terms of behaviors, relationships, or representations? "The essential question isn't that of the relations between fiction and reality; the question is rather to understand how the fiction operates in reality, that is to say in our lives" (Schaeffer 1999, 212). In other words, game, as a metaphor, would seem to evolve from experience but would be, in principle, both valid and wrong because it would be referring to reality while actually not being reality. Therefore, we may wonder what is at stake in the use of such devices in workplaces, as we know that games are not fictitious. Moreover, the kinds of games played in business contexts are still work, and the other players are the player's colleagues.

Considering this "non-game context", what I have studied seems to suggest that the game is a powerful tool for "working the work":

- In the training game sessions I have analyzed, the play frame defines a space where failure is possible. In the work frame, performance and speed are required. In the play frame, one is allowed to fail, to repeat without having to face the consequences it would create in "real" work situations. The play frame is a space for experimentation. Different attempts are experimented about how to do something, what to say, how to behave or act in front of colleagues or employees;
- It also creates a situation of evaluation between peers. In the training sessions, trainees have the same hierarchical level. Evaluation and rating are continuous. You are led to evaluate yourself, to evaluate colleagues

and even if things may become a little acrimonious at times ("I will say that in your 360-degree feedback" says a manager to another), it is better tolerated than in "real life" as evaluation constitutes the game and "naturally" follows the performance;
- Norms are introduced through the game: first, we fail or we succeed. It is the case in all the games I have studied. These failures and successes contribute to the evaluation process. During role-reversal days, in training sessions or in reality shows, the question, "How does it have to be done?" becomes an overriding one. In training sessions, it is possible to do it again and again until it is properly done: actions and beings have to be perfected but standardized.
- Games, as they create a metaphorical or fictional frame, generate a fictionalization of work situations. What is fictional is an executive playing the role of a maid, the reality of the experience (because of the lack of time, for example). But role-playing games are supposed to give access to the "real life" of colleagues or employees. Furthermore, a playful relationship to work is put forward by the management. This can be interpreted in two ways: on the one hand, work contexts and hierarchical relationships are presented as a game; on the other hand, people are required to see interferences with everyone's activity—how do we do, how do we interact—as a game. Games in that sense seem to have a political function. What is transmitted is a political discourse about companies where work is a pleasure, that is to say where we can have fun and where hierarchical relations are smooth. A place where we could play as equals;
- At the same time it presents work contexts as unpredictable, relationships as made up of antagonisms, adversity as fun and business roles as something to be performed or played;
- I have noticed in a previous paper (Savignac 2011) how games, enacting as they do an inversion of roles and hierarchical places, are similar in structure with fairy tales. It is particularly noticeable in TV reality shows where the executives courageously face the hidden reality of their companies and reverse preconceptions and situations. They always succeed, at the end of the show, in gaining the gratitude and admiration of their employees;
- All this points to the transformative power of games. Games would be performative: it would help change people's behaviors and especially their representations of one's role, of the hierarchy, and of the undervalued jobs. By playing simulation games, it would also help people to move from ignorance to knowledge, from distance to proximity and from authority to equality.

In conclusion, one could say that there is a shift between the map and the territory and that the freedom and creativity supposed to be part of games are somewhat modified in business contexts. What appears is that games sometimes seem to generate more constraints than reality: the rules of the game and the rules of status interact. The role given to someone has to be rigorously followed, work processes showed in the game may be publicly controlled and commented on, trainers are allowed to jostle the players, managers may fiddle unrestrainedly with their subordinates' computers and the way roles are swapped means a lot about who, in companies, is replaceable or not.

By Way of Conclusion: A Discussion about the Links between Gamification and about What Games Are Supposed to Produce

After having shown that role-playing games are intrinsically a performative or operative structure, I wish to return to the thought underlying the gamification thesis that games are productive. For Jane Mc Gonigal (2011), for example, game is a "solution", a "remedy", a "way to intervene in" social issues as work issues. According to her, games are supposed, when they are good, to be "a unique way of structuring experience and provoking positive emotion. It is an extremely powerful tool for inspiring participation and motivating hard work" (McGonigal 2011, 33). She adds that games create involvement, coordination qualities and long-time concentration and open access to the "flow" experience[10] (Csikszentmihalyi 1996). The question of engaging employees' attention underlies much of the literature about gamification in business. Games have supposedly the advantage of giving unconscious skills to the players: "Games can provide a new way to engage employees while teaching them, even when they are not aware that they are being taught" (Edery and Mollick 2009, 97).

These arguments about what games may produce underlie the thought that companies should use gamification for their management or business. It is consistent with previous research in the sociology of work about the uses of games in the workplaces. Several researchers[11] have pointed out that workers played on their workplaces. For Michael Burawoy (1979), it is the games organized by workers in the manufacturing plant he studied that creates the conditions of productivity. Games give to the workers the opportunity of escaping routine and boredom. It gives them "relative satisfactions" (Burawoy 1979, 80) that repress the workers' potential desire to stop the process of production. It maintains their productivity or even increases it (that explains why the management tolerates these games). Other social sciences researchers have shown how games might be a resource for the activity of work. Christophe Dejours (1993) and Dominique Dessors (1991) showed how playing a game of scrabble created for the workers in a petrochemical industry the proper conditions for controlling the machines they had to monitor (as it lowers the level of psychological stress and creates the proper conditions for hearing the machines). In these two examples, games are organized by the workers and the management tolerates it.

In the case of the games I have studied, they have the specificity of being "mandatory games" (with reference to the concept of "Mandatory fun" developed by Mollick and Rothbard 2014). They are not controlled by the employees. Therefore, having fun, developing positive emotions or being committed to one's work all depend on the individuals' goodwill, something that is far from being guaranteed.[12] As Mollick and Rothbard (2014) showed in their field experiment, "If workers consented to the game, gamification significantly increased their positive affect. A failure to consent to the game, moreover, resulted in a decrease in positive affect, as well as a marginal decrease in job performance, indicating that mandatory fun created a double-edged sword. (. . .) Consent is not just about participation and engagement, it is also about the belief that managerial goals are legitimate, appropriate and just and entails an active acceptance of such goals" (Mollick and Rothbard 2014, 35–37).

Moreover, what education sciences researchers have shown is that the links between games and learning are far from obvious. First, a learning process cannot be merely considered as something that is transmitted, as it requires the active participation of the learner (Albrecht 2009; Lavigne 2013). Second, what is learnt in games may fall short of what has to be learnt. Researchers as Brougère (1997) or Berry (2009) argue that the kind of learning gained is informal and refer to the concept of "situated learning" (a kind of learning that is included in the experience of game but that does not exceed it).

Considering these arguments and my own research, what can we infer about the effectiveness or even the meaning given to the implementation of games mechanisms into a nongame context such as a work context? What was obvious to me when studying the role-playing games mechanisms, such as the frame, the role and the fiction, is that games provide a symbolic system of representation. This system, made possible by the secluded space of the play frame, defines what is a team, a competition, a person suffering from burnout or a manager. What is "naturally" introduced in this "acting as if" system are rules, evaluation, showing to one's colleagues one's own way of doing things as well as models. Games impose their own paradigms—about what is at stake (and what is left out of the picture), what is one's proper role, or what is the right or the wrong way of doing things or behaving. They tell a story about competitors who have become game players with whom we play or about hierarchies abolished in the game. It provides an additional space to the workplace where transgressive desires and social norms could combine.

Notes

1. Madrid, November 2015.
2. To such extent that some of them urged their colleagues to "stop obsessing over the definition of gamification" ("and instead focus on making lives better and jobs more efficient")—Siddesh Bhobbe, CEO of a gamification platform.
3. Co-led Research at the Disruptive Media Learning Lab (DMLL), Coventry University, UK.

*   GWC2015 speaker
4. I may observe that "fun" is part and parcel of the assumptions about what a game is supposed to be like, which leads us back to the debate about game theories.

*   GWC2015 speaker
5. Business theatre companies were created in Canada in the 1980s, and provide training sessions. The "concept" of this business is to perform a play based on work situations such as conflicts, negotiation, recruitment . . . in companies for people who need to be trained to management, selling, etc.
6. "La gueule de l'emploi" (2011), Didier Cros, Zadig productions.
7. "La mise à mort du travail" (2009), Jean-Robert Viallet, YAMI Production.
8. I met one case where the CEO left his place to one of his employees. But a certain number of names were taken off beforehand from the random draw. The employee had a task list and was prevented from accessing the CEO's computer and files.
9. As such, I suggest that the order of the hierarchical places is reasserted.
10. One could define the flow as a state of full concentration, involvement and satisfaction in doing an activity.
11. As for example Roy (1959), Burawoy (1979), Dessors (1991), Dejours (1993), Sherman (2007), Dujarier (2015).
12. It was obvious in my observations that a certain number of the people who participated in the games voiced some reservations about the games. I was able to observe a marked physical distance and silence during the role-playing games sessions. For example, in two cases, two persons ostensibly evinced their rejection of the game by reading a newspaper or working on their computer. Another one told me his feeling of "humiliation." During a reversal day, one of the employees told me that she felt angry to have to take part in this.

References

Albrecht Florence. 2009. "Autorité et liberté: la ruse pédagogique", Les conférences philosophiques de l'IUFM de Nice, Université de Nice Sophia Antipolis.

Bateson, Gregory. 1972. *Steps to an Ecology of Mind: Collected Essays in Anthropology, Psychiatry, Evolution, and Epistemology*. Chicago: University Of Chicago Press.

Bogost, Ian. 2014. "Why gamification is bullshit" in *The Gameful World: Approaches, Issues, Applications*, edited by S. P. Walz and S. Deterding. Cambridge: The MIT Press, 65–79.

Brougère, Gilles. 1997. "Jeu et objectifs pédagogiques: une approche comparative de l'éducation préscolaire". *Revue française de pédagogie* 119: 47–56.

Brougère, Gilles. 2005. *Jouer/Apprendre*. Paris: Economica.

Burawoy, Michael. 1979. *Manufacturing Consent: Changes in the Labor Process under Monopoly Capitalism*. Chicago: University of Chicago Press.

Caillois, Roger. 1967. *Les jeux et les hommes*. Paris: Gallimard.

Csikszentmihalyi, Mihaly. 1996. *Flow and the Psychology of Discovery and Invention*. New York: Harper Collins.

Dejours, Christophe. 1993. "Intelligence pratique et sagesse pratique: deux dimensions méconnues du travail réel." *Éducation permanente* 116: 47–70.

Dessors, Dominique. 2009 [1991]. "L'intelligence pratique". *Travailler* 21: 61–68.

Deterding, Sebastian, Dixon, Dan, Khaled, Rilla, & Nacke, Lennart. 2011. "From Game Design Elements to Gamefulness: Defining Gamification". *Proceedings*

of the 15th International Academic MindTrek Conference: Envisioning Future Media Environments. ACM: 9–15, Tampere.
Dubar, Tripier. 1998. *Sociologie des professions*. Paris: Armand Colin.
Dujarier Marie-Anne. 2015. *Le management désincarné*. Paris: La Découverte.
Goffman, Erving. 1959. *The Presentation of Everyday Life*. New York: Anchor Books.
Goffman, Erving. 1961. *Encounters: Two Studies in the Sociology of Interaction*. Mansfield: Martino Publishing, CT.
Goffman, Erving. 1974. *Frame Analysis: An Essay on the Organization of Experience*. Cambridge: Harvard University Press.
Groos, Karl. 1898 (1896). *The Play of Animals*. New York: Appleton.
Hamayon, Roberte. 2012. *Jouer. Une étude anthropologique*. Paris: La Découverte.
Henriot, Jacques. 1989. *Sous couleur de jouer. La métaphore ludique*. Paris: José Corti.
Huizinga, Johan. 1951 (1938). *Homo ludens. Essai sur la fonction sociale du jeu*. Paris: Gallimard.
Lavigne, Michel. 2013. "Jeu, éducation et numérique—Approche critique des propositions logicielles pour l'éducation, du ludo-éducatif aux serious games". *Approches critiques des TIC éducatives* 14: 49–71.
Linton, Ralph. 1936. *The Study of Man*. New York: Appleton-Century-Crofts.
McGonigal, Jane. 2011. *Reality is Broken: Why Games Make Us Better and How They Can Change the World*. New York: Penguin books.
Mollick, Ethan R. and Rothbard, Nancy. 2014. *Mandatory Fun: Consent, Gamification and the Impact of Games at Work*. The Wharton School Research Paper Series, University of Pennsylvania, Philadelphia.
Mollick, Ethan R. and Werbach, Kevin. 2014. "Gamification and the Enterprise". In *The Gameful World*, edited by Steffen P. Walz and Sebastian Deterding, 439–458. Cambridge: The MIT Press.
Piette, Albert. 1997. "Pour une anthropologie comparée des rituels contemporains. Rencontre avec les batesoniens". *Terrain* 29: 139–150.
Raessens, Joost. 2006. "Playful Identities, or the Ludification of Culture". *Games and Culture* 1: 52–57.
Robertson, Margaret. 2010. "Can't Play, Won't Play". *Hide & Seek* 6. hideandseek. net/2010/10/06/cant-play-wont-play/.
Roy, Donald. 1959. "'Banana Time': Job Satisfaction and Informal Interaction". *Human Organization* 18/4: 158–168.
Savignac, Emmanuelle. 2011. "Il était une fois . . . mon patron à ma place. Renversement des hiérarchies et morphologie du conte". *Jeunes et médias* 1: 79–93.
Schaeffer, Jean-Marie. 1999. *Pourquoi la fiction*. Paris: Seuil.
Sherman, Rachel. 2007. *Class Acts: Service and Inequality in Luxury Hotels*. Oakland: University of California Press.
Winicott, Donald W. 1975 (1971). *Jeu et réalité. L'espace potential*. Paris: Gallimard.

2 Feeding the RedCritter
The Gamification of Project Management Software

Raul Ferrer Conill

During the last decades there has been a steady reconfiguration of production processes in which large and medium-size companies have evolved into project-based organizations (Evaristo and Van Fenema 1999; Jansson and Ljung 2004), often working with geographically dispersed employees, or as Lipnack and Stamps (1997) call them, virtual teams. This global transformation derives from technological advancements and the need for flexible units that are capable to address decompartmentalized working processes across space and time (Bell and Kozlowski 2002). Yet, as managerial and administrative organizational processes have majorly turned dislocated and digital, the efforts to engage and motivate employees have become a challenge (Crawford, LePine, and Rich 2010). The issue of employee satisfaction and engagement has become a vibrant topic within organizational management and has produced extensive scholarly debate (Harter, Schmidt, and Hayes 2002; Gubman 2004). Increasingly, studies link employee engagement to performance and productivity (Saks 2006; Lockwood 2007).

Against this challenge there have been efforts to incorporate game mechanics into working processes with the attempt to increase employee motivation. The gamification of everything movement as advocated by several champions (see McGonigal 2011; Paharia 2013; Zichermann and Linder 2013; Herger 2014) is often offered as the panacea that is meant to solve engagement problems in all fronts. This rhetoric is often accompanied by celebratory, pompous, and overly optimistic vibes, having an impact on the way we perceive work and leisure, and inviting the pervasive adoption of gamification within several aspects of daily life. And while project management—and most specifically virtual project management—finds in motivation a true challenge and thus is a great candidate of gamified approaches, several other voices raise the question of gamification as a causal force of potential negative effects on employees. As new norms and casual rewards are transferred to the workplace, a procedure and mode that become a pattern of control can be imposed (Robertson 2010; Bogost 2011; DeWinter and Kocurek 2014; Poltronieri 2014).

This chapter argues that the celebratory narrative on gamification, especially when applied to business and management processes, suffers from a biased managerial perspective focusing on potential benefits and very seldom addresses the issues deriving from gamifying working environments. Most notably, the gamification rhetoric promises a world in which the borders between work and play are blurred, and where users and employees are more engaged, more satisfied, and most importantly, more productive (McGonigal 2011). Yet the problem of worker engagement *vis à vis* the circles of inclusion and alienation that working dynamics imprint in employees is often absent within the main body of literature. The focus here lays in the clash of logics that support gamification, as well as the (un)intended consequences of gamifying business processes. Thus, this chapter aims to provide a nuanced analysis of gamification and to critically reflect on how some of its promised virtues are contradicted by its actual implementation, raising the question of resistance, surveillance, and control. To achieve this I turn to the gamified project management service RedCritter Tracker as a critical case study, by studying its use of gamification techniques as an attempt to enhance employee engagement and motivation, but ultimately to increase productivity. The aim is to bring a critical discussion on the tensions between the business gamification logics by analyzing promised rhetoric, business objectives, and actual implementation.

Motivation in Agile Project Management

Increasingly, technology-driven organizations and particularly software-developing companies have started to opt for a streamlined adaptation of project management called Agile Project Management (Hass 2007). Agile methodology aims to reduce the scope and complexity of a project by dividing each project into small segments, focusing on continuous and iterative improvement as well as maximizing flexibility and team input within the process (Schwaber 2004). Incidentally, the concerns in which Agile dwells draw parallels with video games and the way in which most video games represent the narrative of the game: breaking down a story into stages or levels, provide feedback on the player's progress throughout the story, and enhance the experience (or become better) as the player advances in the game (Fernández-Vara 2015). Further in gaming parallelisms, the team is run by the scrum master, who is responsible for supporting the development team and maintaining the collaboration process active, as well as steering the group within the frame of the project (Highsmith 2009; Gustavsson 2014).

When looking at the actual practices of agile project management, the most surprising feature revolves around daily short meetings in which post-it notes are frantically moved around a board. These meetings are one of the cores of Agile and provide almost constant feedback and a picture of progress within the project as well as a hub for enhancing team dynamics. The mere action of moving post-its acts as main motivational drive (Jansson 2015). This is such a landmark characteristic for agile project management that software intended to run agile projects digitally has tried to mimic the post-its transitions. However, dislocated projects—also known as virtual project management—have found that the high impact that meetings have on the cohesion and motivation of the team is difficult to recreate digitally, which poses a serious threat for dislocated organizational cultures (Sutherland et al. 2007).

This challenge becomes particularly important in the global economy, where the adoption of virtual projects has constantly increased. The global scope as a basic drive for business development supposes a large set of inherent organizational benefits, such as a larger pool of workforce skills, access to talent, long active working shifts with dispersed teams, internalization of software, centered virtual knowledge base, smaller sites, reduced international investment, and lower labor costs by reaching lower-wage markets (Hertel, Geister, and Konradt 2005). The internal capitalist logic of choosing a dislocated organization boosts needs for redefining motivational approaches.

The idiosyncrasies of virtual projects allow organizations to surpass the constraints of geographical distance, time zones, and cultural differences; however, they are not deprived of specific challenges. It is harder for virtual teams to be successful than traditional teams (Reed and Knight 2010). One of the reasons is the difficulty to create an inviting environment and to foster cohesion and motivation within the team, directly affected by the lack of face-to-face interaction (Pazderka and Grechenig 2007). The positive motivating effects of agile procedure are lost due to dislocation, even if displacement carries certain benefits for employees. A 1,000+ respondent survey created by Wrike, Inc., shows that the top three benefits identified are time savings (41 percent), increased productivity (29 percent), and the opportunity to focus on work, rather than office politics (10 percent). On the other hand, the main challenges identified by those respondents are lack of direct communication (38 percent), hindered data accessibility (21 percent), and bad visibility into colleagues' actions (19 percent) (Filev 2013). These challenges can be operationalized as lack of engagement and motivation within dislocated teams, since direct communication, data feedback, and overall project progress are some of the main motivators for workers (Amabile and Kramer 2011).

The Motivation of Progress

The problem with conceptualizing the idea of motivation lies in its multifaceted nature. Several studies on workforce motivation discuss a complex mixture of psychological, behavioral, cognitive, and social features (Tampoe and Thurloway 1993; Gordon Rouse 2004; Dwivedula and Bredillet 2010; Jansson and Ljung 2011; Oyedele 2013). Modern theories of working drive include other aspects, such as goal-setting (Latham and Locke 1991), organizational justice (Greenberg 1990; Latham and Pinder 2005), participatory decision making (Latham, Locke, and Fassina 2002), and social cognitive theory (Bandura 2002). Deci and Ryan's (1985) self-determination theory (SDT) conceptualizes motivation as a state affected by a dual typology of motivational sources: intrinsic motivators and extrinsic motivators.

One of the overarching themes in the literature is a clear relationship between performance and efficacy, and the acknowledgment of progress within the workplace, triggering higher states of motivation (Seiler et al. 2012). This theme is the center of Amabile and Kramer's (2011) *The Progress Principle*. Through the examination of hundreds of diary entries by workers who detailed the happenings of everyday work life, the authors conclude that meaningful work and the sensation of progress are the major motivators for employees. The sense of accomplishment leads to a positive inner work life, creating a loop of progress that feeds itself through self-reinforcement. When progress is acknowledged more often and in smaller iterations—what the authors call *small wins*—it has a longer-standing effect in boosting inner work life. Amabile and Kramer conclude that external rewards and punishments, in the current context of the knowledge economy, are ineffective motivators. Employee needs have evolved; the motivational style of most organizations has not (Ariely, Bracha, and Meier 2009; Pink 2009). Thus, the evolution in working processes, facilitated by the advancements in technology, has rendered traditional forms of motivating dispersed teams obsolete for a good part of the industrialized world. Once again, parallels between the business logics and the rewarding systems incorporated within video games can be traced (Zackariasson and Wilson 2012). Providing the sensation of *progress*, as Amabile and Kramer sustain, and fostering the notions of *autonomy*, *mastery*, and *relatedness* as self-determination theory propones are practices that video games have incorporated in their narratives for a long time. The current organizational trend tries to incorporate those motivators through gamification.

Alarmingly, research on the effects of gamification in project management settings is almost nonexistent (Aseriskis and Damasevicius 2014). Nevertheless, the parallels between the challenges of virtual project management and the capacities of video games serve as a linear narrative to support the use of gamification within project management. However, as it is discussed in the following section, merging the spheres of work and play does not happen frictionlessly, and it is a much more problematic endeavor than what is hinted by the proponents of enterprise gamification.

All Play and No Work . . .

It is difficult to imagine Jack Torrance swaying into the emotional state that sets off the tortuous developments in Stanley Kubrik's adaptation of *The Shining* had he been playing instead of working. If anything, the lines on his text might very well have been, "All play and no work make Jack an irrelevant boy".

The negotiations between play and work have been present in scholarly writing long before the new interests on modern gamification emerged. Dutch historian Huizinga, in his seminal book *Homo Ludens* (1938), theorizes about the role of play in human culture. The controversial *magic circle* delineates the borders between game and everyday life as a temporary arena that transcends the usual aspects of life. While Huizinga used the notion of the magic circle as the physical space for playing, or the demarcation in which mundane activities are incorporated with special meanings, Salen and Zimmerman (2004) discuss the magic circle as a transformation of place as it becomes embedded with the rules of the game, thus departing from the rules that apply outside of the game, as a fluid space that can be applied in different contexts. This is where the ubiquitous definition of gamification by Deterding et al. (2011:a) as *the use of game design elements in non-game contexts* incorporates the notion that play can be embedded in any environment, including work. However, the liminality of play, as a symbolic representation of explicitly arbitrary symbols that summon pleasure within the magic circle, presupposes play as a temporary ritual significantly differentiated from reality (Murray 2013). Play and work influence each other, providing meaning to each other, and in a way they could not be understood independently as two unrelated frameworks, or harmonized as one single entity. The logics that drive both frameworks collide. According to Huizinga, on the one hand play is a free-willing activity, not imposed or coerced (2013: 7), while on the other hand when play becomes a mere utility and *business concerns deliberately instill the play-spirit into their workers so as to step up production (. . .) play becomes business* (2013: 200). Thus, both aspects strive for diametrically opposed experiences. The former, the playful logic attempts to enhance joy of playfulness, or what Csíkszentmihályi (1990) conceptualized as *flow*. The latter, the business logic uses playfulness to accomplish business objectives. It subjects play to commercial goals by appropriating game stimuli and inducing playful sensations to employees. This problematizes the use of gamification within business processes and raises questions of the potential benefits and dangers of gamification. The question raised here is which is the logic that predominantly guides the gamified design?

It is worth mentioning that the conflicting nature of these logics does not necessarily mean they are purely binary. While the purpose of this chapter is to investigate the core of each logic, it is acknowledged that the tensions between logics are often negotiated in a way that both are coexistent in different degrees. Therefore, this discussion is done at two levels: on the one hand by looking at the overt intended effect of gamification on the worker, which is normally advertised as empowering; and on the other hand on the covert effect of gamification from the organization's perspective, which is not openly advertised and is often subjected to organizational goals.

Playful Work with Gamification

The optimist reasoning behind the application of gamification in web-based systems is to enhance engagement, grant choices, reaffirm progression, and provoke social habit (Zichermann and Linder 2010; Werbach and Hunter 2012). Applied to virtual project management software, incorporating game elements in a system attempts not only to engage team members, but also provide a sense of progress as well as helping members create the habit of using the software regularly. Successfully designed gamified software has the potential to overcome some of the main challenges that virtual projects face: facilitating communication and keeping information about other team members' actions available (Aseriskis and Damasevicius 2014). In addition, a gamified system could provide the arena where automated features as well as other team members can motivate each other, creating a sense of camaraderie. This is particularly important, as it widens the sources by which an individual receives motivational inputs by granting technology nonhuman agency and considering it a persuasive social actor (Fogg 2002) by utilizing affordances that enhance user agency (Van Dijck 2009).

Games provide specific gratifications, but most importantly they immerse the users within experiences that fulfill psychological needs that intrinsically motivate them to seek more interactions with the medium (Przybylski, Rigby, and Ryan 2010; Tamborini et al. 2010). Translating the capacities of games into other tasks is what gamification attempts, reinforcing different motivators to daily activities (Werbach and Hunter 2012). Reviewing a series of experiments on extrinsic and intrinsic motivators, Deci, Koestner, and Ryan (1999) encountered three common factors that induce intrinsic motivation, which is the motivation that is enacted internally as a reaction to performing an activity. These factors are competence (the users' sense of ability, they are accomplishing something), autonomy (the users feel in control, providing a sense of meaningful choices), and relatedness (the activity is related to something beyond the user's self). These traits are found specifically in virtual environments and games (McGonigal 2011; Deterding et al. 2011:b). Contextualized within virtual teams, a user is expected to be competent to perform the tasks at hand, but also to use the technology involved in the process. The employee is expected to be autonomous, as the face-to-face interaction is minimal or nonexistent. Finally, each team member is expected to have a sense of relatedness, as the team has bigger objectives than those of the individual members.

This premise is a powerful one. It gives room for a potentiality of an amplification of Amabile and Kramer's (2011) concept of small wins. By applying gamification techniques to projectware, every small win remains small, but the effects are amplified by gamification. The recurrent experience of small wins is expected to generate engagement, prompting the social habit of using the system more often, and thus progress is experienced exponentially. The narrative behind this iterative development is generating a loop of progress, which in itself drives motivation.

Furthermore, besides fostering motivation, one of the most interesting features of gamification is that it tends to mix intrinsic and extrinsic motivators, relying on constant feedback, focusing on the users' actions, and adding a balance of rewards and fun that fosters intrinsic motivation (Nicholson

2015). When designed meaningfully, it uses all the spectrum of motivators in a playful way to provide a fun and engaging experience, all included within the system itself. This particularity has the potential to distribute some of the responsibilities of motivating the team from the team leader to the members and the software.

Controlling Work with Gamification

The recent popularity of gamification can be understood within the context of technological advancements that allow for quantifying users' behaviors, collecting and analyzing data, and automatically presenting feedback to the user, accompanied by a societal change in which the ubiquity and pervasiveness of games have been incorporated as elements of everyday life. This implies a systematic proliferation of digital networked devices such as mobile devices that attempt to capture younger generations' responses to new stimuli and motivations, such as video games.

In this sense, precisely as Fuchs (2014) argues, gamification is becoming an ideology in which processes that are anchored within the ruling system are streamlined and enhanced by the use of unconscious motivational conducts. With the promise of fun, the current established neo-liberal economic principles and routines are perpetuated with a congratulatory cheer. Paraphrasing Foucault (as cited in Van Dijck 2013) "operation is not ensured by right but by *technique*, not by law but by *normalization*, not by punishment but by *control*" (p. 19), the sociotechnical norms created by the perpetual connectivity is embedded in daily practices as new habits and affordances slowly erode notions such as privacy, monetization, and freedom.

The ethnographic work of Czarniawska (2011) illustrates how, in the case of knowledge workers, the transition to digital networked environments has transformed the factory into a new often-dislocated working paradigm (*cyberfactories*), which resembles chain production, with its norms and modalities embedded in the sociocultural system: taught in universities and reinforced in the job market arena. The structural capitalist appropriation of play leads to reframing working culture anchored in a new mode of scientific management, or as DeWinter, Kocurek, and Nichols (2014) call it, *Taylorism 2.0*. Data-driven interfaces based on quantification intertwine labor logics with gameplay logics with the attempt of merging the roles of workers and players into one unified model. The problem here is the underlying reason for bringing both logics together. On the one hand it could be understandable that organizations care for the well-being of their workforce; on the other hand it is even more reasonable to believe that the commercial drive of companies sees gamification as an opportunity for increasing productivity, and at the same time incorporating automatic surveilling strategies that feed data back into the production processes enhancing managerial control.

Not incidentally Huotari and Hamari (2012) insightfully define gamification as:

> *"(. . .) a form of service packaging where a core service is enhanced by a rules-based service system that provides feedback and interaction mechanisms to the user with an aim to facilitate and support the users' overall value creation."*

This definition, taken from the perspective of service management, abides by a discourse tightly connected to business logic, deprived from the notion of games, play, or fun. The question of allegiance of the gamified initiative is rapidly determined, a fact that is usually underrepresented in the current gamification discourse. However, the idea of using game mechanics within a working environment for the sole purpose of pushing a productivity agenda carries in itself certain morally grey areas. The overt attempt to pair work and play is met with the covert introduction of enhanced surveillance (Whitson 2013), as well as potential exploitative practices by rewarding coworkers for performing better than their counterparts (Terranova 2000), as well as mixing playful practices as a part of the working processes, also known as *playbor* (Kücklich 2005; Rey 2012). Instead of using game techniques to meaningfully redesign working processes, these are incorporated in order to reinforce the business goals and enhance employee control.

RedCritter and the Gamification of Project Management

In order to investigate the tensions between the business objectives of agile project management software and the motivation goals of gamification, this book chapter examines the case of RedCritter. RedCritter Tracker is the first project management software that introduces gamification techniques as a main feature to engage team members and to tackle issues of employee motivation and productivity. Prior to the appearance of RedCritter, one of the few specifically motivational features of project software was a third party add-on to project management software Podio, the *Happy Pack* app. This app, created by Kjerulf (2012), includes features like the High-five, We rock, and the Happy-o-meter, which is meant to be *a simple way to gauge if people are happy or unhappy at work*. Kjerulf's description of his own app denotes a sincere attempt to motivate and brighten workers' daily tasks, no matter how naïve the approach is. It is up to debate whether a *Happy-o-meter* would have a relevant impact in an environment where workers could feel discouraged to openly show discontent with the organization. This is particularly relevant at a time when controversy over poor labor conditions stem from sociotechnical interactions that make workers feel diminished and alienated when "playful" interactions are incorporated to the working environment; protests against programs like Amazon´s *Mechanical Turk*

(Harris 2014) or Disney's use of the so-called *electronic whip* (Allen 2011) challenge the notion that playful and game-like affordances will lead to an empowered workforce. In fact, such techniques are internalized by workers as a corporate overreach, reinforcing the feeling of being watched, controlled, and oppressed.

Deconstructing the RedCritter

RedCritter Tracker follows the architectural design of an integrated system, in which the software combines and merges project management target functionality as well as game mechanics. It is not surprising that RedCritter advertising accentuates the fact that the tool is the only project management service based on gamification. *It works for multiple teams or even individuals. RedCritter Tracker is the only project management service with badges, rewards, leaderboards and real-time Twitter-style feeds* (www.redcrittertracker.com). However, there is little explanation on how these elements are embedded in the system, or how these features are meant to motivate users.

Setting up a RedCritter account has a relatively steep learning curve. Interestingly, the first feature that needs to be set up is the Reward Store. This approach presents certain problems, which stem from the fact that it is unclear what the rewards are for. Regardless, rewards are central to the system, and they are divided into Reward Points, which can be exchanged for physical rewards offered by each company, and digital artefacts in the forms of badges. There are fifty badges created by RedCritter that are given to team members as they accomplish specific tasks within the system. Once the reward system is set up, the program functionality becomes standard project management software. Each team member is assigned with skills that are quickly displayed in the list of employees along with the achievements obtained after completing tasks. This is an attempt to create a quick graphical representation that aids team formation.

The interface attempts to resemble an agile board, reinforcing the affordance of moving tasks as they are being developed within drag and drop lists. Communication and coordination are taken care by twitter-style message feeds. The dashboard view offers a quick overview of project and organizational progress, and other features, such as approval workflow, synchronized displays, task-level time tracking, report view, and email configurations. These features are usually found in project management software, and thus, are not specific to RedCritter. Communication flows and team coordination, as well as project progression, are integrated in the interface. Interactive reports and the automatic time-tracking feature facilitate the managerial task. However, while sprints and tasks are dealt in the traditional manner, the scrum master deals with team cohesion on a virtual space, which can take a toll on the team motivation. This is where the gamification layer comes in, becoming RedCritter's distinctive feature.

Badges, Rewards, and Incentivation

The defining feature of RedCritter Tracker is the gamification interface promising to engage workers. A set of fifty badges and Reward Points are the two reward systems aim to incentivize behaviors and performance of employees in exchange for automatic tokens of appreciation.

The badges are triggered by specific actions and become graphic representations of an achievement. They aim to provide status within the team and offer a quick overview of top performers. Incidentally, the fifty badges are predefined by the system and are non-customizable. This suggests that the design of this gamified feature is connected to the working processes and not designed to fit the workers' needs. RedCritter does an innovative take on badges, having expiring badges, which need to be earned regularly in order to retain them. The system also incorporates single-owner badges, which can only be owned by a single employee at a time. This characteristic affords the competitive drive in the system, introducing the game narrative usually associated with leaderboards (Werbach and Hunter 2012).

The tasks or activities awarded with badges are very different. Best practices are awarded with badges such as Champion, Persistent, Multi-tasker, Chatter box, or Idea guy. Personality-based badges aim to personalize users with badges such as Night owl, Early bird, Photogenic, or Fashion conscious. Additionally, there is a group of badges that incentivize activities that are questionable for the interests of the employee, for example Shark (for taking tasks from the backlog), Goto Guy (for completing more tasks than anyone), Weekend warrior (for working on weekends), Hot Pockets (for working through lunch), Marathoner (for booking the most hours in the last 7 days), or Dedicated (for working 60 hours or more in the last 7 days). Finally, there are badges linked to activity within the Reward Store, like the Shopper newbie (for buying the first Reward Store item) or the Cheapskate (for buying the least expensive Reward in the Store).

The Reward Store is directly linked to the second reward system of RedCritter, the Reward Points. Managers can incorporate specific value in points for particular tasks. Successfully completing each task will be rewarded with cumulative points. These points can be redeemed for actual real-life prizes or perks displayed in the Store. The prizes in the Store are administered by the organization. This means that the eventual motivating capacity of the Reward Points would be positively related to the actual prizes the users can attain. According to Werbach and Hunter (2012), prizes that appeal to the user can certainly motivate them to engage with the system and be more productive, with increased morale. Prizes that are perceived as condescending and uninteresting, or that are not realistically attainable, can have the contrary effect, demoralizing users and giving the image of an unfair rewarding system.

An additional feature to the RedCritter's reward system is the Accomplishments Directory, which consists of a public display of badges and skills acquired by the worker. This feature can be exported to different platforms, actively embedding work accomplishments and skills into other fora like LinkedIn, Facebook, websites, blogs, or even email signatures.

The Endgame of RedCritter and a Clash of Logics

By looking at how the system incorporates game mechanics, the endgame of the software can be explicated, especially in relation to the tensions and power frictions between organizational goals and team workers' well-being. The concept of "endgame" within game studies refers to the point within the system in which the user has reached the end of the grind and where even if the game actually does not end, continuing playing does not motivate or engage the player. In a gamified system, the endgame is the process by which the user transcends from the gamification reward system into the non-game environment (Nicholson 2014). Without a properly laid out endgame strategy, the user remains entangled in processes that require extrinsic stimuli to remain motivated, always embedded in the grind of the system. Instead, a meaningful approach incorporating reflection, exposition, choice, information, play, and engagement (Nicholson 2015) based on the user's need can lead to intrinsic engagement with the activity, leading to a successful endgame of the gamified strategy. Thus, if gamification is to uphold its celebratory promises, I argue that the endgame of gamification should meaningfully redefine an activity so that performing the activity itself becomes a playful experience.

And this is the problem with the current trend in gamification of business. The endgame is not the objective. The objective is the grind. The stimulus of the reward is the effect intended and not really the creation of affordances that create gameful experiences (Deterding 2014). In the example of RedCritter, points and badges are only rewarded after a task has been achieved. The intention is to create a stimulus after a trigger instead of making the actual tasks playful. Which brings us back to the discrepancies between work and play. Meaningful gamification, as it has been commented, requires a choice taken by the player, but when working within an organization that runs RedCritter, the choice disappears and the player is *forced* to play. The opt-out waiver tends to lead to unemployment.

This happens because there is a clash of logics. The business of gamification prioritizes business objectives. The decision to gamify business processes is often taken by management, not employees. Sales, revenues, and profit are the logic that supports the enterprise. Even for an organization that is truly concerned about the well-being of the workforce, the endgame of their *engagement* strategies is to maximize productivity and keep performance inventory of its human resources. However, the playful logic of gamification prioritizes different values closer to autonomy, mastery, and relatedness, which are the core of SDT (Przybylski, Rigby, and Ryan 2010). Empowerment through meaningful, gameful experiences fosters user agency

(Nicholson 2015). But when the game is not a choice but a chore, user agency cannot be enacted. In fact, as Conway (2014) supports, a diminished agency caused by coercive participation endangers the notions that the very game mechanics attempt to generate. Tasks are assigned to team members by managers, which questions autonomy; skills and achievements are compared between team members, generating conflict that may not be fair nor friendly, which questions relatedness; competing against overworked team members, a regular employee can feel that what is required to succeed is out of reach, questioning mastery. The precedence of priorities is usually biased towards metrics and performance rather than satisfaction and self-realization.

Returning to RedCritter, several examples taken from the badges selection clearly clarify this point. Let's take the Marathoner, Dedicated, or Weekend Warrior badges. The motivation here is aligned with the companies' objectives, not necessarily with the well-being of the employees. The positive reinforcement received by a reward for an accomplishment is overpowered by an achievement that is paradigmatically against the interests of a worker. If an employee wants to collect all badges, she knows that eventually she will have to work more than sixty hours a week, work during lunch, weekends, and at least one hour more than her colleagues. Admittedly, overtime is an incidental byproduct of project labor, and it happens with or without badges. However, perpetuating and reinforcing the business logic of overworking employees while trivializing it and turning it into a motivational practice seems frivolous and unethical, bordering on exploitative. However, within the discourse of a playful game, such an unethical practice becomes normalized with minimal resistance. Similarly, badges like Cheapskate, which attempts to playfully shame users for redeeming reward points in low-price items, could be easily misinterpreted and lead to frustration. Once again, the reinforcement is covertly pushing employees to opt for expensive items that require more points, and hence, more completed tasks.

The homogenization of rewards aims to introduce a degree of transparency and self-reflection that speaks equally to all employees. At the same time it conforms to the narratives within the working tasks and expectations, instead of reframing them and reconceptualizing them to transform the user experience. Once again, this exemplifies the frictions between the goals of a user-oriented gamification and the allegiance to the business objectives. In a similar fashion, the use of graphical representations of workers' achievements may motivate and engage users, providing an instant representation of the users' progress within the project and in the organization. However, this results in a factual trade-off in which workers need to accept a level of surveillance over their work by the organization. Management can track and assess individual labor quantified by RedCritter by micro-analyzing tasks in terms of time, as well as certain social behaviors within the organization. Conversations are recorded and stored at the expense of employee privacy. Furthermore, the content generated and quantified within the system is normally logged by the workers themselves. Once again, the normalization of these practices revives the debate of new scientific management and the emergence of *Taylorism 2.0* (DeWinter, Kocurek, and Nichols 2014). RedCritter as a system becomes a forced and perverted version of Huizinga's (1938/1949) magic circle. Everything that happens within the demarcation of the system receives a new special meaning, embedded with a playful ideal. Following Salen and Zimmerman's (2004) argument, the transformation of place should be substantial so that the rules change the context within the circle. But in RedCritter, the changes are only a mere decoration to practices that remain the same. Thus the fluidity or liminality of RedCritter's digital working space does not separate work from play in order to enact the playful environment. The intrinsic rewards bear too much resemblance to the regular working practice.

One final aspect that illustrates the multifarious values underpinning the gears of RedCritter is the implementation of the accomplishment directory, which not only is present across all the tools and services offered by RedCritter (beyond project management), but also aims to extend the reward system to other networked frameworks used by the employee. This move reinforces the trend of work life trespassing into other fora of everyday life, exemplifying the blurring of boundaries between work and leisure. This feature has three fundamental effects: the open display of the workers' achievements and skills that serve as a personalized real-time portfolio, a showcase of the capacities of the organization using RedCritter as a framework for project management, and most importantly, it is free advertising for RedCritter spread by its users.

In the light of the features discussed in this section, it is difficult to assess who benefits from the gamified layer of RedCritter. I argue that this can be done at three levels. First, the dynamics of labor politics suggest that the main beneficiary is RedCritter as a software service organization. Second, the game mechanics in which users are rewarded for working too hard or too long as well as the micro-controlling practices afforded by the software presupposes that the organization using RedCritter is the one reaping the benefits. Finally, the celebratory rhetoric surrounding gamification would point out that the benefits are placed on the user who has a more rewarding work experience (DeWinter and Kocurek 2014). It could be argued that a gamified system could appease both logics, by empowering users while raising productivity. However, it is hard to argue that RedCritter's framework of rewards and incentives, with badges that celebrate overworking, points that push you to buy expensive items, and a system of surveillance that rewards free advertising, does anything to empower employees.

Conclusions

In this chapter I have attempted to problematize the dynamics of work and play. By using RedCritter Tracker and project management as a case to study the business of gamification, I argue that when the business logic and the playful logic collide, the managerial bias of gamification imposes its rules. The strategies and affordances incorporated in RedCritter Tracker perform admirably in terms of reproducing the work dynamics of agile project management into a digital environment. However, the software merely mimics and reproduces the practices and processes of project management. It has no intention to reformulate working dynamics in a fundamental way so that they appeal to workers, bringing better enjoyment while performing a task as a central core value of the application. Thus, the rewards and gratifications deriving from the gamified structure of RedCritter are layered on top the usual business practices, losing the opportunity of creating valuable and lasting meaning for the employee. Furthermore, surveilling and exploitative strategies emerge, which hint a serious potential for discontent and rejection of the system. The values, norms, and ethics of neoliberal working logic often collide with the logic of play and fun. One could argue that an honest gamified approach would attempt to combine both logics into a mutual endgame where the system engages and empowers employees while at the same time drives behaviors that increase productivity. Redefining working process to suit the motivational needs of workers could lead to multiple real beneficiaries of gamified approaches. Alas, after analyzing RedCritter, it is difficult to make that assessment.

In the current engagement economy, gamification is becoming the cornerstone of organizational employee engagement strategies (Paharia 2013). Services offering gamified enterprise solutions, like RedCritter Tracker, abound, combining several different tactics with the promise of nurturing a happy and motivated workforce. However, this simplistic view on the dynamics between work and play is rather problematic. The fact that work can be fun is undeniable. One could even admit that certain working practices and achievements can lead to Csíkszentmihályi's state of flow if the task is highly challenging and the skill is remarkable. However, this usually requires passion and an intrinsic motivation towards a job. It is questionable that the use of gamification can lead to enhanced and extended sense of motivation for routine labor, especially after considering working dynamics and the modes in which game mechanics are incorporated to current working processes.

Still, it is surprising that a significantly large portion of the gamification rhetoric still conceptualizes gamification as a practice with the end of motivating and engaging users. Similarly, the vast majority of online reviews on RedCritter celebrate the application as an achievement that revolutionizes project management software motivating users with game mechanics. It is rare to find of voices of dissent among the commentators, and the managerial bias of the literature is prevalent. Achieving engaged workers or clients that become more motivated with the organizations' products, services, or working processes is the ultimate objective. However, when defining the goals of gamification, the current rhetoric usually places the user as the beneficiary of the gamification process. Those interacting with the system are supposed to become more engaged, more empowered, and happier.

This case study exemplifies the trend of adopting the notion of gamification as a bandwagon concept in which the use of game mechanics alone is supposed to redefine an activity and engage users (Zichermann and Linder 2013). The trend of gamification has led to rushed implementation that is accepted and welcomed because *it is supposed to be fun*. The positive reputation of games is automatically transferred to business, by which organizations can covertly conduct questionable business processes, under the gamification banner. As long as gamification yields to business logic, the concept will most probably lack the empowering values that most proponents claim. While the mechanical constituents of gamification are in place, it is doubtful that they manage to endow working practices with the intrinsic motivation that Deci and Ryan (1985) propose. Instead, an approach that leans towards the business logic has a higher chance to produce what Lieberoth (2015) calls shallow gamification.

In the future, researchers and practitioners need to work together if they are to foster serious, long-lasting engagement from employees. Frameworks and approaches for meaningful gamification like those suggested by Raftopoulos (2014) or Nicholson (2015) need to be implemented, tested, and studied. If the promise of gamification bringing motivation and meaning to the workforce is to materialize, then new approaches departing from adding meaningless rewards to old practices need to be implemented. Furthermore, a critical analysis of gamified systems is required to discern which logic is most prominent, instead of simply assuming that gamification aims to motivate and engage employees. Otherwise, business gamification will remain as a method that incorporates ephemeral and frivolous rewards in order to keep the workforce feeding the RedCritter.

References

Allen, Frederick E. 2011. "Disneyland uses 'Electronic Whip' on employees." *Forbes*, October 21. Accessed March 15, 2015: http://www.forbes.com/sites/frederickallen/2011/10/21/disneyland-uses-electronic-whip-on-employees/

Amabile, Teresa and Steven Kramer. 2011. *The progress principle: Using small wins to ignite joy, engagement, and creativity at work*. Boston: Harvard Business Review Press.

Ariely, Dan, Anat Bracha, and Stephen Meier. 2009. "Doing good or doing well? Image motivation and monetary incentives in behaving prosocially." *American Economic Review*, 99:1, 544–55.

Aseriskis, Darius and Robertas Damasevicius. 2014. "Gamification of a project management system." In *Proceedings of ACHI 2014, The Seventh International Conference on Advances in Computer-Human Interaction*, 200–7, Barcelona, Spain.

Bandura, Albert. 2002. "Social cognitive theory in cultural context." *Applied Psychology*, 51:2, 269–90.

Bell, Bradford S. and Steve W. J. Kozlowski. 2002. "A typology of virtual teams: Implications for effective leadership." *Group and Organization Management*, 27, 14–49.
Bogost, Ian. 2011. "Gamification is bullshit." Accessed March 5, 2015: http://www.bogost.com/blog/gamification_is_bullshit.shtml
Conway, Steven. 2014. "Zombification? Gamification, motivation, and the user." *Journal of Gaming & Virtual Worlds*, 6:2, 129–41.
Crawford, Eean R., Jeffery A. LePine, and Bruce Louis Rich. 2010. "Linking job demands and resources to employee engagement and burnout: A theoretical extension and meta-analytic test." *Journal of Applied Psychology*, 95:5, 834–48.
Csíkszentmihályi, Mihály. 1990. *Flow: The psychology of optimal experience*. New York: Harper and Row.
Czarniawska, Barbara. 2011. *Cyberfactories: How news agencies produce news*. Cheltenham: Edward Elgar Publishing.
Deci, Edward L., Richard Koestner, and Richard M. Ryan. 1999. "A meta-analytic review of experiments examining the effects of extrinsic rewards on intrinsic motivation." *Psychological Bulletin*, 125:6, 627–68.
Deci, Edward L. and Richard M. Ryan. 1985. *Intrinsic motivation and self-determination in human behavior*. New York: Plenum.
Deterding, Sebastian. 2014. "Eudaimonic design, or: Six invitations to rethink gamification." In *Rethinking gamification*, edited by Matthias Fuchs, Sonia Fizek, Paolo Ruffino, and Niklas Schrape, 305–33. Lüneberg, Germany: Meson Press.
Deterding, Sebastian, Dan Dixon, Rilla Khaled, and Lennart Nacke. 2011:a. "From game design elements to gamefulness: Defining gamification." In *Proceedings of the 15th International Academic MindTrek Conference: Envisioning Future Media Environments*, 9–15. ACM, Tampere, Finland.
Deterding, Sebastian, Miquel Sicart, Lennart Nacke, Kenton O'Hara, and Dan Dixon. 2011:b. "Gamification, using game-design elements in non-gaming contexts." In *PART 2 -Proceedings of the 2011 Annual Conference Extended Abstracts on Human Factors in Computing Systems*, 2425–28. ACM, Vancouver, Canada.
DeWinter, Jennifer and Carly A. Kocurek. 2014. "Games, gamification, and labour politics." *Journal of Gaming & Virtual Worlds*, 6:2, 143–57.
DeWinter, Jennifer, Carly A. Kocurek, and Randy Nichols. 2014. "Taylorism 2.0: Gamification, scientific management and the capitalist appropriation of play." *Journal of Gaming & Virtual Worlds*, 6:2, 109–27.
Dwivedula, Ravikiran and Christophe N. Bredillet. 2010. "Profiling work motivation of project workers." *International Journal of Project Management*, 28, 158–65.
Evaristo, Roberto and Paul C. van Fenema. 1999. "A typology of project management: Emergence and evolution of new forms." *International Journal of Project Management*, 17:5, 275–81.
Fernández-Vara, Clara. 2015. *Introduction to game analysis*. New York, NY: Routledge.
Filev, Andrew. 2013. "Expansion of remote teams: What drives it forward, and how is it shaping the future of project management?" *PM World Journal*, 2:3, 1–3.
Fogg, B.J. 2002. "Persuasive technology: Using computers to change what we think and do." In *Ubiquity*, art. 5. New York: ACM, pp. 89–120, doi: 10.1145/764008.763957.

Fuchs, Matthias. 2014. "Gamification as twenty-first-century ideology." *Journal of Gaming & Virtual Worlds*, 6:2, 143–57.
Gordon Rouse, Kimberly A. 2004. "Beyond Maslow's hierarchy of needs: What do people strive for?" *Performance Improvement*, 43:10, 27–31.
Greenberg, Jerald. 1990. "Organizational justice: Yesterday, today, and tomorrow." *Journal of Management*, 16:2, 399–432.
Gubman, Ed. 2004. "From engagement to passion for work: The search for the missing person." *People and Strategy*, 27:3, 42.
Gustavsson, Tomas. 2014. *Agile—Konsten att slutföra projekt*. Stockholm, Sweden: Liber.
Harris, Mark. 2014. "Amazon's Mechanical Turk workers protest: 'I am a human being, not an algorithm." *The Guardian*, December 3. Accessed March 14, 2014: http://www.theguardian.com/technology/2014/dec/03/amazon-mechanical-turk-workers-protest-jeff-bezos
Harter, James K., Frank L. Schmidt, and Theodore L. Hayes. 2002. "Business-unit-level relationship between employee satisfaction, employee engagement, and business outcomes: A meta-analysis." *Journal of Applied Psychology*, 87:2, 268–79.
Hass, Kathleen B. 2007. "The blending of traditional and agile project management." *PM World Today*, 9:5, 1–8.
Herger, Mario. 2014. *Enterprise gamification: Engaging people by letting them have fun*. Mario Herger. ISBN: 1470000644.
Hertel, Guido, Susanne Geister, and Udo Konradt. 2005. "Managing virtual teams: A review of current empirical research." *Human Resource Management Review*, 15, 69–95.
Highsmith, Jim. 2009. *Agile project management: Creating innovative products*. Boston, MA: Pearson Education.
Huizinga, Johan. 1938/1949. *Homo ludens: A study of the play-element in culture*. London: Routledge.
Huotari, Kai and Juho Hamari. 2012. "Defining gamification—a service marketing perspective." In *Proceedings of the 16th International Academic Mindtrek Conference*, 17–22. Tampere, Finland: ACM.
Jansson, Tomas. 2015. *Agila projektledningsmetoder och motivation: Varför man blir produktiv av att flytta lappar på en whiteboard*. Doctoral dissertation. Karlstad, Sweden: Karlstad University Press.
Jansson, Tomas and Lennart Ljung. 2004. *Projektledningsmetodik*. Studentlitteratur AB: Lund.
Jansson, Tomas and Lennart Ljung. 2011. *Individer, grupper och ledarskap i projekt*. Studentlitteratur AB: Lund.
Kjerulf, Alexander. 2012. "The happy pack: App market at Podio." *Podio*. Accessed March 20, 2015: https://podio.com/market/packs/438-the-happy-pack
Kücklich, Julian. 2005. "Precarious playbor: Modders and the digital game industry." *The Fibreculture Journal*, 5. Accessed, November 5, 2016: http://five.fibreculturejournal.org/fcj-025-precarious-playbour-modders-and-the-digital-games-industry/
Latham, Gary P. and Edwin A. Locke. 1991. "Self-regulation through goal setting." *Organizational Behavior and Human Decision Process*, 50:2, 212–47. Elsevier.
Latham, Gary P., Edwin A. Locke, and Neil E. Fassina. 2002. "The high performance cycle: Standing the test of time." In *The psychological management of individual*

performance: A handbook in the psychology of management in organizations, edited by Sabine Sonnentag, 201–28. Chichester: Wiley.
Latham, Gary P. and Craig C. Pinder. 2005. "Work motivation theory and research at the dawn of the twenty-first century." *Annual Review of Psychology*, 56, 485–516.
Lieberoth, Andreas. 2015. "Shallow gamification: Testing psychological effects of framing an activity as a game." *Games and Culture*, 10:3, 229–48.
Lipnack, Jessica and Jeffrey Stamps. 1997. *Virtual teams: People working across boundaries with technology*. New York: John Wiley & Sons, Inc.
Lockwood, Nancy R. 2007. "Leveraging employee engagement for competitive advantage." *Society for Human Resource Management Research Quarterly*, 1, 1–12.
McGonigal, Jane. 2011. *Reality is broken*. New York: Penguin Press.
Murray, Janet. 2013. "The ambiguity of game studies: Observations on the collective process of inventing a new discipline." In *Presentation at the 6th Digital Games Research Association (DiGRA)*. Atlanta, Georgia. August 26–29, 2013.
Nicholson, Scott. 2014. "Exploring the endgame of gamification." In *Rethinking gamification*, edited by Matthias Fuchs, Sonia Fizek, Paolo Ruffino, and Niklas Schrape, 289–303. Lüneberg, Germany: Meson Press.
Nicholson, Scott. 2015. "A RECIPE for meaningful gamification." In *Gamification in education and business*, edited by Torsten Reiners and Lincoln C. Wood, 1–20. Basel, Switzerland: Springer International Publishing.
Oyedele, Lukumon O. 2013. "Analysis of architects' demotivating factors in design firms." *International Journal of Project Management*, 31, 342–54.
Paharia, Rajat. 2013. *Loyalty 3.0: How to revolutionize customer and employee engagement with big data and gamification*. New York: McGraw-Hill.
Pazderka, Martin and Thomas Grechenig. 2007. "Project management maturity models: Towards best practices for virtual teams." In *Engineering Management Conference, 2007 IEEE International*, 84–9. Austin, TX. IEEE.
Pink, Daniel. 2009. *Drive: The surprising truth about what motivates us*. New York: Riverhead Books.
Poltronieri, Fabrizio. 2014. "Communicology, apparatus, and post-history: Vilém Flusser's concepts applied to video games and gamification." In *Rethinking gamification*, edited by Matthias Fuchs, Sonia Fizek, Paolo Ruffino, and Niklas Schrape, 165–200. Lüneberg, Germany: Meson Press.
Przybylski, Andrew K., Scott Rigby, and Richard M. Ryan. 2010. "A motivational model of video game engagement." *Review of General Psychology*, 14:2, 154–66.
Raftopoulos, Marigo. 2014. "Towards gamification transparency: A conceptual framework for the development of responsible gamified enterprise systems." *Journal of Gaming & Virtual Worlds*, 6:2, 159–78.
Reed, April H. and Linda V. Knight. 2010. "Project risk differences between virtual and co-located teams." *Journal of Computer Information Systems*, 51:1, 19–30.
Rey, P.J. 2012. "Gamification, playbor & exploitation." Accessed March 6, 2015: http://pjrey.wordpress.com/2012/12/27/gamification-playbor-exploitation/
Robertson, Margaret. 2010. "Can't play, won't play." *Hide & Seek*, October 6. Accessed March 4, 2015: http://hideandseek.net/2010/10/06/cant-play-wont-play/
Salen, Katie and Eric Zimmerman. 2004. *Rules of play: Game design fundamentals*. Cambridge, MA: MIT press.

Saks, Alan M. 2006. "Antecedents and consequences of employee engagement." *Journal of Managerial Psychology*, 21:7, 600–19.

Schwaber, Ken. 2004. *Agile project management with Scrum*. Chicago: Microsoft Press.

Seiler, Stefan, Bogdan Lent, Malgorzata Pinkowska, and Melanie Pinazza. 2012. "An integrated model of factors influencing project managers' motivation: Finding from a Swiss survey." *International Journal of Project Management*, 30, 60–72.

Sutherland, Jeff, Anton Viktorov, Jack Blount, and Nikolai Puntikov. 2007. "Distributed scrum: Agile project management with outsourced development teams." In *Proceedings of the 40th Annual Hawaii International Conference on System Sciences, 2007: HICSS 2007*. IEEE, Waikoloa, HI.

Tamborini, Ron, Nicholas David Bowman, Allison Eden, Matthew Grizzard, and Ashley Organ. 2010. "Defining media enjoyment as the satisfaction of intrinsic needs." *Journal of Communication*, 60:4, 758–77.

Tampoe, Mahen and Lynn Thurloway. 1993. "Project management: The use and abuse of techniques and teams (reflections from a motivation and environment study)." *International Journal of Project Management*, 11:4, 245–50.

Terranova, Tiziana. 2000. "Free labor: Producing culture for the digital economy." *Social Text*, 18:2, 33–58.

Van Dijck, José. 2009. "Users like you? Theorizing agency in user-generated content." *Media, Culture & Society*, 31:1, 41–58.

Van Dijck, José. 2013. *The culture of connectivity: A critical history of social media*. Oxford, UK: Oxford University Press.

Werbach, Kevin and Dan Hunter. 2012. *For the win: How game thinking can revolutionize your business*. Philadelphia: Wharton Digital Press.

Whitson, J.R. 2013. "Gaming the quantified self." *Surveillance & Society*, 11:1/2, 163–76.

Zackariasson, Peter and Timothy L. Wilson. 2012. "Marketing of video games". In *The video game industry: Formation, present state, and future*, edited by Peter Zackariasson and Timothy L. Wilson, 57–75. New York: Routledge.

Zichermann, Gabe and Joselin Linder. 2010. *Game-based marketing: Inspire customer loyalty through rewards, challenges, and contests*. New Jersey: Wiley & Sons.

Zichermann, Gabe and Joselin Linder. 2013. *The gamification revolution: How leaders leverage game mechanics to crush the competition*. New York: McGraw-Hill.

3 Gamification as Ideological Praxis
On Play, Games and the Modding of Management

Alf Rehn

Introduction

Lawley is an American insurance company. Just like many other similar companies, they struggle with sales, and particularly with their sales pipeline (i.e., their system for generating and following up on sales leads). And just like many other companies, they use Salesforce, a popular SaaS-provider, for their CRM (Customer Relationship Management) system. The problem, however, is that all such systems are only as good as the data put into them, and putting in correct information for, for example, sales leads is neither fun nor easy. As a result, Lawley ended up with a pipeline for sales that was a mess, including but not limited to leads with incomplete information or leads that were too old to be viable. Gamification to the rescue!

What Lawley did was to, in collaboration with a consulting company (LevelEleven, from whom information regarding the case has been gathered), create an application that turned the cleaning up and clearing up of the pipeline into a game. In effect, behaviors that had earlier been seen as tedious were now recast as point-worthy plays and moves. Updating timeframes was worth 50 points. Logging a phone call was worth 25 points. Setting up a meeting got you a whopping 75 points. And so on.

As a result of this recasting, during the two weeks the contest ran, workers at Lawley logged 257 percent more activities than in the comparable timeframe precontest, ensuring both better activity on existing sales leads and cleaning up false leads from the pipeline. Put somewhat differently, turning what was previously seen as a tedious task into a game created a marked improvement in Lawley's internal business processes, at least for a time.

The case above represents a very typical telling of a gamification tale (cf. McGonigal 2011). It has a problem, recast as a game, which in turn solves (or at least ameliorates) said problem. It is in this sense an archetypal innovation tale, one where the introduction of a new technology brings a boost to a company, but it could also be seen as a form of magical thinking. In the case above (as in the material that presents the case that the text draws on), it is never made completely clear *why* people became more dedicated to clearing up a sales pipeline just because it was cast as a game. Instead, as is often the case when writing about gamification, the technology is presented as having a self-evident yet not very well described power to change the way people act.

Broadly defined, gamification is the deployment of game mechanics and logics in areas where these have previously not been used. The assumption is that by making things more fun (however this is measured) and by introducing elements of collection and contest, gamification could conjure up motivation and productivity as out of thin air. No wonder, then, that the concept has won such favor in the corporate culture. At the same time, this often uncritical acceptance of game logics as the magic bean for bettering the company (and its bottom line) has left the concept of gamification insufficiently queried, including queries from an avowedly critical perspective.

For what did it really mean when people started playing the game at Lawley? Did it represent a true change in how business is conducted, or was it at best an updated version of the sales contest, a motivational technique used since time immemorial? What's really behind the shiny, happy face of gamification?

Understanding Gamification in Business

As a concept, gamification represents both a case study of the successful introduction of a new vocabulary into management thinking and the manner in which ideology can be smuggled in under the most unthreatening and benevolent of guises. On the surface, there seems to be little to take offense at in gamification. Quite the contrary, the immediate reaction to the concept seems to be one of appreciation, one where attention is drawn to issues such as acknowledging the innate playfulness of human beings (i.e., the *homo ludens*-argument from e.g., Hùizinga [1955]), as well as associations with an assumed childlike innocence, now transplanted to an environment in dire need of the same. Further, advocates of gamification have taken pains to align the concept with similar notions of how one with minute redirection (a.k.a., "nudges" [Thaler & Sunstein 2008]) can positively affect human behavior. Gamification thus promises a dual improvement—making work (or any human action) more fun/pleasant, all while ensuring that people are engaged in activities that are beneficial to them. More specifically, gamification has promised more pleasant work together with improved results (Perryer et al. 2012, Oprescu et al. 2014), or making, for example, fitness both easier and more productive (Brauner et al. 2013). Good things all.

At the same time, we might query whether this shiny surface is all there is to gamification. Whilst we've been inundated with the promise of the same, as well as with curated case studies purporting to show its magnificence and its glory, some questions remain. One such is whether gamification isn't at heart a case of McDonaldization (Ritzer 1993). By making everything measurable and, in a sense, "chunkable", gamification can be understood as a radical form of normative control (cf. Fleming & Sturdy 2011, also see

Fisher & Fuchs 2015), one where specific, predetermined, and even programmed behaviors are rewarded under the guise of "play" and "fun". In this way, gamification can support the age-old ideological praxis of keeping a fundamental alienation hidden by wrapping up the same in the accoutrements of entertainment.

Taking this line of argument somewhat further, we might in the contemporary vogue for gamification see a special case of a more general tendency, namely that of the modding of management. What I mean by this is that management, originally thought to be a specific (if somewhat vague) function within the confines of a corporation, increasingly needs to be seen as something other than itself in order to function. In much the same way as a game can be "modded" and "skinned" to present the user with a new experience even when the underlying logic remains the same, management increasingly needs to look like something other than management, without losing its capacity for control. Here, gamification represents an almost perfect vector through which this can be achieved, turning it into a specific kind of ideological praxis.

With this I refer to the manner in which ideology can be understood not merely as a mental meta-construct but also, in line with Gramsci's notion of cultural hegemony, as a set of actions and behaviors that become valorized and repeated in a culture, and which through this solidify and naturalize specific meanings and interpretations therein. Ideological praxis thus denotes the way in which our actions make an ideology more viable, often without us understanding how (e.g., repeating a term or a set of actions becomes ideological). Or to keep in line with the notion of gamification, that the striving to rise higher and higher on a leaderboard, or to collect as many stamps/stars/decals/whatever as possible, can in fact be *constitutive* of an ideology.

Within the tradition of, for example, labor process theory (Burawoy 1979) and critical management studies (see e.g., Hancock & Tyler 2004) the underlying ideological structure of much of contemporary working life has frequently been analyzed in such a manner, noting how the way in which "organizational man" becomes accustomed to and involved in everything from self-surveillance (see McKinlay & Starkey 1998) to mandatory "cultures of fun" (Fleming 2005). I would contend that gamification extends upon this, but further that it does so through a double move.

Whereas the first ideological move of gamification—turning what would otherwise be seen as a chore or a task into "fun"—is designed to turn employees into self-controlling managed subjects, the second move in effect creates a mask for or a distancing to the very nature of management. The first move is managerially efficient in that it can supposedly make people more keen to act in a manner that supports corporate aims—collecting power-ups rather than resisting control, as it were—but the second is ideologically efficient as it for all intents and purposes camouflages management.

By making calls to gamification, ostensibly to benefit workers, management (seen here as the agency utilized by an owner) attempts to achieve the same things—getting people to work harder—without being seen as trying to do so. The entertainment value of games are thus used to mask the true desire of management. As play and games are often seen as innately positive things, and as human beings are, by and large, attracted to the same (Henricks 2006, Sutton-Smith 2009), gamification can thus be understood as management through other means, with the added bonus of making resistance against the same more difficult to engage in.

For how is one to resist the introduction of more fun in the workplace? Who can argue against the joy derived from playing a game? Gamification is far harder to mount strong resistance against both as it is symbolically connected to things we often view as sacrosanct (childhood, fun, playful competition), and thus acts as a distancing technique for management—you can almost hear the manager now: "It's not control, it's the rules of the game! It's not extra work, it's fun, fun, fun! I'm not a manager. I'm a fucking *gamemaster!*"

On Games as McDonaldized Experiences

George Ritzer published *The McDonaldization of Society* in 1993, and it has remained in print ever since, having reached its eighth edition in 2014. In this, he argued that Western society can increasingly be understood as adopting the logics of the eponymous fast-food restaurant (i.e., turning everything into something akin to a McDonald's). More to the point, he argued that the four characteristic components of the fast-food business model existed and increasingly dominated in other areas of society as well. In doing so, he did not claim that this was a cultural form that was born in McDonald's but more that the company and its (well-known) methods could be used as a metaphor for broader societal change.

The four key aspects of McDonaldization that Ritzer highlights are efficiency, calculability, predictability and control. Here, efficiency refers to the way in which society continuously strives to achieve more faster, with less inputs. At heart, this is a logic of reduction, so while McDonald's is one of the most efficient ways to get sated quickly and relatively cheaply, this is achieved at the cost of both taste and nutritional value. Efficiency is all about stripping away things that stand in the way of achieving preset goals, but this is in part achieved by way of the second aspect, calculability. In a McDonald's, everything is quantified and measured, in order to be calculable. Every dollop of ketchup is known and accounted for, and the company can assess the dollar value of each client as soon as he or she enters the system. For Ritzer, this represents the tendency of contemporary society to turn everything into calculable units. In the modern kindergarten, babies are turned into profit centers, and baby carrots are duly accounted for. In the modern university, contact hours are jealously counted, and the value of every professor can be ascertained and put into an Excel sheet. Calculability supports efficiency, but it also introduces its own logics.

Efficiency and calculability come together in the third aspect, predictability. In order to maximize efficiency and make everything calculable, it is necessary to create a standardized, predictable system. This is why a fast-food restaurant sticks to more or less the same menu in all of its outlets, and also why most foods in them are variations on a central theme, with, for example, the same steaks and the same cheese used in a plethora of burgers. Similarly, we can in the world of universities see a striving towards things such as standardized modules and e-learning, ensuring that the same course can be given at any number of schools, even globally. All this is of course done to ensure the fourth of Ritzer's aspects, namely control. McDonaldization is about creating systems of control, systems where the overseer can use the predictability and calculability of the process to ensure efficiency and enact dominance. A McDonalidized world is a world that is ever easier to control, as the tools to do so are built into the system.

Now, the spectre of McDonaldization looms large over the process of gamification, although this link hasn't always been explicitly stated. To understand why, we need to return to the issue of what a game is. A game, stated simply, is a proto-narrative in which a player tries to achieve internally logical goals following assigned rules in order to drive the narrative onwards. I say proto-narrative, as a game's narrative might in fact be quite basic—the narrative of *Tetris*, for instance, might be understood as "clean the screen". A game is always a reduction, defined by a set number of rules that have to be accepted in order to play. In *Pac-Man*, it matters not that ghosts really shouldn't be able to consume you, nor you them, as this is simply the rule set you have to follow to play this specific game.

Further, games are at the very least internally highly efficient. Many games will not allow for almost any nonessential activity, but will instead keep you doing whatever it is you need to be doing to continue in the game. Whilst open-world games like *Grand Theft Auto V* do to a degree allow for more exploratory playing, they too tend to incentivize players to continue the narrative as it is laid out. Game design also tends to go for an optimization of experience, so that, for example, players are not to be let to travel for too long or otherwise get stuck in unproductive activities.

Games are also eminently predictable. Most games have one or at best a few final points towards which the player is directed, or then no end-point at all, but the predictable death that comes from increasingly difficult levels. Whilst there are games that give you freedom to create, even these have great levels of predictability. You cannot play a fighting game in a manner that makes your opponent realize the futility of violence, embrace you as a brother, and then go make tea for you. Nor can you play *FIFA 15* in a way where you give up your career as a football player in order to become an actor. Also, even if a creative games designer did create such possibilities, they would become predictable through this very fact. Games are in a sense closed systems, where the number of possible actions have been preordained. Even in a game as free as *Minecraft,* where enterprising players have built worlds and machines that the designer couldn't have foreseen, these worlds and machines are limited by the tools created by the game's designer (or those made possible by the army of modders creating new possibilities, albeit ones with their own, necessary limitations).

Continuing from here, it is clear that games, by and large, are set out according to a calculative logic. With the exception of some indie games that veer into interactive art, and a few "sandbox games" such as *Minecraft*, most games have tasks to be achieved to continue, not to mention a scoring system. Be it points, kills, achievements or stars, most games give very explicit systems for calculating your progress and your success (or lack thereof). Monsters have a set number of hitpoints, enemy strongholds have specific amounts of ammo and loot, and enemy armies have defined numbers of warriors of defined strength. Most everything in a modern game can, and will, be counted.

It shouldn't surprise us, then, that gamification can be studied as a case of McDonaldization. Such a reading should of course not be seen as a totalizing claim, but it can open up perspectives on gamification that can otherwise become obscured. Where much of what is written on gamification is done in a decidedly triumphalist vein (see Zichermann & Linder 2013, Burke 2014), arguing that the same can cure most if not all of society's ills (see e.g., McGonigal 2011), the reading I'm arguing for here starts from the assumption that games are not necessarily neutral phenomena untouched by ideology, nor are they by necessity "good". This should not be read as a condemnation of games, but rather as a call for observing the same objectively.

It shouldn't surprise anyone that games, as a cultural expression, are a result of the culture they emerge in, so gaming as it emerges in a market society with a marked penchant for competitiveness and quantitative measures will show a bias for the same. That said, a remarkable amount of what is written on gamification at least implies that gaming is connected to things such as a "play instinct." For instance, Janaki Kumar (2013) states that it takes "advantage of people's innate enjoyment of play", thus referring to innate states that would be preideological. This, however, is a simplification and then some. Whilst games might draw upon an innate playfulness in the human species, they are also systems that need to be learnt and understood through socialization, and are aligned with the culture they emerge in. This also means that while games are often viewed as emerging directly out of play, they are presented as if they are products of a field with positive moral connotations. Play is good, and games are play; therefore games are good—or so the implied argument goes.

But this is of course a very dangerous simplification. Whilst it might be true that play at least isn't evil—although it might be more correct to state that play is beyond good and evil—this does not mean that we can infer that games hold any *a priori* ethical position. Whilst games and play have been afforded positive moral connotations in much of contemporary public discourse, and have thus acquired what we might refer to as "moral capital", this does not mean that turning something into a game is automagically a way to make that activity better, nicer or more aligned with a humanist morality. Still, the tensions inherent here are obvious. Looking to a recent research report by Gartner, a consultancy that is quite open about serving corporate interests over that of, for example, employees, we can in this for instance read:

> Organizations such as the Department for Work and Pensions in the U.K. and Allstate have already leveraged more sophisticated game mechanics to inspire employee engagement in the innovation process, and we expect that the trend will continue.
>
> (Burke 2012)

The language is carefully chosen. Mechanics are "sophisticated", and they are not used, they're "leveraged". Employees are further "inspired" to engage in the innovation process. However, just a few lines later, the same report states:

> More sophisticated game design techniques supported by technology can be applied to design employee behaviors—fine-tuning activities to support organizational goals.

And

> Gamification uses the currencies of social capital, self-esteem and fun overtaking extrinsic rewards as motivations for improved performance.

Even though the report also cautions against making employees "feel manipulated or intimidated", the intent is clearly there. Gamification is here presented as a design maneuver, utilizing and capitalizing upon intrinsic rewards to improve performance and to fine-tune the manner in which employees behave. Whilst fun is referenced, it is done so as a tool, not as a way to connect work to something more meaningful. In effect, this is the McDonaldization of fun—making games an efficient and calculable tool of control.

The Power-Games of Culture and the Culture-Games of Power

Let us return to the case of Lawley, and the gamification of the sales pipeline. The key issue for Lawley was the lack of control over the same. For lack of a better term, employees were expressing their agency rather than that of management by filling in leads in the manner of their liking and opting to not unduly burden themselves with pipeline upkeep. This was the problem to be solved. The first step towards doing so was to make the system more predictable. By reframing the problem as a contest, the company could both raise awareness of this as a problem, and also incentivize people to participate in solving the same. The incentive here was double. By casting it as a competition, there was a positive incentive to win said contest, regardless of the actual value of the prizes. Winning such a contest would ensure visibility in the organization and at the very least prove to upper management that one was a good worker. But there is also a negative incentive at play (sic) here. By introducing a gamified app, the company can send a clear signal regarding the necessity to participate. It is, in a way, the company saying, "You have no reasons left not to do this. We even turned it into a game for you. Playing said game is now mandatory". Thus the gamification process could ensure that the pipeline cleaning became more predictable.

Second, the process turned tending to the sales pipeline into something much more calculable. By giving points to different engagements (setting up a meeting gives you three times the number of points a mere phone call will), the systems both creates an internal hierarchy of tasks and nudges users towards such behaviors that have been predefined as the most desired ones. Further, simply by setting up the system, all aspects of the pipeline can be assigned values, or at the very least positioned in a value network. For instance, it becomes easier to follow who is using the app, and one can even reward people simply for checking in daily (one point for opening the app!).

All this is highly efficient, from a management viewpoint. By turning what was before merely a task into a game, one can with far greater granularity reward or punish people for different things. Where one earlier might just have said, "You should tend to the sales pipeline", one could now assign clear values to tasks, and trust that the competitive nature of the game ensured that people put in at least a moderate amount of effort, so as not to look bad on the leaderboard. The "game", then, is more of a control mechanism for management, wrapped up in a far more attractive package than was previously thought possible.

As commentators such as Willmott (1993) noted early on, notions such as culture are far from positive infusions of assumedly more humane aspects into the corporate logic, and can instead act as a reinforcement of the very same. A notion of "company culture" can become a controlling ideology, one where members feel free within the scope of actions the culture allows (cf. Lukes 1974). Following this we can see that whilst it in the case of Lawley is obvious that the aim of management hasn't changed at all, the method through which it achieves its aims have. The activities demanded of employees are the same, but now with the addition of the "fun" that is assumed to come from playing a game. Fleming (2005, p. 297), in his analysis of "cultures of fun", remarks as follows:

> The management of work and nonwork boundaries was translated by a number of employees into problems of self (integrity, dignity, self-esteem, self-respect, etc.), with cynicism being particularly salient.

Further, in the same article, he comments on how the attempt by management to bring in "fun" elements such as party themes or making references to family or school can by employees be viewed as being both pretentious or artificial. That the same could be inferred within gamification is not much of an intellectual stretch. However, this artifice may extend beyond the turning of tasks to games.

The Modding of Management

Even though it is clear that gamification in business includes the tendency to utilize objects and logics from (popular) culture as a handy distancing mechanism for management, there is more at play here than corporate control through other means (cf. Fleming & Sturdy 2011). The literature on, for example, control through culture has usually focused on the way in which an existing power-structure is set up in such a way that it either dupes workers or at the very least shields its true intention (see e.g., Alvesson & Kärreman 2007). I would however contend that this is only part of the story of what occurs when gamification is turned into a management tool.

What is particularly challenging in attempting to understand the role of gamification in business is the role played by management. This has, particularly in the popular literature on the subject (Zichermann & Linder 2013, Burke 2014), been cast mostly as an issue of managers "getting it" and allowing gamification to bring its particular brand of magic to the organization. In so doing, the discussion has often downplayed not one but two forms of agency.

One, the debate has often implied that the implementation of gamification would be something akin to purchasing a piece of software and thus ignored the agency of those realizing gamification engagements. In the case of Lawley, the agent of gamification was a consulting agency, who obviously wielded an amount of power over the process. Within this, there are the actual designers of the game, who, on the basis of their assumed expertise, are tasked with things such as how many points a task receives and so on. These wield a considerable amount of power over the actual shaping of gamification, and the role of this is often studied only insofar as one can try to mine this for "best practices". Matters such as how the worldview of, for example, game designers through gamification becomes a power dimension within the organizational everyday are often downplayed or completely marginalized.

Whilst the above might be explained away by stating that probing the details of game design for ideological markers is taking critical inquiry a step to far—which might or might not be true—the same cannot be said for the second level of agency myopia within the gamification debate. Here, I refer to the manner in which the role of management is affected as well. Whereas much of what has been implicitly or explicitly noted regarding how gamification and similar attempts to frame existing tasks in novel ways (we might, e.g., compare to the quantified self-movement) affect workers, employees and users (see e.g., Morozov 2012, Carr 2014), little similar scrutiny has been afforded to managers. What becomes of the masters, when the underlings are turned into gamers?

On one level, we might se this as managers abdicating part of their power to the aforementioned game-designers, and the consultants who position their wares within the confines of the corporate logic. Where there before were managers, we now have purchasers of gamification projects, who might retain some say-so as to what should be achieved with the same, but who are still forced to accept another layer between themselves and the activities of the firm. A quirky marxist might even go so far as to say that this might institute a form of "management alienation", as managers become dependent on game designs as a new kind of tools of production—tools that they only partially control.

On another level, this recasting could be understood as a form of "modding", borrowing directly from the parlance of the gaming community. A mod is a piece of code that is used to change aspects of a software-based game. For instance, *Minecraft* can be modded to include everything from advanced aircraft and tools to changes in how item storage or maps work, to the point of radically altering the game. Similarly, one can in many first-person shooters add "skins" and "textures" in order to change the aesthetics of the game, which might be understood as a special case of modding. The logic here is that the game itself is merely a template or a platform upon which one can layer various kinds of modifications. What I'm doing here, then, is to use the notion of modding as a metaphor for how we might understand management in an age of gamification.

As already argued, with gamification, the locus of managerial control doesn't necessarily change, but it is at the same recast. The role of management might still be seen in the rules of the game, as it were, and in the way games are introduced and positioned, but it would also be given a new *visage,* as it were. What games do afford employees is a novel way of seeing the management. They are in a sense now moved away from having overarching authority towards being stewards of the game and overseers that the rules of this is followed. The rules and the logics of the game may well have been drafted by management, but once we've moved into the playing of the game, player-employees are at the very least given the chance to probe the newly gamified constructs and attempt to find ways to game (sic) these.

What I at first described as an extension of managerial power through the co-option of more friendly tropes might then be turned against itself. As managers become game-masters, they will need to increasingly pay heed to the fact that it is part of the gaming culture to find weaknesses in game design, flaws to be taken advantage of. Thus the exploited may well become the exploiters—particularly seeing as a clever way to utilize a bug or an unforeseen use in a game is often referred to as an "exploit". The irony of this would not have escaped Marx. At the same time, this isn't merely a question of changing the rules. It is also tied in with how the identity politics of management changes with the introduction of gamification.

In the gaming community, management often takes the form of either a gamemaster, a clan leader, or a moderator (by any other name). The first of these comes to us from the culture that arose around roleplaying and emphasizes the need for someone to act as a warden of the game, to enable it to go along. A gamemaster has a degree of power over the game but needs to wield this in a way that makes the game interesting enough to play and without major hitches. The second form, the clan leader, references the way in which many games can be played more efficiently only if people collaborate, and this often requires for one or more of the team to take on the role of a leader. Here, however, this is done *within* the game. Our final form, the moderator, refers to how the community that can arise around a game may need to be shepherded, often through the use of online media, and the role moderators for, for example, discussion boards then come to play. Here, the salient point is that such moderators can manage the community, but only with the implicit agreement and support of at least a majority of the same. In all three roles, management is possible, but is inexorably linked with the game itself.

What this comes to, then, is that where management gamifies work, it will also end up gamifying itself. Or to put it more bluntly, sometimes you play the game, and sometimes the game plays you. What management may well end up in is a situation where they need to either accept that they may (will?) be outplayed by their employees, or to own up to how they only allow the game to go on for as long as they are in control thereof. In a strange, almost Žižekian turn, then, management might be the thing that is truly gamified, as it so easily becomes hoisted on its own petard. What at Lawley seemed like a great way to clean up a sales pipeline may in fact at heart show a critical weakness in management, in that it creates a most dangerous transparency, one where management is reduced to setting up a series of arbitrary rules, and then throwing a fit if these lead to undesired consequences. The mask of management as rational, logical and fair may well be torn asunder as the agents thereof attempt to utilize the logic of a world in which testing limits is the primary directive.

For what did happen at Lawley? Was the level of 257 percent more activities seen as anything besides another largely arbitrary measure? Did the game make sense to the players, or did it merely showcase to the employees how management viewed them and viewed their jobs? Come one, come all, points to be had if you play the game . . .

Beyond Fun and Games

The *clou* of this text, then, is the following: Gamification should not and cannot be treated merely as the introduction of a new mechanic into a new context. Rather, it always already enmeshed in an ideological context, one that ensures that gamification in business remains wedded to the key functions of market capitalism. Disturbingly, at least in the instances where this isn't made explicit, it might even function as an ideological shielding mechanism. By exploiting notions of fun and games, it can function as a way to make us see less of business, not more.

However, in turn, this attempt to make opaque may end up as its own inversion and in fact highlight the arbitrariness of management. It might further make it more difficult for managers to enact their accustomed position, as to the classical management alien logic of gaming—not to mention the not necessarily controllable input of games designers—embroils it in a context where it might not be able to extend its control beyond the rules as they've been established. So the attempt to bring in normative control under the guise of fun and games may be challenged that the latter actually delimits normative control, stating that anything that isn't explicitly forbidden or made impossible is in fact allowed! What, exactly the rocket jump (a well-known and often utilized exploit by which one in a first-person shooter can utilize the propulsive force of a rocket in order to jump to places not originally intended to be reachable, as made popular by players of the game *Quake* (1996), although introduced as early as in *Doom* (1993)), of gamified business will be is not yet clear. What we do know is that as employees become seen as players, they will do what players always have done—attempt to beat the game.

Here, then, we might speculate on the future of the gamification of business, both when it comes to the potential for workers' emancipation and when it comes to re-theorizing the role of management. Assuming that gamification, by any other name, is something more than a fad—and the McDonaldized logic underlying it suggests it is—we can expect to see more and more complex attempts at the same, in more and more facets of organizational life. In much the same manner as, for example, the project as a form of working in modern organizations has spread to create a projectified society, gamification might undergo a process of both professionalization (Muzio et al. 2011) and diffusion (see Heusinkveld et al. 2011). These processes may well impact both workers and managers.

When it comes to workers, this process is likely to follow the path of other similar management notions (i.e., become increasingly well masked and taken for granted) (cf. Alvesson & Kärreman 2015). Similarly, it is entirely possible that gamification becomes something akin to project management (i.e., something that a modern manager is supposed to have at least some skills in), to the point where many will train in this knowledge. Just like many modern managers have diplomas in project management, and some even are certified in the Project Management Institute's global standards and body of knowledge, we might see the rise of a Gamification Institute with the right to issue professional credentials. Whether one then sees this as the continued process of exploitative capitalism or just the development of a powerful management model is in the eyes of the beholder. However, I wish to raise a second possibility.

Specifically because of the processes of exploit-searching and the modding of management that I've tried to outline above, I want to argue that there is another, potentially more interesting path all this might take. As managers, at least so far, have limited skills in gamification, and at the same time, increasingly game-savvy generations are entering the workforce, the potential for new kinds of workers' resistance emerge (see Courpasson et al. 2012). Taking a look back at the case of Lawley, the figure of 257 percent more activities might now be queried a little. Clearly, this sounds like a great thing, especially for management, and the typical critical analysis of such cases has focused on whether all this has been fair to the workers. However, another question that could be raised is how meaningful such measures ever are. As you may have noted in the initial description of the case, updating timeframes was awarded with no less than 50 points, almost as much as setting up a meeting. Now, what we do not know is whether the workers at Lawley saw this as a potential exploit, continuously updating timeframes. If so, they could manage to seem both busy and as playing along, whilst in effect sabotaging the entire exercise. Managers, again, would have been reduced to merely observing as no rules had been broken, simply hacked.

If gamification truly becomes more popular, such shenanigans could go from being small aberrations to business as usual. Managers, recast as gamemasters, would have to battle endless attempts to disrupt and circumvent the business games created, ultimately becoming little more than parts of the game themselves. Gamification would thus become an arena of resistance, one where the attempt to utilize cultural hegemony to make work appear as play becomes subverted, as the game truly becomes play, albeit a distinctly different one from what was intended.

Fraught and Fragile Games

McDonaldization is often portrayed as a monolithic and oppressive move, one where the powers of, for example, calculability and control narrow the life space of those who enter into it. What is often forgotten in this is that such reductions also introduce a fragility into a system (cf. Taleb 2012), and that such fragility can be exploited. In much the same manner as the McDonaldization of higher education has given academics new ways of "playing the game", gamification could be studied as the reduction of work to something hackable. Many would state that replacing judgement and meaningful discourse with points and levels is a classic case of alienating the worker from the work, but it has to be noted that this also goes for the manager. In fact, it might even be that it is management that becomes the truly fragile thing, locked into perpetuating an increasingly hollow idea of "this is fun, gang!" and having to pretend that game-rigging isn't occurring.

In a gamified business world, the manager might thus find him- or herself in the position to ideology Sloterdijk (1987) referred to as cynical. The manager knows full well that gamification is an attempt at control, and thus part of the wider ideological praxis of capitalism, but at the same time s/he knows that this control is not nearly as complete or as obvious as it might seem. Management must both pretend that the game is a game, but then also pretend that work is work.

So it would be an error to assume that gamification in business is merely a case of increased control and diminished agency among workers, as it might well give these new forms of agency. It might be the managers who become truly McDonaldized, having to keep up the fantasy of work as play and skinning themselves to make management continuously look like something other than management. It is in this move that management becomes a distinctly fragile system, dependent on the upkeep of a specific image whilst at the same time being subverted by novel ways of playing the game.

In *The Pervert's Guide to Cinema*, Slavoj Žižek argues against one of the most common notions of why we enjoy playing video games, namely the idea that games allow us to disappear into a fantasy. This, Žižek argues, misses the entire point of gaming. Rather, he says, in games we are freed from the shackles of ideology and societal norms, and can express our true selves, so that the games can show us a "reality within fantasy itself". Something similar could be said about gamification in business. It is clearly an attempt to create a fantasy, a wondrous world where there is no work, only fun-fun-fun, and this is why gamification is a form of ideological praxis. But there is a turn here, for as we turn work into games, we're also showing the hollowness of work and management in late capitalism, and creating possibilities to challenge the very same ideology. Or at least turn its own logic against itself, all 257 percent of it.

References

Alvesson, M., & Kärreman, D. 2007. "Unraveling HRM: Identity, ceremony, and control in a management consulting firm." *Organization Science*, 18(4), 711–723.

Alvesson, M., & Kärreman, D. 2016. "Intellectual failure and ideological success in organization studies: The case of transformational leadership." *Journal of Management Inquiry*, 25(2), 139–152.

Brauner, P., Valdez, A. C., Schroeder, U., & Ziefle, M. 2013. "Increase physical fitness and create health awareness through exergames and gamification." Holzinger, A., Ziefle, M., Hitz, M., Debevc, M. (Eds.) In *Human factors in computing and informatics* (pp. 349–362). Berlin: Springer.

Burawoy, M. 1979. *Manufacturing consent: Changes in the labor process under monopoly capitalism*. Chicago: University of Chicago Press.

Burke, B. 2012. *Gamification 2020: What Is the Future of Gamification?*, Retrieved from http://www.gartner.com/doc/2226015?refval=&pcp=mpe on April 2nd 2015.
Burke, B. 2014. *Gamify: How gamification motivates people to do extraordinary things*. Boston, MA: Bibliomotion, Inc.
Carr, N. 2014. *The glass cage: Automation and us*. New York: WW Norton & Company.
Courpasson, D., Dany, F., & Clegg, S. 2012. "Resisters at work: Generating productive resistance in the workplace." *Organization Science*, 23(3), 801–819.
Fisher, E., & Fuchs, C. (Eds.). 2015. *Reconsidering value and labour in the digital age*. Basingstoke, UK: Palgrave Macmillan.
Fleming, P. 2005. "Workers' playtime? Boundaries and cynicism in a 'culture of fun' program." *The Journal of Applied Behavioral Science*, 41(3), 285–303.
Fleming, P., & Sturdy, A. 2011. "'Being yourself' in the electronic sweatshop: New forms of normative control." *Human Relations*, 64(2), 177–200.
Hancock, P., & Tyler, M. 2004. "'MOT your life': Critical management studies and the management of everyday life." *Human Relations*, 57(5), 619–645.
Henricks, T. S. 2006. *Play reconsidered: Sociological perspectives on human expression*. Champaign: University of Illinois Press.
Heusinkveld, S., Sturdy, A., & Werr, A. 2011. "The co-consumption of management ideas and practices." *Management Learning*, 42(2), 139–147.
Huizinga, J. 1955. *Homo ludens: A study of the play-elememt in culture*. Boston, MA: Beacon Press.
Kumar, J. 2013. "Gamification at work: Designing engaging business software." In Aaron Marcus (Ed.) *Design, user experience, and usability: Health, learning, playing, cultural, and cross-cultural user experience*, 528–37. Berlin: Springer.
Lukes, S. 1974. *Power: A radical view*. London: Macmillan.
McGonigal, J. 2011. *Reality is broken: Why games make us better and how they can change the world*. New York: Penguin.
McKinlay, A., & Starkey, K. (Eds.). 1998. *Foucault, management and organization theory: From panopticon to technologies of self*. London: Sage.
Morozov, E. 2012. *The net delusion: The dark side of internet freedom*. New York: PublicAffairs.
Muzio, D., Hodgson, D., Faulconbridge, J., Beaverstock, J., & Hall, S. 2011. "Towards corporate professionalization: The case of project management, management consultancy and executive search." *Current Sociology*, 59(4), 443–464.
Oprescu, F., Jones, C., & Katsikitis, M. 2014. "I PLAY AT WORK—ten principles for transforming work processes through gamification." *Frontiers in Psychology*, 5, art. 14.
Perryer, C., Scott-Ladd, B., & Leighton, C. 2012. "Gamification: Implications for workplace intrinsic motivation in the 21st century." *Asian Forum On Business Education Journal*, 5(3), 371–81.
Ritzer, G. 1993. *The McDonaldisation of society: An investigation into the changing character of contemporary social life*. Thousand Oaks, CA: Pine Forge Press.
Sloterdijk, P. 1987. *Kritik der zynischen Vernunft*. Frankfurt: Suhrkamp.
Sutton-Smith, B. 2009. *The ambiguity of play*. Cambridge, MA: Harvard University Press.
Taleb, N. 2012. *Antifragile: Things that gain from disorder*. New York: Random House.

Thaler, R., & Sunstein, C. 2008. *Nudge: The gentle power of choice architecture.* New Haven: Yale University Press.

Willmott, H. 1993. "Strength is ignorance; slavery is freedom: Managing culture in modern organizations." *Journal of Management Studies*, 30(4), 515–552.

Zichermann, G., & Linder, J. 2013. *The gamification revolution: How leaders leverage game mechanics to crush the competition.* New York: McGraw Hill Professional.

Part II
External Organizational Perspectives

4 Game of Gamification

Marketing, Consumer Resistance and Digital Play

Lena Olaison and Saara L. Taalas

Introduction

Gamification, as a strategic resource, "makes a game out of something" and has been deployed by corporations since the early 2000s "as a way to influence online and real-world behaviour" (Dale 2014, 82). The hope of gamification specialists is that increased engagement from employees or customers will lead to innovation and collaboration (Taalas and Hirsjärvi 2013). The definition of gamification varies across industries, and the theoretical work is scarce (Seaborn and Fels 2015). However, most scholars seem to agree on Deterding, Dixon, Khaled and Nacke's definition of gamification as *"the use of game design elements in non-game contexts"* (2011, 10, italics in original). As a marketing tool, gamification has been portrayed as a method for commercial actors to engage with potential consumers online, with the goal of achieving "engagement, loyalty, brand awareness, motivation, purpose and/or ownership over tasks" (Lucassen and Jansen 2014, 194). This strategy is assumed to enhance marketing efforts, particularly in services (Huotari and Hamari 2012). Although gamification is a relatively new phenomena, gamification is today a huge business. The consultancy firm Gartner, Inc., estimates that in 2014, the budget for gamification strategies amounted to 2.8 billion USD (1.7 billion GBP) and that "gamified applications" will be used by over 70 percent of the "Forbes Global 2000". Another consultancy firm, Markets and Markets, predicts that the gamification industry will be worth up to 5.5 billion USD (3.4 GBP) by 2018 (Dale 2014, although Lucassen and Jansen [2014] point out that research is needed to support such claims).

Specialists have noted, however, that the gamified business industry tends to be portrayed as a relatively unproblematic, technical add-on to any strategy, while it in fact is a strategy for communicating at the "emotional level" (Burke 2014; Dale 2014). Gartner Inc. goes so far as to claim that 80 percent of launches of gamified initiatives in 2014 will fail (Burke 2014). The reason for this is "bad design" (Burke 2014; Dale 2014) because most gamification executives fail to align

> the personal goals of a company's customers, employees, and communities . . . with the organization's business goals. Like two sides of the same

coin, shared goals may have different faces, but they are merely different views of the same thing.

(Burke 2014, 9)

Therefore, "aligned goals between players" and the business's objectives is the "sweet spot" of gamification (Burke 2014; Dale 2014).

In this chapter, we contribute to the view that gamification might not be as straightforward and unproblematic as marketing advocates would like to hope, and that perspectives other than those connected to various technical features might be needed to understand the logic of gamified practices. However, our analysis differs from theirs precisely in the notion of "aligned goals" between businesses and players. While gamification strategists seem to believe that "the secret here is for organizations to work towards aligning their goals with those of their employees and customers" (Dale 2014, 90), we have observed that despite marketeers' best intentions, the audiences whom these campaigns are targeting will inevitably follow their own logic, as suggested from the perspective of video game research (Escribano 2012). Online communities invariably resist overt marketing strategies by altering or even perverting strategic meanings, in the forms of circulated iterations, references within references and digital memes. Our empirical cases—the "I love shopping at Waitrose because . . ." Twitter competition; the low-cost airline Norwegian's Airplane Tailfin Hero Competition; "My New 10 Euro" Banknote Selfie Competition by the European Central Bank; and Nutella France's viral marketing campaign—were all perceived as strategic failures from the perspective of "aligned company and consumer goals". Management control gave way to embarrassment on the corporate side. In these "failed" campaigns, consumers and media fans seem to have taken over and started to play the game features in unintended ways. However, rather than interpreting such campaigns as strategic failures, where the goals of the business and its audiences were not "aligned" (Burke 2014; Dale 2014), we are inspired by studies of consumer resistance within consumer research (e.g., Dalli and Corciolani 2008; Hemetsberger 2006) and pursue an alternative question: What is happening when marketing campaigns are gamified and when audiences engage in ways that disrupt or contest the strategic marketing protocol?

To analyse our cases, we propose an alternative understanding of gamification, not as technical devices, but as social processes where the boundaries between producers and consumers are blurred and more importantly, rendered open-ended (e.g., Paulsen and Hernes 2003). This argument implies seeing gaming as culture-producing activity rather than rule-following activity (Huizinga 1955, see also Murray and Ozanne [1991] and Ritson and Dobscha [1999], who call for a critical and culturally sensitive analysis of marketing campaigns). Drawing on cultural theorist and literary critic Kenneth Burke's concept of identification (1950) and terministic screens (1966), we investigate the rhetorical technologies of playing rather than the technologies of establishing a technological platform. We base our analysis on two simple game elements in particular: hashtags and algorithms (i.e., the practice of tagging and the many roles of algorithms as game motors). Hence, we analyse hashtaging as a rhetorical resource and game engine filters as sites for rhetorical gaming. We conclude that the "game" of gamification might be better understood as participatory interaction rather than corporate messaging. In this sense, we view gaming as the interplay of different goals rather than the alignment of goals. This process may thus include various forms of resistance: When the audience engages in "digital rhetorics" in game development, the campaign becomes a site for consumer resistance and development of community rather than a simple tool for marketing messaging.

Gamification as Marketing Tool: From Engagement to Resistance

As a marketing method, gamification refers to the use of game elements outside game worlds; in this case, gaming applied to business in order to further business objectives (e.g., Deterding et al. 2011). The academic literature in marketing on gamification, still relatively new, has focused on trying to define the concept (Deterding et al. 2011; Huotari and Hamari 2012), review the existing literature and survey the present and future uses of gamification approach on practice (Lucassen and Jansen 2014; Seaborn and Fels 2015).

Although the term *gamification* emerged around 2003, gaming, as a marketing strategy, has in fact been around for decades. Loyalty programs, educational games and workplace productivity reward systems (Seaborn and Fels 2015) are examples of precedents to the digital game worlds or game applications that we today think of as gamification. The most commonly seen elements are: achievements (experience points, levels, bonuses, etc.); exercises (challenges, discoveries, etc.); synchronizing with the community (leaderboards, collaboration, etc.); result transparency (experience bars, continuous feedback, etc.); time (countdown, speed, etc.); luck (lottery, random achievements, etc.) (adopted from Dale 2014, 82).

The predominant, rather technical view of gamification has been challenged within service marketing, arguing for a user-driven perspective. This perspective defines gamification as "a process of enhancing a service with affordances for gameful experiences in order to support user's overall value creation" (Huotari and Hamari 2012, 22, see also Conaway and Garay 2014, who support this view). On the other hand, another set of researchers argue for bringing further dimensions into the definition, most notably the "emotional level" and the alignment of various objectives (Burke 2014; Dale 2014) They operate with a definition of gamification as: "the use of game mechanics and experience design to digitally engage and motivate people to achieve their goals" (Burke 2014, 6). Both these views have noted that despite the growing interest in the phenomenon, most of the research has focussed on the technical aspects, despite the fact, as most scholars agree, that the success criteria for a gamified application is its ability to understand the user. As Dale observes:

> implementers . . . place more focus on aspects of the technology and the mechanics (bells and whistles) of gamification applications than engaging with (and understanding) its potential users. After all, technology is relatively simple to understand whereas people are far more complex. The long and painful history of failed projects usually stems from the tendency to focus on technology first and people (users) second.
> (Dale 2014, 89)

The difficulty of understanding "people" also highlights the dubiousness of the play offered in a gamified campaign. While being presented as a playful open interaction in which producers and consumers mingle with each other, marketing departments are working hard behind the scenes to manage and steer these open-ended spaces. Gamified marketing campaign strategies build on the successes of contemporary digital gaming "as massively multiplayer online games (MMOGs) make interaction with others a central component of playing the game, rather than privileging the insular and solitary experiences that can typify single-player gaming" (Paul and Philpott 2009, 1). Similarly, contemporary gamified marketing efforts build upon participatory interaction and game development rather than traditional marketing messaging. Putting gamification in a broader marketing context, the interest in gamified consumer engagement is a continuation of an ideology of marketing that has been in place for quite some time, from relationship marketing, service marketing and one-to-one marketing to the idea of the prosumer (Arnould, Price and Malshe 2006; Vargo and Lusch 2004, 2008). Gamification is further rooted in the logic of marketing practice that seeks to promote a product or a corporate brand and can be seen as a source of credibility via its ability to make marketing viral, authentic and "real" (e.g., Holt 2002; Sköld and Rehn 2007).

A more nuanced understanding of consumer participation as a socio-relational process and culture-producing activity can be found in research on consumer resistance (e.g., Dobscha 1998; Ritson and Dobscha 1999). The consumer resistance research takes its point of departure in the inherent tensions between consumers and markets, focusing on how consumers cope with but also resist, avoid and pervert marketing messaging (Hemetsberger 2006). This research has demonstrated that consumers "do not passively adapt to market offerings and mass communication: they are able to react and develop personal, counter-cultural forms of consumption" (Dalli and Corciolani 2008, 2). Typical coping behaviours include minimizing commercial messaging by distancing from its sources and avoiding marketing content, limiting the flow of marketing material physically or through legal consumer rights measures. These are generally seen as passive forms of avoidance. Active forms of resistance could be practices such as complaints, boycotts and renouncing consumerist roles in society, but also attempts to bypass traditional market actors and cocreate new forms of consumption, such as the open-source movement (c.f. Hemetsberger 2006). There are also studies that seek to understand consumers' communal and more subtle ways of altering, perverting and actively misinterpreting marketing messages for uses in the community, and the effects of this activity (Dobscha 1998; Ritson and Dobscha 1999).

As an example, Ritson and Dobscha (1999) describe how consumers try to rearticulate the messages offered in corporations' advertisements. Thus, consumers act as coauthors of the texts suggested by advertisers and marketers. The rules of advertising have been decoded by consumers, who actively and subversively put these rules into play and in doing so, redefine the very rules of the game. It is the way in which consumers intercept and (re)circulate marketing messages that makes us interested in consumer resistance research. Something similar takes place, we suggest, in what appear to be "failed" gamified marketing campaigns. However, there is a tendency to address consumer resistance only as a form of rebellion against dominant marketing messaging. Although focus is placed on consumers' "lived experience" of resistance (Dobscha 1998), these studies fail to address the productive sides of audience response in popular culture, which has been the focus of audience and fan studies (Taalas and Hirsjärvi 2013; see Hemetsberger 2006 for an exception). Hence, while game-playing can be seen as either rule-abiding or rule-breaking behaviour, it could similarly be understood as "kicking the ball" in terms of circulation as central to gaming cultures.

In order to develop a framework for understanding participant interaction in gamified practices, we now turn to Hans-Georg Gadamer and Johan Huizinga to further explore gaming as cultural practice, and to Kenneth Burke, who addresses human beings as symbol-using and -misusing animals who live and construct cultural worlds using rhetorical play of circulations and utterance in its centre.

Gamification and Digital Rhetorics

Hans-Georg Gadamer (1975) proposes that play is not an empty vessel into which meaning is poured. Rather one is already a player if the game rules make sense. In a marketing campaign, the game of consumer-producer relationship in the form of a market is played. From the perspective of game theory, the characteristic of game playing is that the game stands outside of everyday life, which makes it not serious but nevertheless, intensely engaging (Huizinga 1955, 13). According to Johan Huizinga's definition, on which Gadamer builds, a game is not played for profit. The gamers follow and interpret rules as they play the game, and the rules of play allow for formulation of social groupings that make sense within playing the game itself.

The interplay between gaming and the everyday life outside gaming is of interest to us. Recent game researchers have been exploring gaming in digital spaces as it is situated in the interplay of game rules and everyday experience, "in the complex relationships between social practices and technologies" (Paul 2013, 2). In the large-scale online games and complex multiplayer game communities, games typically incorporate elements that require multiple players and complex interaction among gamers that are not always known outside the game frame. This has led to the study of gaming cultures and their organization. More important to our current enquiry, gamers' understanding of game rules is what distinguishes designed games and everyday life (Huizinga 1955).

The concept of rules is central in the game design itself. Game researchers observe that digital games are generally based upon an idea of game balance (Paul 2013). Balance refers to a set of game functions, rules and progression designed in ways that all players would have an equal chance of progression, not based on arbitrary luck or present status differences. Generally, gamers appreciate, and game designers aim for, digital multiplayer games as meritocracies, where the most skilled players will excel. This makes players' experience of the game fair, giving all an equal chance at the start (ibid.). In the case of a gamified marketing campaign, it is clear that gamification is driven by market logic. It is the campaign producers who set the rules and goals of progression. A gamification design is seldom as balanced as a genuine game. Quite the contrary, the game rules in gamification are rooted in relationships largely existing outside the game, in the marketing communication nexus. This inherent imbalance opens up an opportunity for the analysis of gaming as culture-producing activity, with alternative rhetoric as a way to evoke balance in the gamified marketing campaign. Gamification is therefore not outside everyday life. Unlike "real games", it is precisely situated in the interplay of technology and social practices, making rhetoric the "equipment for living" for digital audiences (Rutten, Vrijders and Soetaert 2014).

Traditionally, rhetoric has been connected to the forms of persuasion and influence within language use and text. Literary critic Kenneth Burke's work on rhetoric (1950, 1966) sought to explore and expand the ties of language and culture in ways that were referred to as "new rhetorics", extending rhetorical analysis to symbol-uses and -misuses, to broader cultural context as a necessary part of living (Rutten, Vrijders and Soetaert 2014). The rhetorical perspective has recently attracted the attention of researchers in game studies (Dale 2014; Paul 2012; Thompson 2014). We employ Burke's rhetoric as a means of understanding the unbalanced dynamics of gamification from the perspective of consumer response.

We would like to supplement the common definition of game as "rule-following activity". While following rules is a means of focusing on strategies fixed in time and place, the rule-based definition tends to frame gaming "as it is seen". A scientific analysis of a game views it as an actual "reality" where the rules are similarly fixed. We suggest an alternative enquiry into gaming tactics whereby the very rules of the game are manipulated or evaded, making the rules themselves the target of the rhetorical play of persuasion. While the marketing campaign remains in the hands of the producers, its meanings can be altered and focus shifted to serve purposes other than the corporate messages. We show examples of this rule-bending and -breaking in gamified marketing campaigns where gamers introduce rules of symbolic action inherited in language games based on natural language. In all our cases, to be described below, traditional interaction between a single gamer and gamified frame has been largely replaced in favour of the interaction between players in multiple digital social media platforms.

Instead of the logological tradition of game play, we seek to engage with the more playful and creative aspects of game play, not as part of culture but as *culture-producing activity* (Huizinga 1955). In this quest, we join recent game studies scholars to explore games and gaming from the alternative perspectives in humanities (e.g., Paul 2012; Thompson 2014), as well as the recent writing on organization as game playing (e.g., Butler et al. 2011; Butler and Spoelstra 2011; Sørensen and Spoelstra 2012).

In our analysis, the starting point of game rules as reality outside everyday life is contrasted with a view of game rules as subject to rhetoric play that is a necessary part of life. Kenneth Burke (1966) describes the difference between reality and play as two approaches, much like the difference between scientific analysis that is concerned with the idea of "reality as it is experienced" and gaming as human interaction and symbol use in game progression as play. In Burke's view, the two approaches have a dialectic relationship in historical development. Burke proposes that we treat game playing as governed not by rules but by historicality, that constitutes Burke's social-rhetoric, "dramatist", analysis. Burke's game playing is never separated from other aspects of life. On the contrary, Burke sees game playing as an historical and inescapable aspect of life, where the playing subjects are rhetorically produced and constituted in time and place. While Burke proposes historicality as the authority in ongoing gaming, his concepts are geared for the study of the progression of playing, and further, the "constitutional games of changing the rules of the game" (Wess 1996, 27). If we accept Burke's notion of human action as symbolic, and in Burke's terms persuasive, it implies that symbolic action like play constitutes human relations and meaning. Applied to digital gaming, social play can be understood as producing continuous associations among players, game frames, producers and the wider society. This view positions game playing as persuasive action within symbolic systems, opening alternative ways to negotiate gaming and in our case, allows us to view the rules in gamified marketing campaigns as continuous rhetoric negotiation.

We seek to explore this culture-producing aspect of game play through the historical unfolding of gaming and draw on two of Burke's concepts to make our move. The first concept is "identification" (1950), which is central to

Burke's rhetoric and intrinsic to all forms of persuasion. The second concept is that of "terministic screens" (1966), which in Burke's analysis refers to the filtering out of selected terms that directs attention in a particular way, much like the colour filters fitted over a camera lens.

To sum up, our work focuses on the shift in marketing from producer messaging to participatory interaction. We understand gamification in marketing campaigns as a cultural practice of the intersection of producers and consumer networks. This means that consumers do not just play the game. They take an active part in the reformulation of the very rules of the game. They engage in the game of gamification that allows not only the tools to play by the strategic rules but also the progression of gaming that allows for breaking the strategic rules and identification to join a community of players. Our intention is to take the playful option of looking at game playing by investigating what is allowed in a particular game and what is not, what is "given" as a way to "directing interest" (Burke 1966, 44). This allows us to observe gamification as an interplay between different goals rather than just the alignment of goals (compare Burke 2014; and Dale 2014), and consumer game-playing is thus rendered as a kind of rhetoric. It presents itself as evading or skirting the rules of the formal play by introducing rhetorical rules of word play and interrupting the corporate goals as a form of resistance.

Research Design

Our research design is inspired by netnographic research strategy and methods, used to study online communities and digital consumer cultures (Kozinets 2002, 2010). The cases are constructed with the help of multiple online media sources, such as blog posts, digital newspaper entries, social media discussion, Twitter feeds and hashtags trending in social media. The data collected was used to construct several campaign stories. The selection criteria was twofold: 1) "Exemplary cases": The campaigns all employ game elements. The gaming has in various ways run wild, beyond the control of the producer. Contrary to corporate intent, the audience participation has turned into ridicule of the producer or even evolved into a hijacking of the original marketing campaign. The campaigns have also received media attention due to the unexpected turn of events and embarrassment on the part of the producers. 2) Only campaigns that are conducted on open forums and social media sites are included. Campaigns inside gaming platforms or MMOGs have been excluded because we want to explore gaming by a larger public rather than a specific gaming audience. While it would certainly be clearer to stay within such controlled environments, we seek to study the progression of playing in gamified campaigns that typically seem to involve all-out violating the formal game rules (contra Paul and Philpott 2009).

The data collected was used to construct four main campaign stories: 1) the low-cost airline Norwegian's "Airplane Tailfin Hero Competition"; 2) the "I love shopping at Waitrose because . . ." Twitter competition; 3) the

"My New 10 Euro" Banknote Selfie Competition by the European Central Bank; and 4) Nutella France's viral marketing campaign to explore the effects of gamification in marketing. However, throughout the analysis, we also refer to other similar campaign dynamics for comparison, such as NYPD and McDonalds.

We base our analysis on the uses of two game elements: hashtags and algorithms (i.e., the practice of tagging and the many roles of algorithms as game controller). Instead of treating these two elements as technological tools to apply, we are interested in their rhetorical powers in the interaction and communication among gamers in our gamified campaigns and in the process of forming a gaming community. In this sense, we are interested in the rhetorical technologies of playing rather than the technologies of establishing a technological platform. In our cases, the game enters into life: the game is taken outside the rules of the playing court through gaming community exchange enabled by the game elements available. We suggest that an analysis of gamification as an interplay of different cultures and goals can elucidate organizational processes whereby it has become difficult to control the game, and where the control exerted by the game's (corporate marketing) masters can quickly shift and be overthrown. The game "runs away" from its owners, as it were.

Analysis

Gaming Corporate Messaging: Consumer Resistance in Digital Networks

The basic idea in a gamified campaign is to activate your audience and let them provide both content and the circulation of the campaign. This means that for a campaign to go "viral" (i.e., for it to be shared and circulated by a high number of participants), the campaign must attract attention in high-density networks and in media space. A basic requirement for achieving recognition in media space, be it a gamified campaign or other event, is to create a particular hashtag (#). The hashtag has a dual purpose: the name of the hashtag will identify the event, and the event can be tracked, monitored and followed by the recurring hashtag or the technical mechanism of a hashtag search.

Identification is one of the key concepts in Kenneth Burke's rhetoric (1950). Identification is a necessary element in Burke's understanding of persuasion and therefore one of the cornerstones of his rhetoric. For identification to be possible, people must be able to recognize other players in the media space, or more specifically, to be able to find a common theme of play. Burke's rhetoric centers on "we" as constituting the playing audience, and the resulting playing subjectivity. "By constituting subjects as participants in a distinctive culture, identifications on a sub- or unconscious level make possible the activity of persuasion on a conscious level" (Wess 1996, 200). Identification is a central aspect of community and circulated responses.

For example, a hashtag is used as technology to follow a storyline or to follow an ongoing or unfolding event, in Twitter and Instagram. In the media space, hashtags became known to the large audiences during recent media events connected to natural disasters and events that have gained much attention to members of the audience on multiple media sites. Famous hashtags were employed during events such as the Arab Spring across Northern Africa in 2010 and the Occupy Wall Street movement in 2012.

In a similar way, gamification campaigns are strategically designed to draw attention. They call for participation as a persuasive and engaging form of marketing, while remaining intensely controlled. In Kenneth Burke's treatise, persuasion is supplemented by identification as a necessity for it. "To persuade a man only insofar as you can talk his language by speech, gesture, tonality, order, image, attitude, idea, identifying your ways with his" (Burke 1950, 55). Thus, hashtags can be an effective technology to achieve media attention by relatively simple means, at a low financial cost. Hashtags are a marketer's dream, as a campaign can be launched on a social media platform where the targeted consumers will be active anyway. The marketer need only catch their attention, as Dale (2014) has expressed it, to temporarily align their goals with the goals of the users. The question of what it is the user will identify themselves with, and what their goals might be, however, is open-ended and not subject to control by corporate messaging. It is left to the engagement in peer interaction. The corporate messenger launches the message, but after that, the message is "free".

In our first example, we will look at a marketing campaign on Twitter, where the high-end British food retailer Waitrose launched a competition under the hashtag #WaitroseReasons. On September 12, 2012, at 05.43 in the morning, Waitrose posted a Twitter launch of the campaign:

> Finish the sentence: "I shop at Waitrose because _____. #Waitrose Reasons".
>
> (Twitter.com/hashtag/waitrosereasons)

This campaign was part of Waitrose's branding effort to broaden the brand from its "posh reputation" (Ledwith 2012). Twitter users reacted swiftly, but not in the intended way. In a matter of hours, Waitrose's Twitter campaign resulted in hundreds of responses making fun of the retailer's image of a place where wealthy people go shopping, its expensive prices, the higher social status attached to people shopping at the brand's shops, and a cultural distinction expressed in the consumption choices of the Waitrose clientele:

> I shop at Waitrose because Tesco doesn't stock Unicorn food @inkognitoh
> I shop at Waitrose because the toilet paper is made from 24ct gold thread. (Unless its the Essentials range) @taitto40

> I shop at Waitrose because the produce is simply sublime darling, leave the peasants to shop at Lidl, haraar!! @ZainHassan786
> I shop at Waitrose because it's the shopping equivalent of burning fivers to keep warm. @Mike__Hodges
> I shop at Waitrose because the M&S "2 dine for £10" attracts the proles. @JoeBradbury1991
> I shop at Waitrose because darling, Harrods is just too much of a trek mid-week. @parapism
>
> (Twitter.com/hashtag/waitrosereasons)

That same afternoon, at 14.41, Waitrose posted a comment in Twitter, trying to end the campaign with some form of dignity:

> Thanks for all the genuine and funny #waitrosereasons tweets. We always like to hear what you think and enjoyed reading most of them.
>
> (Twitter.com/hashtag/waitrosereasons)

Needless to say, the Waitrose campaign had become unstoppable. The seemingly endless creation of memes kept circulating, and in the days that followed the campaign, Waitrose received major media attention (e.g., Chapman 2012; Ledwith 2012; Smithers 2012; 'Twitter jokers ruin' 2012) all recycling the "best" spoof recommendations to shop at Waitrose for the most fanciful luxury goods such as gold-plated toilet paper and unicorn food; or shopping there to avoid "being surrounded by poor people"; or referring to the personal experience of shopping at Waitrose as being surrounded by pretentious people. It was called one of the "best examples of social media goes wrong" (Stones 2012). Waitrose's efforts were also compared to other Twitter campaigns, based on simple tagging with sharing of stories and completing of phrases and with similar unconventional consumer response, such as that of McDonald's restaurants (January 2012) and the New York Police Department (April 2014).

Hashtags are used as an element in marketing campaigns to enable tracking of developments of the game, particularly with the aim of "going viral" (i.e., becoming widely circulated). Following Burke, identification is a necessary process in social games, and hashtags can be observed by any audience member and interpreted as identification, not only with the particular campaign but as an entry to the social gaming community, not like kicking the ball over to someone else in a game of soccer but as a an input to an ongoing tapestry of conversations. In the act of passing on memes or humorous entries, one becomes identified as a player in the game. It is notable that being a player does not necessarily indicate the team or the goals in the game. In the Waitrose case, the entries keep circulating for days, accumulating into a growing number of entries that could be defined as "class bashing" (Chapman 2012). Burke suggests that identification allows for a study of the rhetorical nature of human relations and how social cohesion is performed. In our cases, hashtags were used by the consumers and active audiences in their play to tag those who were participating in the gaming, (i.e., to identify who was "in the game").

Hashtags also allow for the development of the game with multiple iterations and for the development of common themes among the participants. In the Waitrose campaign, game participants used the hashtags as a sign of alternative interpretation of game content and bending rules while attaching nongame content and references to the campaign gaming. This progression of making memes and playing to find common themes was encouraged by community acceptance and by the lists of best entries published in the mass media. The hashtag was used by the active audiences to mark their "breaking away from the rules" set by the official producer game hashtag and used as identification. Tracing the hashtags trending in social media like Twitter, Instagram and Facebook allows other players to follow developments of the gaming in social media in ways that create multiple meanings. The can associate or disassociate from the hashtag, generating multiple unpredictable content and relationships. As one of the #myNYPD Twitter campaign commentators put it: "Lesson number 1 about hashtags: just because you created one doesn't mean you own it. #myNYPD" (Twitter.com/hashtag/myNYPD).

Gaming Meta-Game of Community Building

Our first example of active identification through hashtagging and resisting the corporate control of messaging stayed close to the gamified content. In our next example, we will see how a gamified campaign was hijacked by fan audience through the social practice of hashtagging.

Norwegian Air Shuttle's online competition "The Tailfin Hero" was launched in 2012 by the communication bureau Trigger. Norwegian's goal with the campaign was to "involve the public in the celebration of their 10-year anniversary in a way that would reinforce their position as a challenger in the airline industry, while also strengthening people's preferences for the brand in its four most important regional markets" (Trigger 2012a).

On their website, Norwegian listed potential candidates for the title and their intent with "The Tailfin Hero" in the following way: "it felt only natural for us to adorn the tails of our aircraft with personalities who have pushed the boundaries, challenged the established and inspired others" (Norwegian 2012).

The Tailfin Hero campaign was highly successful in attracting media and audience attention. It received several marketing industry competition nominations and prices: 2012 European Excellence Awards (nomination for Travel and Tourism); the HSMAI's annual marketing awards (won gold medals for best campaign in social media, best digital campaign and best use of multi-media); and the 2013 SABRE Awards (gold medal for best campaign in excising products) (Trigger 2012b). Trigger lists one of the achievements of the campaign inventing a new word for the Norwegian language:

> Who would have the honour of gracing Norwegian's new Tailfins? In only four weeks Norwegian's Tailfin hero election led to more than 500 stories in the media and several hundred thousand online votes. The word 'halehelt' (Tailfin hero) was placed number six on the Top Ten Words of 2012 list, developed by the Language Council of Norway and NHH—the Norwegian School of Economics.
> (Trigger 2012a)

The game element of this campaign was simple. Crowdsourced suggestions for Tailfin hero nominations were entered into a game site in social media.

On the game site, audience members could both nominate candidates for the competition, as well as vote on their favourite candidates. Various travel prizes were offered at the site Halehelter.no as motivation to participate. In addition to the actual game site, the competition used the hashtag #Tailfin and #halelet to tag campaign developments (see for example Twitter.com/hashtag/halehelt or Instagram.com/explore/tags/halehelt).

In Oslo, capital of Norway, the competition soon started breaking national news when Øystein Aarseth, also known by his stage name Euronymous, was entered into the competition to fly with Norwegian as a national hero. Aarseth was a former black-metal musician who started a legendary death metal band Mayhem in 1984. Aarseth was murdered in 1993 by a fellow band member, Varg Vikernes, who served 15 years in prison for the crime. When the "Tailfin Hero" competition closed, March 28, 2012, Aarseth was leading the popular vote over other top candidates, such as navy officer Trond André Bolle, who died in Afghanistan 2010, and Lutheran reformer Hans Nielsen Hauge. Aarseth's high number of votes came from heavy metal music fans who were campaigning for Aarseth's candidacy in social media. These fans managed to mobilize international fandom networks of death metal music.

While the game element is a familiar feature of popular social media voting contests, the Tail Heroes campaign distinguished itself through the mobilization of international networks of death metal fan community, with the systematic production and circulation of internet memes in fandom networks, sites, zines, e-zines and fanzines. Competition hashtags were circulated with memes on international death metal fan sites, resulting in a large participation. Death metal fans took the campaign outside Norway, utilizing hashtagging for making connections at will. Death metal fans connected hashtags in their social media communication, continuously linking #Norwegian, #Tailfin, #Aarseth, and #Euronymous hashtags in various combinations.

Although later collecting multiple prizes as a roaring success, the campaign was embarrassing for Norwegian's management while the competition was running. Norwegian was faced with a challenge of whether to enter the most popular suggestion to their short list of candidates for the final round of votes. The company was saved from the embarrassment when on March 31, 2012, the national newspaper *Dagbladet* published an interview with Aarseth's family, who did not wish for the rock musician to be entered into the short list for the final round of votes (Ottosen and Fjellberg 2012).

The death metal networks that participated in Norwegian's contest, of course, had no real interest in the air carrier's campaign as such. They participated for reasons of their own. Community building through symbolic action is a central feature of fan cultures, and the competition proved an opportunity to contribute to the community building and the sense of "we". This case demonstrates the community-building aspects of gaming that is central to fan networks, where the game is used to serve a purpose other than that intended by the marketing campaign strategists (e.g., Taalas and Hirsjärvi 2013). Drawing from Ludwig Wittgenstein's (1965) notion regarding building games, we argue that while it is typical for natural games of language to build on adding and circulating as building a language and community, it would be a misunderstanding to interpret gaming as playing within the rules of the gamified marketing campaign. Rather, such exchange and accumulation is a form of communication that is part of the natural language within fandom community exchange and intended for the fan audience, not primarily targeted at the outside audiences (Taalas and Hirsjärvi 2013). In this sense, popular media fandom participation is only marginally focussed on contributing to marketing campaign games. Rather, it interrupts or appropriates such messaging and utilizes the game elements to build its own community. The game is simply community-building. The identification option offered by hashtagging—shouting out "here we are"—allows the audience in gamification to construct a performative "we".

To understand meta-gaming for community in gamification, as demonstrated in the case of "The Tailfin heroes" case, we will dig deeper into the use of hashtags for identification in digital networks. Burke (1966) emphasizes his approach to language in terms of (symbolic) action, not as descriptive naming. We thus turn our attention to tagging as deliberate action of engagement with the game motor algorithms for communal gaming, not only as back stage features supporting a game frame.

Social Gaming and Rule-Breaking

In the Waitrose campaign, Waitrose themselves proposed a game in Twitter using a hashtag that was subsequently appropriated and used to resist the corporate messaging. In the case of the "Tailfin hero", fan networks were mobilised in Norwegian's competition with the help of active hashtagging. In both cases, the gaming was intended for a networked fan audience. In our third example, we move to the European Central Bank, where tagging is used to mobilise resources that shift the focus of the campaign entirely: the rules of the competition rules are breached, and hashtagging is utilised in the meta-gaming to contribute to the sense of "we" for the larger public. Here we will see how the European Central Bank's "selfie-competition" took an entirely different spin, allowing for a change of terminology that began with a simple banknote but "ran away" to become a critical commentary on a the banking system as a whole.

In September 2014, the European Central Bank (ECB) launched a "selfie-competition" in an effort to gain attention to the new 10-Euro banknotes (Chibber 2014). Havas Media France was responsible for the technical operation of the competition platform on behalf of the ECB, operating the competition website http://www.new-euro-banknotes.eu/. Havas had predicted that some participants might attempt to resist or disrupt the intended message, so the competition rules strictly forbid any improper use of the competition theme, the 10-Euro banknote, or the ECB, and such selfies would not be published on the game site:

> Selfies must not under any circumstances show the new €10 banknote in a situation that may adversely affect the reputation and honor of the ECB, is considered to be insulting, defamatory, racist, an affront to morals and public decency, pornographic or discriminatory or to constitute an incitement to crimes, offences and hatred based on race, religion, gender, appearance or of any other kind. Any selfie deemed improper by the Provider will not be posted, and thus will result in the disqualification of the Participant.
>
> ('New-euro-banknotes' 2014, 2–3)

To attract attention and to circulate the messages, the selfie competition used the hashtag #mynew10. While the content on the actual game site was highly moderated and censored, content outside the controlled space was in the hands of the consumer audiences. The results were, as Quartz reported "The hijacking of the ECB's euro selfie competition was swift and brutal" (Chibber 2014). The public policies in the Eurozone countries have put many people across Europe into a difficult financial situation, with high unemployment and growing tax burdens. The Twitter and Instagram messages carrying the official competition hashtag #mynew10 included entries mocking the Euro currency and the ECB. The selfies circulated on Twitter reflected everyday realities of Europeans today, all placed under the selfie competition hashtag #mynew10 and expressing utter disregard for the competition rules.

In one stream of selfies, the 10 Euro bank note was replaced with previous European currencies calling for the return to French Francs, Spanish Pesetas, Italian Lire and Greek Drachmas. Further, selfies included pictures of European statues with a hand over face in shame, and instructions on how to use the new bank note for consumption of illegal substances or to snort away the letters "Draghi", referring to ECB President Mario Draghi, whose signature is on the note. The audience circulated and tagged entries in social media directed the audience's attention away from the competition object of the bank note, instead linking the #mynew10 tag to everyday experiences, breaching of social norms and performances of shame in connection to national institutions. This directing of attention through accumulation and re-textualisation shows how even controlled campaigns can be changed in context, purpose and connections. In Burke's (1966) terms, this marks a change in terminology in the rules of play. While the game rules can limit the inputs to the actual game site, the social gaming that alters the intended message and connects to a new audience can profoundly alter the meanings associated with the game objectives.

From the perspective of aligning the corporate goals in gamification with the consumer audiences (e.g., Dale 2014), it would imply that the terminology on a subject, the way it directs attention operating as terministic screen, would be somehow fixed within the game framework from which the game rules are derived. In our case, however, we see a clear example of the sheer impossibility of such fixing. We view the case in Burke's optic, constructing worlds by using symbols and observing how language filters through and filters out aspects in our world that is considered real in scientific terms. Burke writes, "Even if any given terminology is a reflection of reality, by its very nature as a terminology it must be a selection of reality; and to this extent it must function also as a deflection of reality" (1966, 45). This logological nature of language and terms used in Burke's symbolic-rhetorical system is always related to the fictional. Hence, there are always other terministic screens possible for framing any given event or object, in various ways. Burke proposes a systematic study of such terministic usages and how they screen, directing our attention in a particular direction, acting much like "colour filters in photography" (ibid.: 44–48). Meta-gaming on rules seems to suggest that gamification opens up any goal rooted in a particular terminology to social gaming to alternative terminologies, screens and filterings in the audience response. We continue our study of the terministic screening at the heart of the gamified marketing campaign with a second illustrative case that focuses on the game motor itself.

Gaming the Game Motor Algorithm

While social gaming customarily seeks to test the limits of game rules, game creators typically anticipate this in the gamification process. What cannot be fully controlled, however, is the destabilising of the terministic screens on which the game rules themselves are based. This leads to the creation of strategically undesired or unexpected associations that can throw the marketing strategists off balance. Algorithms enable game functions in software game motor operations. Algorithms control the possible gaming inputs in terms of what responses are allowed or encouraged. Still, controls cannot be easily incorporated in gaming that is outside a particular game frame or environment, which is the case in most gamified campaigns where play takes place "off the field" so to speak (i.e., in open social media sites and Twitter or Instagram type of networked digital environments). In these cases, algorithms operate to filter responses and game developments according to present criteria and rules. This filtering might be necessary for the strategic control of gaming, but it serves other purposes that are worth special attention. Algorithmic filtering feeds into the game by rewarding participation and blocking out unwanted gaming interactions, as was already illustrated in our first cases of word play. The gaming on the terminology on which the algorithm is based will be our fourth and last case, to which we now turn.

Nutella France's viral marketing campaign offered consumers a chance to enter alternative words to be printed on virtual Nutella spread jars (February 2015). The game algorithm shows that the producer was hoping to restrict game entries with a long list of forbidden words already in the game's controlling algorithm. Some competent programmers in the audience found out that the source code of the game motor actually included a comprehensive list of words that had been ruled out from the game.

The gaming audience on the Internet turned the social gaming into finding and inventing words that would outsmart the algorithm and in doing so, framed the terministic premises that were incorporated in the Nutella game logarithm. While algorithms filter game input by default, they are also based on a particular set of vocabulary that in Nutella's case revealed themes the corporation did not want to discuss, including sexual orientation and religion. The gaming of the campaign, through the exposure of the list of forbidden words, quickly gained media attention, as the words included in the filtering algorithm included all the usual obscenities but also French words that had political connotations:

> . . . *diabetes*, *obese*, *bisphenol*, *phthalates*, *Indonesia*, *palm oil*, and *orangutan* were all banned. (Palm oil—*huile de palme* in French—is an ingredient in Nutella whose harvest threatens the natural habitats of orangutans in Indonesia; phthalates and bisphenols are endocrine-disrupting chemicals commonly found in plastic packaging.) And then there were a few head-scratchers on the blacklist: *lesbian*, *Jewish*, and *Muslim* were also disallowed by the 'Say It With Nutella' algorithm.
> (Anderson 2015; Gillman 2015)

As a response, Nutella changed the competition to fixed word messages, removing the free gaming aspect of the game algorithm. Once the game element is restricted to "keeping it clean", the game loses the dialectic nature of 'keeping it real' (Sköld and Rehn 2007). The consumer participation dynamics changes similar to the traditional mass marketing efforts.

Burke's concept of terministic screens focuses on exactly how language has this filtering effect, in the sense of it being able to constitute matters through screens altering their meanings and appearances. Terministic screens have the capacity to play a decisive role in what we can see, say, think and say that is considered "reality". In digital spaces, the filtering and operation of terministic screens in our gamification cases are located in the source code of the game motor, in the heart of the algorithm. In our cases, consumers become engaged in the gaming in order to bypass and alter the terministic screens incorporated in the algorithm. They try to outsmart the machine-imposed limiting rules. The game is not about Nutella anymore; it is about beating the machine, and using hashtags to let others know how that you did it.

Burke's interest does not lie within the filtering in the language, however. It focuses instead on the performative nature of this filtering aspect in language use and how it directs attention as experienced "reality", to what is allowed and possible in such reality articulated as a process or progress of the game playing. We pick up on this notion of observations of reality being "spinning out of possibilities implicit in our particular choice of vocabulary" (Burke 1966, 46). Social gaming in gamified marketing campaigns opens up the vocabularies of goals and rules into a playing field.

Concluding Discussion

This paper has investigated the phenomenon of consumer resistance in connection to gamification as it is applied to contemporary marketing campaigns. Inspired by studies of consumer resistance within consumer research (e.g., Dalli and Corciolani 2008; Dobscha 1998; Hemetsberger 2006; Ritson and Dobscha 1999), we analysed gamified marketing campaigns where audiences engaged and played in ways that disrupted or undermined the strategic marketing protocols from the perspective of Burkean symbolic action.

Our analysis indicates that these disruptions are a form of consumer activism with the purpose not only of redirecting marketing campaigns but also an engagement in an organizational process of another kind. We view gamification as a culture-producing activity, and what gamers are seeking is not a relation to the producer. They tap into the social space that the producer offers, but they use it as a playground for contesting the goals and rules of the marketplace. They are playing around with the very game they were supposed to play. Gamified marketing campaigns seem to incorporate disruptions, resistance and creating alternative rules for the game, as a meta-game of gamification. We focused here on how communities are produced in the process of gaming through identification and media interaction, the breaching of the formal game rules and even hacking the controlling aspects incorporated in game algorithms in the game development. This rule-bending, skirting and breaking became a form of social identification, an effort to find a common theme among participants, contributing to building of playing community of rule-breakers.

Further, our analysis highlighted the meta-play in gamification as negotiation about the concept of rules and regulations, arguing for alternative readings of marketing campaigns "gone wrong". Based on our findings, we suggest a reading from the perspective of such iteration being part of active audiences' engagement that produces alternative terminologies and forms of communication, and further, performative digital rhetoric community. We suggest that gaming could be more fruitfully approached as "a strategy of interpretation and thus more of a cognitive activity that is then reflected in one's symbol use" (Mahan-Hays and Aden 2003, 35). Gaming, we suggest, should be seen as an attitude in media space, rather than a matter of identity-building or identity confirmation.

Gamification of promotion campaigns should thus be seen as a site for understanding how market relationships are played in meta-games ruled by identification as organization of gaming community in digital space. This approach opens up terministic screens incorporated in strategic messaging and in corporate goals for gaming but which do not seem to be offering much help for influencing them. Game algorithms work as filters that direct interest through screening and policing game play to stay within the rules of gamified campaigns. The algorithm is not simply a game element, however. It is rooted in vocabularies of the embedded market relations. The active audiences are producing community rhetorics to play with, and thereby contest, these relations in the game developments. Our analysis calls into question the logological separateness of the game from other parts of life. We suggest that focusing on the scientific reading of gaming leaves unanalyzed the organizational spaces created by consumer meta-play. When gamification is applied to marketing, it brings to the surface the rules and regulations of consumer-producer relationships. Viral play and breaking the game rules open up the traditional game rules and move them into the sphere of meta-play and struggle for meaning, identity and subjectivities (Cherrier 2009; Mikkonen, Moisander and Firat 2011).

As we have shown, the dynamics of circulations and usages in social gaming can be read differently from the perspective of digital gaming rhetorics. The community-building gaming culture seems to be a growing, becoming a casual activity as a kind of "technology to live by" in digital spheres (Paul 2012). While utterance and circulations are at the centre of this organisation, the "we" is increasingly constructed through playful rhetorical utterances, not as a protest as such but as a community through identification, a hashtag community. In gamified marketing campaigns, the historical development of gaming on meta-play becomes apparent. Historicality becomes the only authority setting the rules of a game that is ongoing. The rules of both marketing and the formal game become the subject of social gaming rather than the contest itself. Games become meta-games. We suggest that the game of gamification might be better understood as participatory interaction rather than corporate messaging, as the encounter of different goals rather than the alignment of goals (compare Dale 2014). This process further includes forms of resistance: When the audience engages in "rhetorics of gaming", the campaign becomes a site for consumer resistance and development of community rather than a simple tool for marketing messaging.

References

Anderson, L.V. 2015. "Nutella's Attempts to Keep People From Calling It 'Poop' Are Valiant but Futile." *Slate*, March 3. Accessed January 27, 2016. http://www.slate.com/blogs/browbeat/2015/03/03/nutella_s_say_it_with_nutella_viral_marketing_campaign_what_we_can_learn.html.

Arnould, Eric J., Linda L. Price, and Avinash Malshe. 2006. "Toward a Cultural Resource-Based Theory of the Customer" in *The Service-Dominant Logic of Marketing: Dialog, Debate and Directions*, edited by Robert F Lusch and Stephen L. Vargo. New York: M E Sharpe, 320–333.

Burke, Brian. 2014. *Gamify: How Gamification Motivates People to Do Extraordinary Things Hardcover*. Brookline: Bibliomotion.

Burke, Kenneth. 1950. *A Rhetoric of Motives*. New York: Prentice-Hall.

Burke, Kenneth. 1966. *Language as Symbolic Action: Essays on Life, Literature, and Method*. Berkeley: University of California Press.

Butler, Nick, Lena Olaison, Martyna Sliwa, Bent Meier Sørensen, and Sverre Spoelstra. 2011. "Work, Play, and Boredom." *Ephemera* 11, no. 4: 329–355.

Butler, Nick, and Sverre Spoelstra. 2011. "Your Excellency." *Organization* 19, no. 6: 891–903.

Chapman, Matthew. 2012. "Waitrose Twitter campaign hijacked by 'upper class' jibes." *Marketingmagazine*, September 20. Accessed January 27, 2016. http://www.marketingmagazine.co.uk/article/1150951/waitrose-twitter-campaign-hijacked-upper-class-jibes.

Cherrier, Helene. 2009. "Anti-Consumption Discourses and Consumer-Resistant Identities." *Journal of Business Research* 62, no. 2: 181–190.

Chibber, Kabir. 2014. "The hijacking of the ECB's euro selfie competition was swift and brutal." *Quartz*, November 18. Accessed January 27, 2016. http://qz.com/298378/the-hijacking-of-the-ecbs-euro-selfie-competition-was-swift-and-brutal.

Conaway, Roger, and Mario Cortés Garay. 2014. "Gamification and Service Marketing." *SpringerPlus* 3: 653.

Dale, Steve. 2014. "Gamification: Making Work Fun, or Making Fun of Work?" *Business Information Review* 31, no. 2: 82–90.

Dalli, Daniele, and Matteo Corciolani. 2008. "Collective Forms of Resistance: The Transformative Power of Moderate Communities." *International Journal of Market Research* 50, no. 6: 757–775.

Deterding, Sebastian, Dan Dixon, Rilla Khaled, and Lennart Nacke. 2011. "From Game Design Elements to Gamefulness: Defining 'Gamification'." Paper presented at *MindTrek11*, Tampere, Finland, September 28–30.

Dobscha, Susan. 1998. "The Lived Experience of Consumer Rebellion Against Marketing." *Advances in Consumer Research* 25: 91–97.

Escribano, Flavio. 2012. "Gamification as the Post-Modern Phalanstère: Is the Gamification Playing with Us or Are We Playing with Gamification?" in *The Video Game Industry: Formation, Present State, and Future*, edited by P. Zackariasson and T.L. Wilson. New York & London: Routledge, 198–217.

Gadamer, Hans-Georg. 1975. *Truth and Method*, tr. W. Glen-Dopel, London: Sheed and Ward.

Gillman, Ollie. 2015. "Lesbian, Jewish, Muslim . . . and orangutan: The bizarre list of words Nutella has banned from jars in France." *Dailymail*, March 2. Accessed January, 27 2016. http://www.dailymail.co.uk/news/article-2975716/

Lesbian-Jewish-Muslim-orangutan-bizarre-list-words-Nutella-banned-jars-France.html.
Hemetsberger, Andrea. 2006. "When David Becomes Goliath Ideological Discourse in New Online Consumer Movements." *Advances in Consumer Research* 33, no. 1: 494–500.
Holt, Douglas. 2002. "Why Do Brands Cause Trouble? A Dialectical Theory of Consumer Culture and Branding." *Journal of Consumer Research* 29: 70–90.
Huizinga, Johan. 1955. *Homo Ludens: A Study of the Play-Element in Culture*, tr. R. F. C. Hull. London: Routledge.
Huotari, Kai, and Juho Hamari. 2012. "Defining Gamification—A Service Marketing Perspective." Paper presented at *MindTrek*, Tampere, Finland, October 3–5. http://www.rolandhubscher.org/courses/hf765/readings/p17-huotari.pdf.
Kozinets, Robert V. 2002. "The Field Behind the Screen: Using Netnography for Marketing Research in Online Communications." *Journal of Marketing Research* 39, no. 1: 61–72.
Kozinets, Robert V. 2010. *Netnography: Doing Ethnographic Research Online*. Thousand Oaks: SAGE.
Ledwith, Mario. 2012. "'I shop at Waitrose Because . . . I Don't Like Being Surrounded By Poor People': Internet Jokers Hijack 'Posh People's Supermarket' Twitter Stunt." *Daily Mail*, September 20. Accessed January 27, 2016. http://www.dailymail.co.uk/news/article-2205975/Waitrose-Twitter-backlash-I-shop-Waitrose-I-dont-like-surrounded-poor-people.html.
Lucassen, Garm, and Slinger Jansen. 2014. "Gamification in Consumer Marketing—Future or Fallacy?" *Procedia—Social and Behavioral Sciences* 148: 194–202.
Mahan-Hays, Sarah, and Roger C. Aden. 2003. "Kenneth Burke's 'Attitude' at the Crossroads of Rhetorical and Cultural Studies: A Proposal and Case Study Illustration." *Western Journal of Communication* 67: 32–55.
Mikkonen, Ilone, Johanna Moisander, and Fuat Firat. 2011. "Cynical Identity Project as Consumer Resistance: The Scrooge as a Social Critic." *Consumption Markets and Culture* 14, no. 1: 99–116.
Murray, Jeff B., and Julie L. Ozanne. 1991. "The Critical Imagination: Emancipatory Interest in Consumer Research." *Journal of Consumer Research* 18: 129–144. http://www.marketing.pamplin.vt.edu/facultyFolder/julieOzanne/01socialwebsite/professional/researchpapers/1991_JCR_critical.pdf.
New-euro-banknotes. 2014. "Terms and Conditions of the 'Selfie with the New €10' Competition". Accessed January 27, 2016. http://www.new-euro-banknotes.eu/press/game-10/selfie/EN-Terms-conditions-competition-Selfie-new-euro-10.pdf.
Norwegian. 2012. "Tail Fin Heroes". Accessed January 27, 2016. http://www.norwegian.com/uk/about/our-story/tail-fin-heroes.
Ottosen, Peder, and Anders Fjellberg. "Boikotter Norwegian: Familien vil ikke at Øystein «Euronymous» Aarseth figurere som en «halehelt» på et fly." *Dagladet*, March 31 2012. Accessed January 27, 2016. http://www.dagbladet.no/2012/03/31/kultur/musikk/norwegian/halehelter/black_metal/20917428.
Paul, Christopher A. 2012. *Wordplay and the Discourse on Video Games: Analyzing Words, Design, and Play*. New York: Routledge.
Paul, Christopher A. 2013. "Resisting Meritocracy and Reappropriating Games: Rhetorically Rethinking Game Design." Paper presented at 'Internet Research 14.0: Resistance and Appropriation', Association of Internet Researchers (AoIR) Conference. Denver, Colorado. 23–26 October 2013.

Paul, Christopher A., and Jeffrey Philpott. 2009. "The Rise and Fall of CTS: Kenneth Burke Identifying with the World of Warcraft." *DiGRA Conference—Breaking New Ground: Innovation in Games, Play, Practice and Theory*. Conference proceedings. http://www.digra.org/wp-content/uploads/digital-library/09287.18568.pdf.

Paulsen, Neil, and Tor Hernes. 2003. *Managing Boundaries in Organizations— Multiple Perspectives*. Houndmills: Palgrave/Macmillan.

Ritson, Mark, and Susan Dobscha. 1999. "Marketing Heretics: Resistance Is/Is Not Futile." *Advances in Consumer Research* 26, no. 1: 159.

Rutten, Kris, Dries Vrijders, and Ronals Soetaert. 2014. "Rhetoric as Equipment for Living: Kenneth Burke, Culture and Education—Reflections on the First European Kenneth Burke Conference." *KB Journal* 10, no. 1. Accessed February 5, 2016. http://kbjournal.org/rutten_vrijders_soetaert_introduction.

Seaborn, Katie, and Deborah Fels. 2015. "Gamification in Theory and Action: A Survey." *International Journal Human-Computer Studies* 74: 14–31.

Sköld, David, and Alf Rehn. 2007. "Makin' It, by Keeping It Real: Street Talk, Rap Music, and the Forgotten Entrepreneurship from 'the 'Hood'." *Group Organization Management* 32, no. 1: 50–78.

Smithers, Rebecca. 2012. "Waitrose Twitter hashtag invites ridicule." *The Guardian*, September 19, 2012. Accessed January 27, 2016. http://www.theguardian.com/business/2012/sep/19/waitrose-twitter-hashtag.

Sørensen, Bent Meier, and Sverre Spoelstra. 2012. "Play at Work: Continuation, Intervention and Usurpation." *Organization* 19, no. 1: 81–97.

Stones, Mike. 2012. "Social media goes wrong: 'I shop at Waitrose because Tesco doesn't stock unicorn food'." *Foodmanufacture*, September 20. Accessed January 27, 2016. http://www.foodmanufacture.co.uk/Business-News/Social-media-goes-wrong-I-shop-at-Waitrose-because-Tesco-doesn-t-stock-unicorn-food.

Taalas, Saara L., and Irma Hirsjärvi. 2013. "Fandom as Mode of Second Production— Active Audienceship of the Rising Shadow." *International Journal of Management Concepts and Philosophy* 7, no. 3–4: 245–262.

Thompson, Jason C. 2014. *The Game Culture Reader*. Cambridge: Cambridge Scholars Publishing.

Trigger. 2012a. "Norwegians Nye Halehelter". Accessed January 27, 2016. https://www.trigger.no/en/arbeider/norwegians-nye-halehelter.

Trigger. 2012b. "Norwegian's new tail fin heroes". Accessed January 27, 2016. https://www.trigger.no/en/arbeider/norwegians-nye-halehelter.

"Twitter jokers ruin 'Why I shop at Waitrose . . . ' promotion." *The Telegraph*, September 19, 2012. Accessed January 27, 2016. http://www.telegraph.co.uk/technology/twitter/9553232/Twitter-jokers-ruin-Why-I-shop-at-Waitrose . . . -promotion.html.

Vargo, Stephen L., and Robert Lusch. 2004. "Evolving to a New Dominant Logic for Marketing." *Journal of Marketing* 68, no. 1: 1–17.

Vargo, Sephen L., and Robert Lusch. 2008. "Service-Dominant Logic: Continuing the Evolution." *Journal of the Academy of Marketing Science* 36, no. 1: 1–10.

Wess, Robert. 1996. *Kenneth Burke—Rhetoric, Subjectivity, Postmodernism*. Cambridge: Cambridge University Press.

Wittgenstein, Ludwig. 1965. *Philosophical Investigations*. New York: Macmillan.

5 Win, Earn, Gain

Gamification in the History of Retailing

Franck Cochoy and Johan Hagberg

Introduction

Gamification is clearly in vogue. Although the term *gamification* was only introduced quite recently (according to Deterding et al. 2011a, the first documented use occurred in 2008), its application in the meaning "use of game design elements in non-game contexts" (Deterding et al. 2011b, 1) has a long history. In this longer history, however, gamification represents "the most recent and visible instantiation of the interpenetration of games and everyday life" (Walz and Deterding 2014, 6). As the definition of gamification suggests, gamification means that something that is "gamified" does not necessarily make it a "full-fledged" game, but rather that many parts of everyday life may include one or more aspects of games (Deterding et al. 2011a). Examples of applications where such game design elements are used range from marketing communication (e.g., Dymek 2014), health promotion (King et al. 2013), risk management (Bajdor and Dragolea 2011), and education (e.g., Kapp 2012), to green consumption (Fuentes, this volume).

One element that is central in the definition of games, and independent of the context in which they are applied, is that they include some form of outcome. Based on his review of game definitions, Juul (2005, 36) identified six specific features of games: 1) they are rule-based; 2) they have variable, quantifiable outcomes; 3) different outcomes are assigned different values; 4) the player exerts effort to influence the outcome; 5) the player feels emotionally attached to the outcome; and 6) the consequences of the activity are negotiable. Thus, outcomes constitute a central element of games; according to Juul, these are variable and quantifiable, assigned different values, and associated with players' efforts and attachment. However, in addition to the variability of outcomes in a specific game, there is also a variety between different games and contexts of what constitutes the particular outcome. Outcomes are particularly prominent in business contexts, where gamification primarily serves as a means used for achieving more important goals in terms of economic success and profit. Therefore, this chapter turns its attention to outcomes as a particular element of games from a faceted approach in terms of what constitutes the outcome and as well as how it is achieved.

This chapter turns towards the field of retailing, which could be seen as an example of such a nongame context where game elements have been used in different ways over the years. The chapter explores four examples of the use of game elements in historical and contemporary practice of retailing in the U.S. In addition to illustrating that the use of game elements has been part of the retailing scene during the last century, the more specific purpose of the chapter is to discuss variation concerning outcomes of games. The examples range from competitions initiated towards the readership of the *Progressive Grocer*, display contests, loyalty schemes and retailer smartphone apps. The first example consists of competitions introduced by the *Progressive Grocer* magazine that were oriented toward the retailers in the 1920s. The second example is a campaign conducted by the Kellogg Company that simultaneously included grocers and their customers in the 1950s. The third example is the so-called loyalty programmes that became popular among many retailers during the 1990s. The fourth and final example is the use of gamification in retailer apps in the 2010s. These four cases will be analysed from two particular points of view, which will be presented next.

Winning, Earning, and Gaining: On Game Addiction in the Retail Context

The main argument of the chapter is that the current discussion about gamification should include a variety of notions of what constitutes the outcome of games. Drawing on our four historical examples from the history of retailing in the U.S., we propose that this development can be furthered, first by relying on Natasha Schüll's recent theory of "addiction by design" (2012), and second by refining this framework even more so by distinguishing between three different meanings of the French word *gagner*.

In her fascinating account of Las Vegas casinos and gambling machines, the American ethnographer Natasha Schüll proposes an implicit theory of "addiction by design". Attaching gamblers to their game addiction, Schüll explains, is not so much a matter of betting on the players' hope to win money as it is a matter of offering them a specific architecture, which helps isolate them from the outer world, as they enter a private "zone" and dive into the somewhat hypnotic practice of gambling. This architecture is both external, embedded in the maze-like and dark design of the casino, and internal, incorporated in the inner design of the gambling machines. Indeed, these machines have the dual ability to: 1) present losses as "near wins" by displaying the missing cards close to the ones obtained; and 2) give the impression that rare cards are as probable as the others. These two features entice the players to repeatedly renew their bets, and all the more so because casinos provide new payment facilities, based on special credit cards and payment systems. Enveloped by the protective atmosphere of the casino, embarked by the near-win incentives, and assisted by payment facilities, the player succumbs to a repetitive gaming practice that results in addiction (Schüll 2012).

Retailing places are both very close and quite different from the casinos' addictive gaming context—even if a major French retailer has taken "Casino" as its brand name! Like casinos, grocery stores aim to addict consumers to a purchasing game, and like in Las Vegas, they play on architectures that lead consumers to review the goods on display rather than interacting with people. The same stores also implement special devices, like contests, promotions, and even games, aimed at "heating" the consumption experience and encouraging repetitive consumption practices. Casinos and grocery stores are both "B to B to C" markets: devices are sold to them (B to B) on the argument that these devices are meant to entice gamblers and consumers to spend more (B to C). This said, it is uncertain if retailing devices are as powerful as casinos' design and machines. In the grocery business, the one who is addicted is not necessarily the end consumer, but rather the professional who wants to addict her or him. Moreover, the consumption experience, unlike the one-dimensional gambling practice, is a fully multidimensional game, playing on a much greater variety of devices and motives.

This will be better understood by referring to another fundamental difference: gaming in the supermarket takes a richer meaning than gaming in the casino. In order to catch this difference, it is useful to refer to the French word *gagner*. This word could indeed be translated to either winning, earning, or gaining. According to the Merriam-Webster dictionary, to *win* implies that one achieves "victory in a fight, contest, game, etc." and also that one gets "something such as a prize" by achieving this victory as well as "to get (something) by effort". To *earn* implies that one receives a "return for effort and especially for work done or services rendered" or "to bring in by way of return". It also has the meaning of coming to "be duly worthy of or entitled or suited to" or "to make worthy of or obtain for" something (such as a promotion). To *gain* implies that something wanted or valued "is gotten: something that is gained; especially: money gotten through some activity or process", or "something that is helpful [such as an] advantage or benefit" or "an increase in amount, size, or number". In the following sections, we will provide four examples of the use of game elements in retailing. These examples are like "snapshots" drawn from different sources and time periods of the history of retailing. The four examples are analysed based on the different emphasis of winning, earning, and gaining that are promoted (i.e., actions that are at the core of games and economic practice and thus help bridge the two). The chapter argues that the distinctions between these terms are important in understanding the history of gamification in retailing. Each of these four examples is further scrutinized below.

Gamification 1. *Progressive Grocer* Competitions

Games were very soon introduced in business, and one of the best ways to monitor such an introduction is to look at the trade press, whose purpose is precisely to perform (describe and advance) innovations in business. Our focus being on retailing, we propose to focus on *Progressive Grocer*, a magazine that promoted innovative techniques among American retailers from the early 20th century. In the subsequent developments, the references to the journal adopt the YYYY, MM, PP format, where YYYY refers to the year, MM to the month, and PP to the pages of each quoted article. Although the *Progressive Grocer* targeted grocers, its clients were actually the advertisers; in other words, all of the companies that marketed supplies for shops, cash registers, and other commercial equipment, but also all the magazine press (*Companion, Ladies Home Journal, Life* . . .), which advertised in *Progressive Grocer* in order to sell their own advertising space, and of course, all food manufacturers, who were trying to persuade grocers to stock their products.[1]

From this point of view, this business was quite successful, if we look at the growth of its readership, the variety and number of its advertisers, its rise in turnover, and its continuously increasing size, first in the number of pages and then in terms of format. How do we know this? Just as earlier, regarding the "establishment" of the readership, we know this thanks to the magazine itself. Their own efforts have provided us with an explanation, formatting, and the staging of signs to prove its own efficacy. This saves us the trouble from having to find this information or count the increase in pages ourselves. Here we have a very particular strategy, consisting in establishing recursive loops between utterances and their enactment, and thus establishing a kind of circular performativity, where the discourse becomes increasingly performative as it encompasses elements "attesting to" its past performance. From the outset, far from being simply recorded and published, these loops were also "provoked" in the sense given to this participle by Fabian Muniesa (2014) as an effect of a performative act.

A particularly clever mode of such "provocation" lay in the organization of various contests that the magazine very quickly and repeatedly presented as a way to attract consumer attention and develop sales. For instance, the magazine—which itself featured a regular "quiz" page to entertain its readers—reported that organizing a contest (probably guessing the weight)[2] increased cheese sales by 90 percent (1936, 11, 118) and claimed that "Sales Prize Spurs Saturday Extras" (1936, 03, 66). Based on such convictions, it gave precise advice to its readers about how to organize such events, by "put[ting] drama into store contests" (1937, 10, 36–41). More precisely, the journal starts from the assumption that: "People like action. Action in competition, whenever possible. Above all, people delight in conflicting action. Because we all love contests or fights, the sporting pages of a paper are closely read". And *Progressive Grocer* quotes various successful implementations of such a conception in the retailing sector: by sponsoring a bicycle race, three beverage makers have "attracted 40,000 people who were not only fed appropriate advertising about the three beverages through the loud speakers but had to buy them in quantities to quench their long drawn-out thirst". Furthermore, a chain store held a contest for the "champion cracker salesman of the week". Far from being oriented to the supply side only, this contest helped increasing consumers' purchases. Indeed, the results were displayed near the cash registers, boosting sales, "for each customer wishes to see her favorite clerk win the prize", and so on (ibid., p. 36). Prize contests for consumers were highly encouraged, along with the argument that, "One of the reasons why people enter contests is the enjoyment they get from anticipation. Aside from the anticipation of either tangible or intangible rewards, there's considerable value to be capitalized. Many types of contests are substantially the same as games sold in toy stores for good American money" (1941, 01, 30).

What is good for retailers is also good for *Progressive Grocer*. One of the most interesting type of such devices is a competition that the journal organized for itself. Beyond an apparent concern to entertain its readership, the contest aimed more to measure the latter's size and involvement. In July 1922 (i.e., only seven months after its inception), the magazine announced that it was holding a competition with $100 in prizes, to be distributed to the readers who provided the best captions to a picture showing a grocer preparing to violently slay a fly with a flyswatter, just above a crate filled with eggs (1922, 07, 24–25). In subsequent years, the same caption competition for the cover was repeated, such as in 1923, with an image showing a young employee so engrossed in reading a magazine on the art of managing a grocery store that he forgets he had come to draw off some molasses from a barrel, which is now overflowing (1923, 04, 20–21). Every year, not only were these competitions the subject of a preliminary advert, but also reminders aimed at maximizing the number of participants (1922, 09, 22–23; 1923, 05, 20–21; 1923, 06, 1; 1923, 07, 58; 1924, 07, 20–21).

Who won these competitions? The question seems absurd given how obvious the answer is: the winners were the winners, of course; for example, the winner of the first prize for the 1923 competition was an employee of a grocery shop in Kansas, whose caption for the picture of the young, distracted employee was the magnificent play on words: "Storing the mind but not minding the store" (1923, 08, 20). However, one has to beware of riddles that are too easy; one winner could conceal another. The magazine was gambling on ensuring that the real winner of these competitions was most often not the receiver of the ten or so dollars for first prize but the organizer of the competition itself. How? By foreshadowing the technique of real-time competitions so dear to today's television channels: as we know, this method consists of promising a flat screen television, a holiday, or a car to a happy winner, drawn by lots from all those who have called a premium rate number and given the correct answer to a bafflingly easy question.

Figure 5.1 How to run a retail store (Progressive Grocer 1923, 04)

Thanks to the tens of thousands of small "phone bets" collected from all the participants, pleased that they know the answer and thus hoping, for a few cents, to obtain an alluring prize, the channel manages to make a net profit of tens of thousands dollars, pounds, or euros. In the *Progressive Grocer* competitions, participation was free and the answers were not as easy, but there was an economic gain, admittedly indirect, and one more "hoped" than "achieved": the number of answers received was in fact a means of measuring the magazine's readership. Therefore, every competition came with the simultaneous announcement of the number of participants. Five months after the 1922 competition, the magazine published a double-page spread of "self-publicity" entitled, "Answering that question: 'DO GROCERS READ?'" The sales pitch that followed mentioned that more than 60,000 answers had been received in response to the recent competition as "proof", meant to dissipate the "common fallacy that grocers don't read" (1922, 12, 2–3). In 1923, the magazine reiterated the process as an advert, proudly proclaiming that "5,649 readers wrote The PROGRESSIVE GROCER in response to a recent contest". The advert itself emphasized that this figure represented "10% of its total circulation", adding that this would have been equivalent to a response from 200,000 readers had it been for a publication with a print run of two million copies. In other words, the coverage of a national magazine, and concluding on a triumphal question, whose (negative) answer is as easy to guess as the overpriced guessing games of today: "Did you ever hear such a response?" (1923, 08, 2–3). The competition was therefore explicitly used as a very clever system for measuring readership, able to allay advertisers' suspicions, not only regarding the possible lack of appetite on the part of the grocers for reading, but more fundamentally, vis-à-vis the free press model, whose distribution did not in way guarantee that it was read, given that it was imposed rather than requested, and at the risk of the most common fate of all adverts, which was not to be read, and thus ignored, or even thrown away. This first case clearly shows how games were soon articulated to business objectives, and even how one business game (having the customers play) plays itself on a secondary one (having the customers play in the hope to *win* is for the magazine a way to *earn* knowledge about its own activity and thus *gain* a distinctive advantage). Natasha Schüll showed that gaming devices can be addictive, but the *Progressive Grocer* example clearly shows that there also exists a corresponding addiction to gaming with these very gaming devices aimed at developing consumer addiction.

Gamification 2. Display Contest

Like contemporary casinos (i.e., archetypal examples of game businesses!) any retail outlet appears as a "captation device", for example, as a special apparatus that plays on consumers' dispositions (here, the pleasure to play) in order to attract them and have them consume, thus spending their money (Cochoy 2007). Significantly, it is no wonder that the name of one major French retailer is Casino! If window displays are a type of captation device (aimed at attracting consumers), display contests about the best display are another (aimed at attracting the ones who pretend to attract consumers):

Figure 5.2 Display contest (Progressive Grocer 1953, 09, 132–133)

On the left portion of the above two images, the Kellogg Company offers a child's mask for each cereal box sold; on the right, the same company organizes a display contest aimed at promoting these same "mask boxes" and sharing $15,000 in prizes between the lucky grocers. The same "gift logic" of rewarding a purchase may be found on both sides, as if one tries to seduce grocers with the same stratagems, which are presented to them as a way of seducing clients. But who is the more naïve here? The child or the grocer? Of course, the values of the gains are incommensurable: while the former gets a cheap mask, the second receives tens, hundreds, or even thousands of dollars. But a closer look shows that the asymmetry of values is counterbalanced by the difference of gain expectations. While the child is certain to get back with a mask, the grocer is in no way sure to win the prize he covets. Here of course lies the trick of the chosen method: since winning is only possible if one joins the race, the organization of the contest allows Kellogg to obtain, for free, the setting up of many more displays than it will have to reward. All in all, everything looks as if the grocer is pushed in the oven of the profit-making machine by paper-children (the masks) waved by a much bigger witch than him.

Therefore, the illusion obviously consists of seducing the grocers in painting in glowing colours the promise of catching clients and the profits, which supposedly come with them, without revealing the aim to catch grocers in turn. In commercial relationships, seductive frames do not only take multiple appearances and try to target all sorts of subjects, but they are also fitted into the others: the packaging house is in the aisle, which is in the shop, which is in the trade mark, which is in the *Progressive Grocer*, etc.! Here, the appetite for a given gain blurs the uncertainties of an uncertain win and thus hides the unbalanced distribution of earnings between the one who organizes the game (who always wins) and the one who plays it (who dreams to gain but who loses in most cases). Once again, gaming patterns are clearly articulated: the trick is about addicting professional gamers to supposedly addictive market devices.

Gamification 3. Loyalty Schemes

The same dynamic of gaining, winning, and earning that could be observed in the past, as evidenced through the particular example of *Progressive Grocer*, has experienced novel developments and is refined today. Whereas in past retailing the spread of service based on credit and delivery arrangements had the power to strongly attach customers to their local dealers, the subsequent development of cash and carry systems and self-service operations favoured competition and thus shifted customer loyalty from a given asset to a business goal.

Now, loyalty programs are also often mentioned as an example of gamification in business settings (see e.g., Zichermann and Linder 2010). Their popularity in various settings have resulted in different terms such as "reward programmes, frequency reward programmes, frequent-shopper programmes, loyalty cards or schemes, point cards, advantage cards, and frequent flyer programmes" (Dorotic et al. 2012, 218), which are herein considered synonyms. A search for "loyalty program" in combination with "gamification" on Google has 30,100 results (15 Dec., 2013). The connection among gamification and loyalty programs is often related to the use of points. However, authors have pointed out that contemporary loyalty programs in general lack important elements in order to serve as good examples of gamification. The Starbucks loyalty program is often mentioned as an example of gamification, but as El-Khuffash points out, "For the Starbucks Rewards program to truly be gamified, it needs to add elements of fun, choice, and challenges for users to accomplish" (2013, 29). In this section, we will describe the evolution and contemporary use of loyalty programs as a type of marketing tool and specifically its application in retailing.

Loyalty programs in marketing were developed from a notion that customer loyalty creates long-term profit. The increased profits are based on reduced cost of recruitment (as there is already an established relationship), because loyal customers tend to purchase more and also make recommendations to other consumers (e.g., Tapp 2008). While it may seem unreasonable that these principles of increased loyalty lead to increased profit, the question of whether loyalty programs do indeed lead to profit growth in reality has been much discussed by researchers since the 1990s (see e.g., O'Brien and Jones 1995; Dowling and Uncles 1997; O'Malley 1998). The introduction of modern loyalty programs was paralleled with a simultaneous academic interest in "relationship marketing" (e.g., Berry 1983; Grönroos 1994; Morgan and Hunt 1994). Loyalty programs were in many ways an operationalization of the ideas of loyal consumers and the notion of relationships between firms and their customers (Araujo and Kjellberg 2015). This operationalization as well as "relationship marketing" more generally became an oxymoron (Ford and Håkansson 2006), because the notion of relationships was based on a symmetrical relationship, but relationship marketing and loyalty programs built on the idea that these relationships could be managed by one side of this relationship (i.e., the seller).

Although the use of various forms of loyalty schemes has a long history in marketing (e.g., preceded by the use of trading stamps in retailing), the modern form of loyalty schemes is usually considered to have started with the introduction of the AAdvantage frequent flyer program, introduced by American Airlines in 1981 (see e.g., Araujo and Kjellberg 2015). However, there had been similar, previous efforts in the airline industry. For example, the AA initiative was preceded by Southwest Airlines' "Sweetheart Stamps" in the 1970s (Gilbert and Hartley 1996; O'Malley 1998). A number of frequent flyer programs among other airline industries followed. Various forms of loyalty programs as a form of marketing spread rapidly to different industries and applications, and in particular in consumer-oriented service industries, such as: "airlines, grocery, apparel, and book retailers; financial service firms; hotels and casinos; and car rental companies" (Dorotic et al. 2012, 220). In retailing, the loyalty programs often took the form of specific "customers clubs" (e.g., Butscher 2002) to which the consumers were enrolled to become members. During the 1990s, there was a rapid growth of loyalty programs among European retailers, estimated at around 25 to 30 percent annually (Ziliani and Bellini 2004). Once they started to spread in a specific retailing industry, competitors soon followed suit (Ziliani and Bellini 2004; Leenheer and Bijmolt 2008; Liu and Yang 2009; Dorotic et al. 2012). As commented by Dowling and Uncles (1997, 71): "Customer loyalty schemes have attracted considerable interest as companies practice one of marketing's most familiar strategies—'If you see a good idea, copy it.'" However, the imitation game came at a price. The growth of loyalty programs affected profitability in the industries in which they were used, but once they were introduced, it became very difficult to quit them (Gilbert and Hartley 1996; O'Malley 1998).

Based on previous literature (Berman 2006; Leenheer et al. 2007; Blattberg et al. 2008), Dorotic et al. (2012) distinguish five characteristics of loyalty programmes. First, their purpose is to foster and reward attitudinal and behavioural loyalty. Second, they are based on a formal membership in some form. Third, they are long-term oriented and not short-term campaigns, etc. Fourth, they reward customers who are members based on their purchase behaviour. Fifth and finally, marketing efforts are oriented towards the members continuously.

Loyalty programs often include benefits that are utilitarian (e.g., economic benefits), hedonic (e.g., personalization), or symbolic (e.g., social status) (Dorotic et al. 2012). According to the review by Dorotic et al. (2012) many studies have shown that consumers attach more importance to utilitarian aspects of the programs. The authors' interpretation is that these benefits are often easier to communicate and evaluate and also that customers who are keen to participate in loyalty programs are often more economically oriented. However, the propensity for these consumers to participate in a specific loyalty program also often means that they are enrolled in many other programs at the same time.

Concerning the use of rewards in loyalty programs, one may distinguish between their orientation in time and how much they are related to the value proposition. Dowling and Uncles (1997, 77) separate between four types of reward schemes based on a two-dimensional matrix. The first dimension is the timing of the reward and whether it is immediate or delayed. The second dimension concerns the type of reward and whether it directly supports the value proposition of the product or if it is indirect. The matrix results in four types of reward schemes: 1) Immediate/direct (e.g., price promotions); 2) Delayed/direct (e.g., frequent flyer programs); 3) Immediate/indirect (e.g., competitions); and 4) Delayed/indirect (e.g., multiproduct schemes). Thus, differences in rewards based on these two dimensions and four resulting combinations are important to take into account.

Dorotic et al. (2012) argue that studies on the impact of loyalty programs show divergent findings. They found that loyalty programs overall had some positive effects on penetration levels, average purchase frequency, and average share-of-wallet. Previous studies indicated positive effects on customer retention rates, as well as on consumer expenditures. They also found that many studies have led other authors to claim that loyalty programs do not change customer behaviour in any substantial way. Concerning the rewards, Dorotic et al. (2012) found two impacts from previous studies. However, they found that rewards seem to be an important component of loyalty programs if they should have impacts on customer behaviour and attitudes.

A partial conclusion thus far is that in a marketing context loyalty programs constitute another precursor to contemporary gamification practices and that most of the components of loyalty programs can be found in modern gamification applications. They also join Natasha Schüll's concern for addiction, since loyalty and addiction are close behavioural patterns that obviously share their respective properties at the risk of trapping people into an inescapable loop: addiction traps gamers/customers into a long-term relationship that ends up with loyalty; and loyalty creates the necessary comfort and routine that helps in developing addiction. Admittedly, Zichermann and Linder (2010) posit loyalty programs, and more specifically frequent flyer programs, as the preeminent and most ubiquitous form of gamification within marketing. With loyalty programs, one gains, earns, and win(g!)s, and for once, the identity of this "one" is not necessarily the actor who organizes the game: as Araujo and Kjellberg recently showed, the history of frequent flyer programs in the airplane business soon led to "multi-loyal" practices that partially ruined the dream of exclusive customer-company relationships. It also favoured the emergence of secondary markets of bonuses, collective customer claims, and other opportunistic behaviours that seriously reduced the efficiency and profitability of loyalty schemes (Araujo and Kjellberg 2015). Thus, the concern for addiction is not restricted to the gamers/customers only but also to the originators of the programs; as pointed out by Gilbert and Hartley (1996) and O'Malley (1998), once they are launched the programs can be difficult to quit even for the retailers, who may fear competing programs or the risk of upsetting consumers who are attached to the program.

Gamification 4. Retailer Apps

Our fourth and final example concerns quite a recent but nevertheless ample development of gamification elements that also involves the retail practice. Since the opening of the App Store and the Android Market in 2008, the world has witnessed a dramatic growth of apps for smartphones and tablets. These apps provide different usages for most aspects of everyday life, such as cooking, exercise, communication, playing games, shopping, etc. Among the increasing amount of apps for different types of usage, most retailers today are providing their own apps to be used for different purposes. Many retailers have introduced the apps as an extension of their merchandising schemes or loyalty programmes (see our three first cases) but also included many new features that go much further beyond what display techniques and loyalty programmes usually entailed. In addition to being used for shopping purposes (such as searching for products, comparing prices, etc.), some of these retailer apps also explicitly include gamification features. One such example is the app Pink Nation provided by the famous retailer Victoria's Secret.

The version history of the Pink Nation app reveals a heavy emphasis on game elements inside the app, for example:

Version 2.3 (July 19, 2012)

Dot Dot Dot, a crazy tool and totally addictive limited edition game! Play for a chance to win a new PINK campus wardrobe. Only available for iPhone® 4/4S. Game ends 9/4.

Version 2.4 (Sep 28, 2012)

A fun (and totally addictive!) new game. PINK-O! Play for a chance to earn PINK Points and unlock exclusive wallpapers.

PINK Points. Rack 'em up to unlock photo filters, earn new Puppy Love badges and more surprises.

Version 2.5 (Nov 20, 2012)

Weeks of WOW: unlock exclusive holiday goodies and surprises and enter for a chance to win one of 100 pink leather Mini Dogs! Limited time only!

Version 3.0 (Apr 29, 2013)

Summer of P-I-N-K contest! Four letters, four weeks, one sweet summer prize.

Version 3.2 (Aug 26, 2013)

PINK's Got Spirit! How 'bout you? Play all-new games to unlock spirited goodies and surprises. Including a sweet PINK Nation exclusive. Trust us: You don't want to miss this one!

As we can see, this app wraps up all of the previous gamification schemes, like the contests ("Summer of P-I-N-K contest"), prizes ("win one of 100 pink leather Mini Dogs"; "sweet summer prize"), and loyalty schemes based on bonuses ("exclusive wallpapers"; "earn new Puppy love badges") we have presented, including the explicit emphasis on being "totally addictive". The introduction of game elements in this retailer app was made in order to "boost consumer engagement and gain new users" (Bernard 2014). It is also intended not to be restricted to the retailer context, but the app includes different mobile games that "customers play outside their natural 'shopping time,' for instance during sports events" (Bernard 2014). The app has been used for several campaigns including the "social in-app scavenger hunt" that distributed promotions and giveaways to the users during Spring Break in 2014 (App Annie Blog, July 11, 2014). The campaign had a contest in the app where consumers were asked to find four icons that represent PINK, with one letter released each week (Lacy 2014). The users who found all of the icons representing the letters "are in 'for a final treat'" and ". . . the first 100 to scan the icon each week 'get a freebie'" (Lacy 2014). When the users scan an icon a message appears with an offer from the company.

The Scratch-it blog describes the Pink Nation app as a combination of gamification and "reveal based marketing" (i.e., marketing playing on curiosity and requiring an action to be visible for its receiver), which is used to "engage visitors and keep them coming back for more" (Flamm 2014). According to the same blog, "the Pink Nation . . . loyalty app has a simple motive—to get users to unlock badges by looking through the brand catalogues and playing branded games. The games such as scratch offers and a 'trace to reveal' drive engagement with the app by playing off of their users' curiosity. Due to the concealment of their messaging, visitors are compelled to interact with the app, leading to high levels of engagement and greater brand awareness" (Flamm 2014).

The PINK-O game works as an incentive for users to get back to the app "even when they're not shopping" (App Annie 2014). Another game in the app converts the smartphone "into a pom-pom, in that it prompts consumers to shake the phone as much as possible within a 10 second time frame" (Amodio 2013). If the three levels of challenge are met, the user may unlock certain stickers. Last but not least, Johnson (2013) describes the game the Panty Jackpot, which resembles a slot machine with icons of products from the retailer. The slots are connected to rewards inside the app, such as a special offers and promotion codes or virtual stickers that can be unlocked in case of winning. The users can spin the wheel 25 times every day to try to win prizes. The loop is looped: the casino and the grocery business exchange their features and design to shift consumption into a game, and possibly give its game all the addictive power that has for a long time been the distinctive power of casino arrangements.[3]

Concluding Discussion

Throughout our four examples, we can see that winning, earning, and gaining has been "part of the game" in a literal sense of the term, along patterns close to what may be encountered in casino settings; nevertheless, it is hard, in the retailing case, to know who really wins, earns, and/or gains along the process. In our first example there was an emphasis on winning in the sense that there was someone to achieve a victory in a contest. Our second example combined this contest (among the grocers) with an element of earning directed towards children, where the former was not sure of receiving anything and the latter had a guaranteed earning of something (a child mask) in return for something else (a cereal box). With the loyalty program the outcome was the transformed rewards in favour of something earned, usually based on consumers' purchase behaviours. With the loyalty schemes there was a clear shift from the winning aspect (if you were lucky to be the only or one of the few winners) into earning in the sense of being more certain of what a particular effort also would bring in terms of points, bonuses, and rewards. It shifted the uncertainty of winning towards the certainty of earning and also challenged managerial control in the process. As with the child masks in the design contest example, the emphasis was on receiving something in return for the efforts performed (in this case, buying a certain amount of goods during a specific timeframe). Retailer apps have proliferated in parallel to the increased interest on gamification, and unsurprisingly game elements have also become part of the development of these apps. Among these, there are examples of winning and earning, but it also moves the gamification aspect of retailing further into the aspect of gaining. In relation to our previous examples, there is also emphasis on gaining that is "internal" to the game itself, the emphasis on "fun" and to earn points inside the game. In comparison with our earlier examples, there is not only a few winners to be chosen, but rather it makes it possible for "everyone" to gain by playing the game.

The emphasis on gaining also calls for a reflection of the opposite side of term (i.e., losing and what is it that is lost during the inclusion of game elements in retailing). Although we can still see major differences between the casino and the retailing context, there are elements of the notion of addiction in Schüll's account that warrants reflection and also in the case of retailing. From the early examples, game elements have been introduced in order to learn about the customers/users/readers in terms of who they are, to engage them into more loyal behaviours and attachments. Over time retailers have included more sophisticated tools and methods by combining elements of winning, earning, and gaining in the attraction of consumers. We have seen that various forms of rewards have been introduced in order to attract engagement, which, although it does not lead towards the form of compulsive engagement restricted to addiction, it still has at its purpose achieving repetitive behaviours. We could also note efforts to move beyond the retail context with the introduction of apps with the intention that these should be played outside of shopping times and that are promoted as "totally addictive". In addition, the inclusion of gamification in retailing may serve like other forms of enticements, leading someone to shop too much or to refrain from switching to another retailer, although it would have benefited them. With these developments and considerations, it is important for future research on gamification of retailing to also move more into exploring the opposite of these terms (i.e., failure, losses, and forfeits that these may bring) and to reflect further on the repartition of gains and losses among the players. Even if our examples first and foremost are based on the case of retailing, we believe that these questions also concern the development of gamification and its application in a broader sense.

Acknowledgements

Financial support was provided by The Swedish Research Council [Digcon: Digitalizing consumer culture, grant number 2012–5736] and The Swedish Retail and Wholesale Council. The authors would like to thank the editors of this volume for their constructive comments on previous versions of this chapter. We warmly thank the *Progressive Grocer* for granting us the permission to reproduce the images this chapter rests upon.

Notes

1. The following developments borrow elements from Cochoy (2008; 2015a). The authors warmly thank *The Progressive Grocer* for granting them the permission to reproduce the images this chapter rests upon.
2. For a detailed analysis of a cheese contest, see Cochoy (2015b).
3. The spread of gamification features through smartphones even goes beyond the costly frame of app design, thanks to the use of third-party services, which offer retailers the possibility to design their own games through mobile websites coupled with bi-dimensional barcodes: for instance, the French start-up Unitag provides a platform that enables any retailer to conceive a web app in five minutes, by choosing several layout options adapted to its brand and needs, by connecting it to social networks, and by retrieving statistics about how the game is played, and so on (https://www.unitag.io/app/contest).

References

Amodio, Michelle. 2013. "The Gamification of Retail: How Victoria's Secret Uses In-App Games for Campaigns." *Mobile Commerce Insider*, September 12.

App Annie. 2014. "Think Outside the Box: Gamification Gives a Boost to Retail Apps." *App Annie*, July 11.

Araujo, Luis, and Hans Kjellberg. 2015. "Forming Cognitions by Investing in a Form: Frequent Flyer Programs in US Air Travel Post-Deregulation (1981–1991)." *Industrial Marketing Management* 48: 68–78.

Bajdor, Paula, and Larisa Dragolea. 2011. "The Gamification as a Tool to Improve Risk Management in the Enterprise." *Annales Universitatis Apulensis: Series Oeconomica* 13 (2): 574–583.

Berman, Barry. 2006. "Developing an Effective Loyalty Program." *California Management Review* 49: 123–148.

Bernard, Oliver. 2014. "Apps are Increasingly Important in Online Shopping." *The Grocer*, October 3.

Berry, Leonard L. 1983. "Relationship Marketing." In *Emerging Perspectives on Services Marketing*, edited by Leonard L. Berry, Lynn Shostack and Gregory D. Upah, 25–28. Chicago: American Marketing Association.

Blattberg, Robert C., Byung-Do Kim, and Scott A. Neslin. 2008. *Database Marketing: Analyzing and Managing Customers*. NewYork, NY: Springer.

Butscher, Stephan A. 2002. *Customer Loyalty Programmes and Clubs*. Aldershot: Gower.

Cochoy, Franck. 2007. "A Brief Theory of the 'Captation' of the Public: Understanding the Market with Little Red Riding Hood." *Theory, Culture & Society* 24 (7–8): 213–233.

Cochoy, Franck. 2008. "Hansel and Gretel at the Grocery Store." *Journal of Cultural Economy* 1 (2): 145–163.

Cochoy, Franck. 2015a. *On the Origins of Self-service*. Routledge: London and New York.

Cochoy, Franck. 2015b. *On Curiosity, the art of Market Seduction*. London: Mattering Press.

Deterding, Sebastian, Dan Dixon, Rilla Khaled, and Lennart Nacke. 2011a. "From Game Design Elements to Gamefulness: Defining 'Gamification'" *MindTrek'11: Proceedings of the 15th International Academic MindTrek Conference on Envisioning Future Media Environments*. Tampere, Finland, 9–15.

Deterding, Sebastian, Rilla Khaled, Lennart Nacke, and Dan Dixon. 2011b. "Gamification: Toward a Definition." *CHI 2011*, May 7–12.
Dorotic, Matilda, Tammo H.A. Bijmolt, and Peter C. Verhoef. 2012. "Loyalty Programmes: Current Knowledge and Research Directions." *International Journal of Management Reviews* 14: 217–237.
Dowling, Grahame R., and Mark Uncles. 1997. "Do Customer Loyalty Programs Really Work?" *Sloan Management Review* 38 (4): 71–82.
Dymek, Mikolaj. 2014. "Gamification in Marketing Communication—Competing for Attention." *SCOS 32nd Standing Conference on Organizational Symbolism—Sport, Play and Games*. Utrecht.
El-Khuffash, Ahmed. 2013. "Gamification." Accessed December 15. http://www.el-khuffash.com/gamification/gamification_report.pdf.
Flamm, Jared. 2014. "Mobile App Gamification: An Example from Pink Nation." Accessed October 28. http://blog.scratch-it.com/author/jared/.
Ford, David, and Håkan Håkansson. 2006. "IMP—Some Things Achieved: Much More to do." *European Journal of Marketing* 40 (3/4): 248–258.
Gilbert, David, and Mary Hartley. 1996. "Airlines." In *Relationship Marketing: Theory and Practice*, edited by Francis Buttle, 131–144. London: Paul Chapman Publishing Ltd.
Grönroos, Christian. 1994. "From Marketing Mix to Relationship Marketing: Towards a Paradigm Shift in Marketing." *Management Decision* 32 (2): 4–20.
Johnson, Lauren. 2013. "Victoria's Secret Gamifies iPad App to Prompt Online, In-Store Sales, Mobile Commerce Daily." Accessed October 28. http://www.mobilecommercedaily.com.
Juul, Jesper. 2005. *Half-Real: Video Games between Real Rules and Fictional Worlds*. Cambridge, MA: MIT Press.
Kapp, Karl M. 2012. *The Gamification of Learning and Instruction: Game-Based Methods and Strategies for Training and Education*. San Francisco: Pfeiffer.
King, Dominic, Felix Greaves, Christopher Exeter, and Ara Darzi. 2013. "'Gamification': Influencing Health Behaviours with Games." *Journal of the Royal Society of Medicine* 106 (3): 76–78.
Lacy, Lisa. 2014. "Victoria's Secret Readies its Pink Nation for Spring Break with In-App Scavenger Hunt." *ClickZ*, February 18.
Leenheer, Jorna, and Tammo H.A. Bijmolt. 2008. "Which Retailers Adopt a Loyalty Program? An Empirical Study." *Journal of Retailing and Consumer Services* 15: 429–442.
Leenheer, Jorna, Harald J. van Heerde, Tammo H. A. Bijmolt, and Ale Smidts. 2007. "Do Loyalty Programs Really Enhance Behavioral Loyalty? An Empirical Analysis Accounting for Self-Selecting Members." *International Journal of Research in Marketing* 24: 31–47.
Liu, Yuping, and Rong Yang. 2009. "Competing Loyalty Programs: Impact of Market Saturation, Market Share, and Category Expandability." *Journal of Marketing* 73: 93–108.
Morgan, Robert M., and Shelby D. Hunt. 1994. "The Commitment-Trust Theory of Relationship Marketing." *Journal of Marketing* 58 (3): 20–38.
Muniesa, Fabian. 2014. *The Provoked Economy: Economic Reality and the Performative Turn*. London and New York: Routledge.
O'Brien, Louise, and Charles Jones. 1995. "Do Rewards Really Create Loyalty?" *Harvard Business Review* 73 (3): 75–82.

O'Malley, Lisa. 1998. "Can Loyalty Schemes Build Loyalty?" *Marketing Intelligence and Planning* 16 (1): 47–55.
Schüll, Natasha D. 2012. *Addiction by Design: Machine Gambling in Las Vegas*. Princeton: Princeton University Press.
Tapp, Alan. 2008. *Principles of Direct and Database Marketing: A Digital Orientation*. Harlow, England: Financial Times/Prentice Hall.
Walz, Steffen P., and Sebastian Deterding. 2014. "An Introduction to the Gameful World." In *The Gameful World: Approaches, Issues, Applications*, edited by Steffen P. Walz and Sebastian Deterding, 1–13. Cambridge, MA: MIT Press.
Zichermann, Gabe, and Joselin Linder. 2010. *Game-Based Marketing: Inspire Customer Loyalty Through Rewards, Challenges, and Contents*. Hoboken, NJ, USA: Wiley.
Ziliani, Christina, and Silvia Bellini. 2004. "From Loyalty Cards to Micro-Marketing Strategies: Where is Europe's Retail Industry Heading?" *Journal of Targeting, Measurement and Analysis for Marketing* 12 (3): 281–289.

6 Inside the Gamification Case of a Mobile Phone Marketing Campaign

The Amalgamation of Game Studies with Marketing Communications?

Mikolaj Dymek

Introduction

This chapter explores the avid adoption of gamification by the marketing communications industry by taking a closer empirical look inside a communication agency's mobile phone marketing campaign using gamification at its communicational core. Introducing games inside the non-game context of marketing communications is indeed a "game changer" in the way it provides potential new strategies of consumer engagement (i.e., marketing communication arenas)—but is it possible to see beyond the fast-paced mediatised game of marketing communications trendsetting, hype, marketisation and inevitable bust? Is it possible to constructively amalgamate gamification with marketing communications from a theoretical point of view?

Gamification as a notion has conquered the marketing communications industry with an impressive swiftness and passionate fervour. The prospect of engaging consumers with marketing communications by (fairly) novel means of game mechanisms (conveniently automated by software technology, as usually framed) presents a promise of dizzying allure since it cuts to the very heart of the marketing communication predicament—how to generate consumer attention by means of mass media, preferably cost-effectively, and as part of universally acknowledged marketing communication discourses of positive connotations, such as fun, play, community, engagement and passion.

This chapter will arrive to the conclusion that the unique communication properties of gamification make it compatible with the domain of public relations. Gamification is analysed according to two frameworks from game studies and marketing communications theory, indicating paths of future research that fuses both. Furthermore, the analysis contextualises the communication modes of gamification in relation to theoretical developments within marketing communications that signal a congruity between the "relational turn" in marketing, with the game communication modes of active participation that characterises gamification.

This chapter is based on empirical data collected at a (consumer) communication agency during a three-year study focusing on gamification in marketing communications. Empirical focus is placed on a specific marketing campaign in the consumer public relations realm for the launch of mobile phone that consisted of an implementation of a gamified promotional campaign in concert with strategic public relations and advertising efforts. The gamification campaign involved consumers (as players), a social network plugin, a geolocation-based game mechanism, a cooperating mobile phone reseller/network operator and a software platform that tied all these elements together as a game experience where the promoted mobile phone model was offered as a final prize and reward. The marketing communications components of the campaign symbiotically used the gamification campaign to raise awareness among prospective consumers/campaign players.

As a starting point this chapter will contextualise gamification and the marketing context within which it exists. These perspectives are enriched by insights brought in from the campaign case from the communication agency's work for a mobile phone manufacturer. Finally, the chapter concludes with a theoretical analysis of the campaign, followed by a broader discussion on the ramifications of the use of gamification of marketing communications and conclusions.

Context: Gamification

The notion of gamification was purportedly coined already as early as 2002 by game developer Nick Pelling but has only gained mass-media attention since 2010. As most chapters in this edited volume recount, the concept is without a paradigmatic definition, a common and tentative viewpoint is that gamification involves the use of game mechanics in "non-game" contexts (Deterding et al. 2011). Although lacking in stringency, this perspective has spawned a global gamification frenzy in numerous industries. A Google Trends query indicates a dramatic surge in popularity at the end of 2010, and interest has continued to grow for years—although a popularity peak was registered in 2014 as 2015 seemed less interested in the term. In 2011 it was termed the hottest digital trend at the immensely influential SXSW festival (Öhrvall and Miller 2012). Exceptionally popular presentations at the prominent TED Conferences by gamificiation gurus such as Tom Chatfield (2010), Jane McGonigal (2010) and Gabe Zichermann (2011), and others, have inspired a plethora of software applications, services, campaigns, products and communication strategies that all claim to be part of the gamification movement. These gamification applications have been implemented in an impressive range of fields, ranging from weight loss, education, journalism, loyalty programmes through marketing campaigns, exercising, language learning to social networks and corporate intranets. More specifically within a business context efforts have been made within marketing, project management, education, internal communication, health care and human resource management.

The gamification trend was initially primarily developed and implemented by the IT industry—often entrepreneurial Internet startups predominantly outside the sphere of the traditional video game industry. A trailblazer in this context has been the immensely successful case of Foursquare—a location-based social network for smartphone users. This application and service has received disproportionate attention from media, IT or marketing industries, as well as scientific inquiry (see e.g., Cramer, Rost, and Holmquist 2011; Foxman 2014)—often assuming the role of the preeminent arbiter of the current state of gamification. Not unexpectedly the chronic inability of Foursquare to turn into a profitable business venture, and its (somewhat confusing for casual users) split into two services in 2014, Foursquare and Swarm, has led some commentators to generally question gamification as such (Urbanski 2014). Gamification is significantly bigger than the fortunes of the Foursquare/Swarm platforms, but suffice to say Foursquare and its global popularity has inevitably acted as a groundbreaker and enabler for the gamification trend within many other industries, where Foursquare's achievements as a social media network, consumer engagement platform and marketing intelligence source has been duly noticed by the marketing communications industry and many other media-centric and trend-oriented industries.

Gamification in Marketing (Communications)

Although "gamification" as a concept has only existed for a decade and as a popular notion half that time, the notion of using game-like elements as part of marketing strategies have existed for a much longer time period. Zichermann and Linder (2010) illustrate how leaderboards (e.g., "Employee of the month"), loyalty programs and other marketing-related game elements have been used in marketing and business context at least since the 19th century. Loyalty schemes are also, in general, a way of framing the business case of gamification—the purported increase in consumer engagement, enjoyment, play and satisfaction by means of marketing efforts created by brands, companies and organisations. The popularity of loyalty schemes in various settings, such as airlines (American Airline's *AAdvantage* in 1981 is credited as the pioneer), grocery, apparel, and book retailers, financial service firms, hotels and casinos and car rental companies have resulted in different concepts such as reward programmes, frequency reward programmes, frequent-shopper programmes, loyalty cards or schemes, point cards, advantage cards and frequent flyer programmes (Dorotic, Bijmolt, and Verhoef 2012). Traditional perspectives state that loyalty schemes are founded on reduced cost of recruitment since loyal consumers buy more and make recommendations to others (Tapp 2008), but others question these (see e.g., O'Brien and Jones 1995).

The current wave of gamification craze and hype in marketing communications is significantly bolder in its claims—gamification generates awareness, activity, engagement, community, loyalty and innovation, and it does so significantly more cost-effectively than other strategies, and sometimes its even fully automated by gamification software that can scale the success to unprecedented volumes. These are just some of the most popular claims raised by gamification gurus, consultants, advertising or PR agencies and countless others that are biased towards a sales-oriented and triumphant rhetoric that positions gamification as a panacea tool for practically all the fundamental challenges of marketing communications and particularly in digital media settings. High-profile cases such as Starbucks, Samsung Nation (analysed in this volume by Harwood and Garry) or the U.S. Army have acted as trailblazers for the magic powers of games within marketing.

Admittedly these hyperbolic claims are not sustainable, or even logical, and need stringent examination. This chapter aims to provide more critical perspectives on this issue.

Context: Marketing Communications

In order to understand the impact of gamification on marketing, a brief contextualisation of the marketing subject is needed—regarding its conceptualisation, framing and manifestations. Marketing is both a philosophy and a function in a company. In that sense the concept both serves as a profession to be carried out and as a way to frame relationships between different actors. In general it is plausible to say that marketing is a function that constructs relationships between different actors. One of the major actors within pragmatic marketing is the American Marketing Association (AMA), who defines marketing as "an organizational function and a set of processes for creating, communicating, and delivering value to customers and for managing customer relationships in ways that benefit the organization and its stakeholders" (Hunt 2007). Despite having an excessive focus towards managerial and corporate-centric pragmatism, this definition highlights the foundation of marketing as a process—one that starts before creating products, or services, and ends after delivering these to consumers. This is initially a very important distinction to make as marketing is many times mistaken solely for sales promotion, and more specifically advertising.

Much can be said about the ramification of this definition and in the context of this study, the overall intersection of marketing, communication/media and technology. However, this falls outside of the scope of this study, which is to investigate the use of gamification in marketing communications. What is relevant, however, in this general context is the fact that marketing as perspective, practice and process is intrinsically *ideological* at its core. Ideological can mean a lot of things, and particularly from a, for example, critical Marxist point of view the ideological dimensions of marketing are immensely permeated with capitalist ideology and constitutes in fact one of its preeminent mechanisms of proliferation (Stavrakakis 2006). This may very much be the case but is again somewhat outside this chapter's scope. Nevertheless, what critical perspectives on marketing can provide is the analysis of marketing as not merely "an organisational process to deliver customer value" (see AMA's previous definition) but primarily as a contested field of ideological and normative practices, with various implicit and unstated values that permeate much of its everyday practice as well as its theoretical conceptualisation. Hence "ideology" is here used in the sense of Marxist philosopher Louise Althusser, whose noted definition of ideology states that it is "the imaginary relation to the real conditions of existence" (Althusser 2006)—an intricately complex statement with vast implications indeed—but leaves us with the insight that ideology is a set of imaginary interpretations of existence, but also a set of beliefs of how existence *should* be interpreted according to imagination.

Ideological tenets (such as, e.g., a quest for the "unique") constitute the underlying driving force of much of traditional marketing ideology, here mainly represented by the Kotlerian marketing management perspective (P. J. Kotler and Armstrong 2010), and subsequent successors in specialised subfields (e.g., Aaker's brand management) (Aaker 2009), which have dominated the marketing field theoretically, as well as practically, since the 1960s. In these ideological perspectives "unique selling points" (USP) (i.e., product/service differentiation) provide a foundation for a marketing strategy (a central tenet in Kotlerian marketing management) that generates a long-term sustainable competitive advantage in the marketplace (the foundation of most *strategic* marketing management models). Kotler claims that "marketing deals with identifying and meeting human and social needs" (P. Kotler 2000) by "getting the right goods and services to the right people, at the right places, at the right time, at the right price, with the right communications and promotion" (P. Kotler 1988). In other words new and unique ways of meeting "human and social needs" will create marketing differentiation, which will generate sales, which will generate profits by means of a superior marketing strategy. The question of marketing strategy is thus translated into a selection of "the right" people (target groups), places (distribution/sales channels), time, price, communication and promotion. In the context of this study, the last two are of pivotal importance since they advance the analysis from marketing to marketing *communications*.

The Kotlerian worldview has for decades delegated communication to a promotional function that extends the remaining three Ps (Price, Product and Place) of Kotler's pivotal 4P marketing mix notion (P. J. Kotler and Armstrong 2010), by instructing, informing and selling through mass-media communication channels. In other words, the role of communication, in a Kotlerian marketing strategy, is to convince as many consumers as possible, by means of mass-media, of the existence of a certain product, at a certain store/reseller, at a certain (attractive) price. Despite substantial r/evolution to the media/technology landscape, but also the theoretical analysis of the role of communication in marketing (see e.g., Grunig 2009, and the influential communication models of a/symmetrical communications modes in public relations), the traditional marketing management perspectives broadly adhere to a sender/producer–message/media–receiver/consumer conceptualisation of communication processes with theoretical foundations in mathematical communication perspectives from the 1960s (Shannon and Weaver 1969). Making a long theoretical argumentation very short, it can convincingly be argued that the marketing management perspective on communication is not in line with developments in communication research from the last several decades. Critical marketing communications theorist Richard Varey provides an updated, comprehensive and elaborate definition based on contemporary perspectives on both marketing and communication:

> Marketing [communication] is a social process consisting of individual and collective communicative activities performed by people as producers, intermediaries, and/or purchasers that facilitate and expedite participation in voluntary chosen satisfying tangible and intangible exchanges in social relationships by creating, maintaining or altering attitudes and/or behaviours in a dynamic environment through the joint and interactive creation, distribution, promotion, and pricing of valued goods and services, and the promotion of ideas, causes, places, and people.
> (Varey 2002, 12)

While the analysis of this definition requires a separate chapter, or more, it suffices to say that this study, in line with Varey's definition, applies a *cultural* perspective on both marketing and communication. Marketing communication is best understood as a cultural process of meaning negotiations, with a much broader perspective stretching far beyond the traditional marketing management entities of corporate marketing managers, marketing "tools", and the (fetishised) individual as consumer.

Analysis: Gamification in Marketing Communications

Empirical Context: The Agency

In order to examine the quasi-revolutionary rhetoric surrounding gamification in marketing communications, this study will take a closer look from the inside of a marketing communications campaign that was almost in its entirety based on gamification. The empirical material of this chapter is based on a three-year, empirical participatory action-oriented "thick description" (Geertz 1973) style study at a leading communication agency in Stockholm ("the Agency"). Furthermore, the empirical data has also been collected at secondary sources such as trade publications, marketing communication industry awards, competitors and generally marketing communications campaigns with gamification elements or concepts.

The Agency was founded in 2003 by four DJs/club organisers who decided to evolve their successful venture as club organisers in the Stockholm club/DJ scene of the late 1990s/early 2000s. The partners evolved the venture into a "communications agency" (as apart from an "advertising" or "public relations" agency) and subsequently slowly, but surely, expanded its operations along with its evolving business proposition to include divisions that handled media relations, creative/design, digital communication, planning (i.e., research/campaign planning), production, fashion showroom (for fashion brands) and lately even a limited corporate relations offering. The Agency is more than a decade in business (which is rare), and the spectrum of client brands is very broad—ranging from car manufacturers, razors, mobile phones, wine brands, through shampoos, low-calorie juices, cookies to cargo boxes, game consoles to mineral water, toilet paper and jeans, as well as its original line of clients from the world of club- and lifestyle-oriented products (i.e., liquors and vodka). The focus of the Agency is consumer public relations, and in particular "lifestyle brands" (Chernev, Hamilton, and Gal 2011) (i.e., brands that attempt to be part of a consumer's identity and lifestyle).

Empirical Case: The Mobile Phone Campaign

One of the Agency's top accounts was a major mobile phone manufacturing brand that was in the midst of launching a new type of smartphone with extensive (mobile) gaming features, which were reflected in the device's name/branding, its hardware design as well as its new software system, which was co-branded by one of the (probably) top three game industry brands of the world. The core message of the campaign was linked to the name of the device, which advertised its heavy focus on gaming and fun. Consequently, the client brief consisted of establishing this link with the targeted consumer segment of smartphone buyers with a knack for gaming, by "activating" them (using the industry parlance) through various channels. The end result was comprised of five campaign components:

1. *Contest*—A digitally mediated (through the social media network of Facebook) official contest where several dozens of the promoted smartphones were offered as final prizes. Official marketing contests are, in Sweden (where the campaign was performed), as well in most countries, regulated by various laws covering marketing, gambling and other related areas and need to fulfil certain specific requirements (statement of terms and rules etc.)
2. *Gamification application*—A geo-location-based (software) component, which "gamified" the contest through Facebook's network by means of a purpose-built software application (created by the Agency) that integrated with Facebook's social network mechanisms.

106 *Mikolaj Dymek*

3. *Marketing communications activation*—A so-called activation (i.e., marketing communications activity) that placed real-life mock-ups of famous video game icons and or personalities in prominent public spaces in Stockholm where the campaign was performed.
4. *Advertising*—Some (limited) bought digital media—mainly consisting of advertising banners on selected websites.
5. *Media relations campaign*—A selected number of suitable media outlets (a so-called media list) that could potentially be interested in publishing news items regarding the contents of 1) to 3), were targeted with a media relations campaign involving standard industry practice of information drives (press releases), coordination/cooperation with media producers and general attempts to influence media producers to generate positive coverage.
6. *Marketing communications campaign*—The sum of 1) through 5) was to generate exposure of the marketing message to targeted consumer audiences, with the intent of creating a positive consumer interpretation whose ultimate purpose is to stimulate a purchasing decision and/or voluntary sharing of this positive opinion to other individuals/consumers, thus creating a "viral mechanism" of "buzz" and "word of mouth". Although the causal link between "(marketing) communication" and "increased sales" is intriguingly challenging to stringently establish in the case of marketing communications, it remains nevertheless the meta-objective of *all* marketing communications. Different sub-objectives (such as creating awareness, brand(ing) building/repositioning/dialogue, reminder advertising, discount promotions, etc.) are, in a business setting of consumer goods marketing, subordinated the ultimate business goal of increasing sales. From the Agency's perspective, this is the primary objective as campaign production is what they are contracted for by clients/brands.

Although it is difficult to stringently separate the gamification dimensions from the marketing communications dimensions in this campaign, this study will in terms of theoretical frameworks explore this campaign from two perspectives: a game studies perspectives focusing on components 1) and 2), and a marketing communications perspective that focuses on 3) to 6). This will be done be analysing the gamification application first as a digital text, and then continuing on to the analysis of its game dynamics, followed by a theoretical contextualisation of this gamification application in marketing communications.

Exploring Digital Gamification: Methodological Challenges

This gamification case consists at its core of a digital game mediated through a "game engine" (a software application that executes the mechanisms of the game) that cooperates with the social media network Facebook by means of its web and mobile phone applications. There are numerous ways of approaching a digital game like this, but this study posits this particular case as a *digital text*, and as empirical data in *itself* (i.e., meanings are created in software as a form of digital text). Although appearing at first instance as a game of limited textual communications (simple check-ins with keywords posted on Facebook), this does not contradict the fact that *meanings* are imbued inside the dynamic game structures. This shifts the analysis to the game structures that the user "*wreads*"—*w*rites and *reads* as conceptualised by Landow (1994). The user/"wreader" writes input (by means of check-ins in this particular case) into a dynamic process of frequent (text) modifications in a feedback loop read and explored by the user. Within new/digital/game media studies the methodological analysis of this loop evolved into polemics between those analysing digital texts as (interactive) narratives (e.g., Laurel 1993;Murray 1997; Ryan 2001) or those focused on the internal dynamics of the game structures. A prominent theory of the latter perspective is Espen Aarseth's (1997) theory of *cybertexts* (*cyborg text machines*—mechanical and material machines that produce ergodic texts) centred around notions of *ergodic texts* (dynamic texts that require mechanical input), providing game/new media studies with alternative insights into digital media. Aarseth does not exclude narrative dimensions but considers it more pertinent to analyse *what* happens on the screens, *what* the user modifies, *how* the (software) mechanisms modify text elements and *how* hidden (not displayed) text elements are accessed. Aarseth basically provides a stringent deconstruction of the mythical notion of "interactivity", replacing it with the concept of cybertexts, which has very broad ramifications for analysis of digital media/texts.

A limitation with Aarseth's perspective is its predisposition towards codex like texts. Contemporary digital texts are seldom purely codex like and contain basically every mode of digitisable communication (i.e., *multimedia*). Basically a methodological extension that embraces other multimodal communication is needed. It is provided by *multimodal discourse analysis* (MDA) (Kress and van Leeuwen 2001)—a framework that integrates various semiotic modes in a discourse analysis adapted to contemporary media. It criticises semiotics for fragmentation into incompatible "monomodal" semotical perspectives, which each tell their side of the story while the *entire* story is missing. Kress and van Leeuwen (2001, 4) define four strata of practice in which meanings are dominantly made. They are *discourse* (socially constructed knowledge of reality), *design* (conceptualisations of the form of semiotic products and events), *production* (articulation in material form of semiotic products or events), and *distribution* (reproduction of semiotic products and events). Implications of MDA stretch far beyond digital texts but establishes the *design* stratum, in the case of digital texts, as the site of multimodal integration of semiotic modes. Discerning the meanings of the discourse strata reflected in the design stratum based on the interplay between various semiotic modes is the objective of the methodological integration of cybertextual and MDA perspectives. Due to the dual nature of software (source/machine code), the strata of production and distribution are of lesser importance. A complete analysis of material articulation in software requires analysis of source code and is impractical in its scope (probably tens of thousands of code lines) and legally impossible (source code is proprietary). Consequently, a cybertextual MDA perspective incorporates textual mechanisms, *as well as* all other semiotic communication modes.

Empirical Exploration of the Campaign's Gamification Dimensions

The gamification components of this campaign will be analysed more thoroughly using the cybertextual MDA perspective. The gamification application of the campaign presents the user with an expressive screen of text elements, graphics (symbol, icons, fields), various colours, intricate graphical organisation, dimensions of movement/animation that provide multimodal communication integrated in the design stratum of this digital text. To investigate the core "interactive" text mechanism—or *traversal function* using Aarseth's notions—a user scenario of the gamification campaign is analysed. It highlights those functions deemed relevant in the context of this campaign and in general gamification in marketing communications.

The gamification application consisted of a purpose-built application on the social networking platform Facebook where users would have to install a Facebook "plug-in application" on their user profiles. This application enabled posts from the mobile phone brand on the user's wall/timeline, which could be seen by all of the user's Facebook friends, thus achieving a message distribution mechanism based on the user's "social graph" (i.e., the user's network of connected Facebook friends). In order to participate in the campaign, the user was instructed according to the following rules of the game:

1. "Check-in" at physical locations using Facebook's then newly introduced check-in feature on their smartphone apps. In other words users were required to launch their Facebook application on their smartphones, and then "check-in", which means to announce, on the wall/timeline, the user's specific physical location by means of the smartphone's built-in GPS functionality.
2. The gamification campaign required specifically users mentioning/writing the name of the promoted mobile phone model in their check-in. This would be on at the user's wall/timeline and hence to all of his/her friends regardless whether they were participating in the game or not.
3. The purpose-built Facebook application (as part of the Facebook back-end infrastructure) would visualise the check-in action by plotting its location on a stylised map of the city. This map was only visible to the Facebook users who had the purpose-built plug-in application installed on their Facebook accounts.

4. The more and further distance between check-ins the user performed, the more points the Facebook application handed out to the user—a line was also drawn between every check in on the map.
5. Creating geographical shapes by means of the user's check-ins ("connecting the dots") gave even more points, thus encouraging users to "draw" by means of the check in functionality.
6. Top lists/leaderboards were then compiled and prominently displayed on the Facebook application. By answering correctly questions regarding the capabilities of the promoted smartphone, the user would be awarded even more points.
7. Checking in at stores of a cooperating mobile network operator (which had exclusive rights for launch sales) was another way to earn bonus points.
8. The top scorers of the game would eventually win a free smartphone at the end of the campaign.

The traversal functions of this gamification application consists of three characteristic instances: the "geo-location list", "map plotting" and "leaderboard" functions. The first "geo-location list" function is based on the user input of keyword triggers in check-ins, but also importantly the user decision to disclose publically its physical location(s). This traversal function allows the user to collect a list of physical locations from check-ins, but it also constitutes the core mechanism of a rule-based mechanism that produces variable and quantifiable results (cf. with Juul's (2005) definition of games) (i.e., a mechanism for play and competition that yields winners and losers). The more check-ins and further physical distances between them, or at specific locations (the cooperating mobile operator's points of sales), the closer a user could come to winning the game. Furthermore, the input mechanism of this "geo-location list" function also constituted the core mechanism for generating attention ("marketing communications") in social media—all the Facebook friends of a user/participant, regardless whether they were participants or not, would see status updates on their own Facebook feed from a participating user's wall/timeline that advertised the name of the brand. This traversal function in itself constituted a simple text-based game, that introduced game mechanisms in a non-game like context of check-ins, but also the voluntary mentioning of a brands name to the user's friend (i.e., becoming, in extension, an independent promotion agent of the gamification contest as well as generally the brand and its marketing communications campaign).

The next traversal function of "map plotting" introduces an array of graphical elements that visualises, in two dimensions, the "geo-location list" function on a city map, thus opening up new dimensions of textual dynamics and exploration. By drawing and "connecting the dots" with check-ins to create figures even more points could be earned, and new elements of competition introduced. This traversal function is only available for participating users via the plug-in Facebook application. Non-participating users do not have access to this added layers of textual dynamics introduced by this traversal function. No added input options are afforded by this traversal function.

The final traversal function is the "leaderboard" function that ranks players according to points that are correlated to achievements. The exact principles of the point system were not communicated to users, and the bonus point system was also unclear. Nevertheless, this is the traversal function that produces quantifiable rankings, final end-results, and prizes, continuously updated and visualised in order to increase feedback, activity and hopefully user activity and competition. As with the map-plotting function, access is restricted to participating users (with the plug-in Facebook application installed), and no added input options are afforded, since input affordances are all contained within the geo-location list function.

With this cybertextually infused MDA perspective, the gamification application has been explored as a dynamic text that involves its users by means of three distinct traversal functions that in various degrees allows the user to introduce textual elements into a dynamic text mechanisms that produce a game with categorical results.

Analysis: Gamifying Marketing Communications

Despite its distributed nature in terms of physical location and communication (multiple users, Facebook feed, Facebook web application, plug-in Facebook application, back-end "game engine", mobile application), the empirical exploration of the previous gamification case illustrated that it can be "read" as a fragmented digital game. In other words this study posits game studies as a pivotal perspective in any study of gamification, and particularly the case of gamification in marketing communications.

As mentioned previously in the methodological discussion, within the field of games studies there has been considerable polemics as regards the interpretation of the digital game medium (Aarseth 1997; Murray 1997; Frasca 2003; Juul 2004): games as games, or as narratives seems to be the abbreviated culmination of this interpretative discussion. The debate has transformed into a truce that posits the opposing perspectives as ontological perspectives on the matter, and as a consequence diverging methodological approaches. In the context of marketing this dyad has also theoretical as well as analytical repercussions as discussed by Dymek (2010) in relation to the strategic marketing of the video game medium. The way we approach the medium of games is also the way we construct, evolve and read it. The versatility of interactivity and the expressive register bestowed by the video game medium is truly impressive, yet the medium in its contemporary commercial form exhibits considerably less than the aforementioned vast spectrum.

The analytical framework from games studies is equally pertinent when applied to the case of gamification and in particular to the case of gamification in marketing and its communication. Ludology (from latin *ludo* meaning game), and its main proponents, Aarseth (1997), Frasca (2001) and Juul (2004), claim that the game medium is most rewardingly analysed *independently* from other forms of media. Games are unique, not because of "interactivity" or "non-linearity" or other forms of vague notions, but due to the requirements bestowed on its reader/user—s/he *must* participate in the game by making decisions. Based on this understanding ludology posits *game rules/mechanisms* as the foundation of game interpretation—games are built on rules that its user(s)/player(s)/reader(s) explore(s) and this produces an experience of *simulation*. If applied to gamified cases of marketing communication, and in particular to the case of the aforementioned mobile phone campaign, we notice that this theoretical framework is still viable—the communication channels (Facebook application, mobile application, Facebook feed) are fragmented, but nevertheless form a fairly cohesive *simulational* game experience. Game mechanisms structure the marketing message and its diffusion. The core message according to this perspective was to increase awareness (and sales) of the product brand (as all marketing campaigns ultimately do), using the three traversal functions of "geo-location list", "map plotting" and "leaderboard", through playfulness, mobility and pervasiveness—qualities that could favourably be associated with the product whose main selling point was its mobile gaming capabilities. By creating a gamified campaign, the Agency designed game mechanisms that attempted to emphasise this core message *as well* as appeasing the various stakeholders of the campaign (mobile brand/primary client, mobile network operator with store/secondary client, Facebook/media infrastructure provider).

Inasmuch as the empirical exploration relied on a cybertextually/ludologically inspired multimodal discourse analysis, this study does not by any means exclude a narratological approach to gamification. It treats games as part of the much older and wider field of narratology, which studies narrative (Genette 1980) and narrative structure (e.g., Propp 1958). Game narratologists such as Laurel (1993), Murray (1997) and Ryan (2001) analyse games as cases of interactive storytelling as part of interactive narratives (i.e., the continuation of a thousand-year-old tradition of storytelling—bards, theatre/drama, literature, film, hypertexts, etc.) with the added dimension of (digital) interactivity. Digital games provide interactivity and immersion that give rise to storytelling and narrative experiences—a perspective focused on the *representational* dimensions of games. Games in this perspective do simulate realities as ludologists claim, but the experiences of readers/users/participants are in essence symbolic narratives that also represent the interpretation of reality by the author of the game. If applied to the mobile phone gamification campaign—there are rewarding insights from approaching it as a (basic) form of interactive narrative. The author (the brand in cooperation with the Agency) has created an interactive and immersive world of (limited) storytelling that communicates messages of playfulness (game aesthetics on Facebook, but also through the cues generated by the marketing communications activations in the cityscape, advertising online, check-ins by other users, and generally the results of media relations campaigning, i.e., media exposure and/or news articles), mobility (mobile application and physical location check-ins) and pervasiveness (it can be played anywhere and anytime within the city with a mobile phone). Furthermore, there are parallels between the mobile phone gamification structure to the story structures of (a hero's) journeys as famously described by narrative theorist Propp (1968), where the travelling between check-ins resonates with the prevalence of journey metaphors in many dominant narratives in the Western world. Narrative similarities exist between the gamification application and competitions/contests, which Murray, based on *agon*—one of the French philosopher Roger Caillois' (2001) four patterns of play—considers one of the must fundamental narrative structures of storytelling as it faces dichotomies against each other.

There are numerous rewarding avenues of future research development for ludolological and narratological perspectives on gamification in marketing communications. From a ludological point of view, gamification could be further analysed at the intersection of virtual (Rheingold 1995) and brand communities (Muniz and O'Guinn 2001) with perspectives from online game worlds (Filiciak 2003; Zackariasson 2007). From a narratological perspective, gamified marketing communications can be aligned with the "narrative turn" of marketing communications—brand storytelling (Mark and Pearson 2001; Brown, Kozinets, and Sherry 2003). Brand narratives could be conceptualized as interactively performed together by brand and consumers through pervasive and expansive gamification platforms.

Analysis: Games in the Non-game Context of Marketing Communications

Gamification in a marketing communications context poses many research questions. Since this study posits games/gamification as a type of dynamic text used for marketing communications purposes, it only seems logical to continue this line of reasoning analysing the actual marketing communications form (i.e., its mass-media form, which many posit as having historically evolved symbiotically together with marketing communications) (see e.g., Smythe 1977). What type of marketing communications mass-media form does gamification constitute?

To explore this subject the categorisation of *bought/paid, earned/non-paid* and *owned* media will be elaborated. Within the broader industry of marketing communications, based on empirical findings of PR research related to this study (Dymek 2013) and on theoretical approaches (Katz 2014), there is an established categorisation framework for the entire spectrum of marketing communications in relation to media channels. This is particularly pertinent when applied to a novel hybrid form such as (digital) gamification. Industry vernacular often refers to the "trinity" of marketing communication media channels: *bought/paid, earned/non-paid* and *owned* media. It is evidently based on a media-centric perspective, but more importantly positioned in relation to media ownership and compensation for temporary use of media space. The following general framework is predominantly based on Katz's (2014) framework.

Bought/paid media is essentially "advertising" (i.e., "messages"—video sequence, image/graphics, text, sound etc.) which are exposed in intermediary channels (media outlets) in exchange for compensation/fees. Advertisers pay one-way communicational media channels for exposure, hence the alternative term "paid media", to an allotted space (time in television/radio, space in print/billboards/point-of-sale, etc.). This is the most established, organised and dominant form of marketing communications, due to its long history, in its modern form, tracing back to the first half of the 19th century (Pincas and Loiseau 2008). Advertising, in all of its diversified forms, has still by far the largest share of the global marketing communications market.

Earned/non-paid media can, in terms of marketing communications, be summarised as "public relations". The logic of the "non-paid media" label is the absence of direct payments/transactions for the use of media space. The typical standard non-paid media scenario is a "message" being voluntarily exposed by various media channels—preferably journalists and/or media producers. The media channel contributes to the diffusion of the message but not due to commercial interests and is instead driven by other reasons (interest, journalistic inquiry, popularity, information needs, etc.). This transforms and reverses the entire traditional advertising-based marketing communication process. While publicity/media relations/PR management was historically used within political communications or by celebrities or other influential individuals, it has only fairly recently, during the last 20 to 30 years, been extensively adopted by the consumer marketing and marketing communications fields. Commercial, consumer-oriented PR is now one of many established "tools" of marketing communication managers, by incorporating any possible communication channel/device/object/movement/social phenomenon that can reach audiences and consumers. The classical one-way "push" logic of bought/paid media/advertising that drives attention to a message from advertiser to consumers by buying exposure in various media channels, is reversed by the earned/non-paid media logic that "pulls" attention from audiences through media channels, or more correctly, the attention is attracted by two-way communication with media producers, which then expose it to audiences/consumers (in one-way communication forms).

Since the term "non-paid media" posits "paid media" (advertising) as the norm, and erroneously indicates the absence of payments/transactions (PR agencies clearly do not work for free)—the PR industry disputes this notion with the replacement notion of "earned media". This notion disposes the transactional focus and instead stresses that PR communication is created by "earning" the attention of media producers and/or consumers.

Subsequently, "paid media" becomes alternatively "bought media", thus implying, slightly pejoratively as riposte, that this type of media exposure is in essence "bought off", somewhat implying classical media ethical issues of ambiguous media independence and opinion maker integrity.

The final categorisation of *owned media* is simply put the media/communication channels owned and/or controlled by the author/brand/company/organisation/entity/etc. and can be used to communicate with a desired audience/consumer/group/receiver. With the rise of digital media, as well a plethora of social media platforms, the number of brand/company owned communication channels have multiplied dramatically. It should be noted that owned media can exist, and has existed for long, in non-digital "offline" media formats (e.g., retail spaces, newsletters, loyalty schemes, such as discussed in the previous chapter, sponsorships and many other forms). The domains of owned media are traditionally part of PR management as owned media audiences are already in a relationship with the brand/company (e.g., newsletter), whereas advertising always has to reestablish a new relationship with audiences for every advertising campaign.

Discussion: Gamified Marketing Communications as PR?

How does this theoretical framework of bought, earned and owned media relate to the role and practice of gamification in marketing communications? A majority of gamification implementations within marketing communications would fall primarily into the categories of owned media, but also into the earned/non-paid category, consequently constituting the realm of public relations and digital agencies. This can be analysed from a strictly communication-oriented games studies perspective, as well as a business/management-oriented marketing communications perspective—as shown in the preceding analyses. However, what can the fusing of game studies and marketing communication perspective produce in terms of insights?

Since a tentative definition of gamification usually tends to include the following, or quite similar, phrasing "the use of game-design elements in non-gaming contexts" (Deterding et al. 2011), this subsequently entails the need for delimitation of the notion of game. While defining a game is a large endeavour, it is adequate for this study to focus on the "interactive" dimension of games that can be more stringently defined as *participatory*—a user/consumer/reader *participates* in a game and consequently is *active* in a way that differs from traditional "linear" media such as most text, video, music, graphics, etc. Game narratologist Murray defines the participatory property (Murray 1997, 71) of games, together with the procedural (rule-driven) property, as constituting the interactive dimension. In other words, games are different from all other forms of media due to the requirement of the user/reader to make active choices that affect the dynamics of the medium. In terms of communication flows this becomes a two-way setting—the user responds to a register of cues generated by the game, by making various input choices that affect the game, which in its turn through a feedback loop continuously affects the user/reader/gamer. While some theorists (e.g., Aarseth) question the characterisation of this feedback process as "interactive"—since truly interactive communication is only possible between real humans in for example, a conversation—others (e.g., Murray, Ryan, Laurel) highlight this conceptualisation. Suffice it to say, games establish communicational relationships between user and medium in ways that radically depart from the traditional, and still dominant, media forms.

The logic of bought/paid/pushed media has historically been, and continues to be, based on static messages that are displayed in a linear fashion to audiences (i.e., the audience is expected to *interpret* the message). Gamification requires interpretation as well—but demands *active participation*. From a ludological perspective, games are consequently ontologically different (Frasca 2003) from traditional linear representative texts. If this perspective is transferred into the communicational organisation of marketing communications practice as described previously, then the interactive component of games/gamification by definition excludes it from any linear type of communication medium, and hence is incompatible with traditional advertising communication (i.e., bought media), since this communication mode relies on static messages being interpreted in linear fashion by the audiences.

This transfer of a digital literary theory/game studies perspective on medium and interactive communication onto a media analysis of marketing communications has some rather fascinating and rewarding perspectives on gamification, but also media dimensions of marketing communications. Although gamification relies on (inter)active participation and two-way communication that is incompatible with one-way push advertising communication—it does *not* by default make it unsuitable for advertising. Quite the contrary—advertising agencies have produced many visible and award-winning cases of gamification in marketing communications. These examples are based on a *pull* logic of earned/owned media whereby game-mechanisms are used as tools to generate consumer attention, engagement and potential customer loyalty—this fact is in and of itself promoted as an innovative and newsworthy message in a separate and additional *push* based campaign in bought media, as advertising. Similarly the oldest forms of gamification in marketing communications—simple loyalty programmes, as described above, date back to the end of the 19th century, as do sweepstakes or caption contests in magazines/newspapers—have been extensively used in advertising campaigns over the years. Nevertheless, the defining feature is that participatory dimensions are done externally of the advertising campaign—which are using the game element to create attention to their message. (Consumer) PR agencies have also passionately embraced gamification, with numerous gamification cases used with *pull* and dialogue-based marketing communications logic.

This is *not*, however, a debate about "turf wars" between advertising and PR, and who ultimately "owns" gamification in the marketing communications. Rather this is a question of contextualising the media communication modes of gamification among the various competing and evolving strands of thought in contemporary marketing communications. A prominent marketing (communications) perspective that has had transforming impact on marketing theory is the turn toward establishing relationships (between companies/brands and customers/consumers) as foundations for marketing communications instead of the Kotlerian emphasis on promotion. Beginning from the 1990s, several frameworks, with various departure points, have attempted to reconceptualise marketing according to this line of relational reasoning: relationship marketing/branding (Grönroos 1994; Fournier 1998), brand communities (Muniz and O'Guinn 2001), service marketing (Vargo and Lusch 2004), prosumer marketing (Ritzer and Jurgenson 2010), among several others.

Partially independently from this, the adjacent research field of public relations studies has since the 1980s been dominated by the so-called excellence theory (Grunig 1992) that posits a historical progression from one-way asymmetrical communication between brand/company/organisation and its publics/consumers (press agentry/publicity), through one-way symmetrical communication (public information) and two-way asymmetrical communication (roughly the equivalent of Kotlerian/marketing management promotional communication), and finally the envisaged two-way symmetrical communication model where publics/consumers are engaged on equal terms with the company/brand in a dialogue of mutual negotiations and understanding. The final stage has been heavily criticised as unrealistic by other public relations scholars (Roper 2005), but this influential communications model nevertheless assumes, remarkably similar to the "relational turn" within marketing (communications) theory, some sort of communicational parity between company/brand and consumers. Consumers are in these various conceptualisations engaged in an egalitarian dialogue-based relationship with the company/brand instead of the transaction-focused Kotlerian marketing management approach of promotional communications by company/brand targeting persuasive instructions towards consumers.

However, these rosy prognostications of consumer empowerment and communicational parity as a result of relational two-way symmetrical (marketing) communications have been thoroughly criticised as being paradoxical and constituting an oxymoron (e.g., by Evans 2003). Simply put, the paradox is based on the invalid assumption that mutual and symmetrical relationships between company/brand and consumers can be managed by only one party, and additionally managed to generate a financial profit for only one party—the brand/company. Symmetrical brand-consumer relationships cannot be asymmetrically for-profit-managed by the brand only. Commercial relationships, such as these, regardless of label and communication model will always become instrumental in nature.

So how does this relate to gamification in marketing communications? Gamification in this non-game context of marketing communications relies on consumer-participatory relation-oriented dialogue-based (not necessarily fully symmetrical) communication model of marketing communications, which falls into the domains of public relations, as analysed previously. This conclusion not only applies to digital application, but even more so to non-digital gamification examples, such as loyalty programmes, since these often somehow involve direct human interactions.

Does this also entail that gamification in the service of marketing communication propagates the same type of instrumental relationships as claimed by critics of relationship marketing? This perspective is supported by some critical gamification research—gamification is "exploitationware" (Bogost 2011a), "Viagra for engagement dysfunction" (Bogost 2011b), or transformers users/players to "playborers" (Rey 2012), to mention a few. From this perspective gamification in marketing communications becomes the latest and newest communicational strategy to obfuscate the instrumental exploitation of consumers by companies/brands in a context of relational marketing communications. Or, does gamification in marketing communications, *ceteris paribus*, contribute with surplus gameplay to consumers? This research question probably constitutes the most pertinent avenue of future research of gamification in marketing communications.

Conclusions

This chapter have arrived to the following insights:

- Gamification has been used within marketing (communications) for decades and is not limited to digital media.
- The empirical gamification in marketing communications case was analysed with two separate frameworks from game studies and marketing communications.
- The game studies analysis, based on cybertextual MDA, identified three traversal functions: "geo-location list", "map plotting" and "leaderboard", which constituted the core game-textual mechanisms of the gamification case.
- Furthermore, the theoretical frameworks of ludology and narratology are rewardingly applicable on the context of gamification within marketing communications, and indicate new avenues of future research, such as the intersection of games with virtual/brand communities or games as brand narratives/storytelling, that can integrate game studies with various marketing communications perspectives.
- The marketing communications analysis of gamification emphasised the unique communicational property of *active participation*, which subsequently resulted in a categorisation of gamification as a type of *pull* communication that is the domain of earned/non-paid and owned marketing media communications, which is part of the public relations modes of communications.

- This gamification property of active participation was aligned with the theoretical turn towards relationship perspectives within marketing communications and public relations theory, indicating a theoretical and practical congruity.
- Finally, the study concluded that an important issue for further research is whether gamification as relational marketing communications is another form of obfuscation of instrumental management brand strategies vis-à-vis consumers, or whether gamification does indeed contribute elements of novel play into the landscape of contemporary marketing communications.

References

Aaker, David A. 2009. *Managing Brand Equity*: Capitalizing on the Value of a Brand Name. New York : Maxwell Macmillan International.

Aarseth, Espen J. 1997. *Cybertext—Perspectives on Ergodic Literature*. Baltimore, MA: Johns Hopkins University Press.

Althusser, Louis. 2006. "Ideology and Ideological State Apparatuses (Notes towards an Investigation)." In *The Anthropology of the State: A Reader,* edited by Abhinav Sharma and Akhil Gupta. Oxford: Wiley-Blackwell. 86–111.

Bogost, Ian. 2011a. "Persuasive Games: Exploitationware." *Gamasutra*. http://www.gamasutra.com/view/feature/6366/persuasive_games_exploitationware.php.

———. 2011b. "Gamification Is Bullshit." *The Atlantic*. http://www.theatlantic.com/technology/archive/2011/08/gamification-is-bullshit/243338/.

Brown, Stephen, Robert V. Kozinets, and John F. Sherry. 2003. "Teaching Old Brands New Tricks: Retro Branding and the Revival of Brand Meaning." *Journal of Marketing* 67 (3). American Marketing Association: 19–33. doi:10.1509/jmkg.67.3.19.18657.

Caillois, Roger. 2001. *Man, Play and Games*. Urbana: University of Illinois Press.

Chatfield, Tom. 2010. "7 Ways Games Reward the Brain." *TEDGlobal*. https://www.ted.com/talks/tom_chatfield_7_ways_games_reward_the_brain.

Chernev, Alexander, Ryan Hamilton, and David Gal. 2011. "Competing for Consumer Identity: Limits to Self-Expression and the Perils of Lifestyle Branding." *Journal of Marketing* 75 (3). American Marketing Association: 66–82. doi:10.1509/jmkg.75.3.66.

Cramer, Henriette, Mattias Rost, and Lars Erik Holmquist. 2011. "Performing a Check-In: Emerging Practices, Norms and 'Conflicts' in Location-Sharing Using Foursquare." In *Proceedings of the 13th International Conference on Human Computer Interaction with Mobile Devices and Services*. ACM, Stockholm, Sweden.

Deterding, Sebastian, Miguel Sicart, Lennart Nacke, Kenton O'Hara, and Dan Dixon. 2011. "Gamification—Using Game-Design Elements in Non-Gaming Contexts." In *CHI EA '11 Proceedings of the 2011 Annual Conference Extended Abstracts on Human Factors in Computing Systems,* Vancouver, Canada.

Dorotic, Matilda, Tammo H.A. Bijmolt, and Peter C. Verhoef. 2012. "Loyalty Programmes: Current Knowledge and Research Directions." *International Journal of Management Reviews* 14: 217–37.

Dymek, Mikolaj. 2010. "Industrial Phantasmagoria—Subcultural Interactive Cinema Meets Mass-Cultural Media of Simulation." PhD diss., Royal Institute of Technology. Stockholm, Sweden.

———. 2013. "Spectacles as Communication Industry—the Rise and Fall of the Consumerist Avant-Garde." In *31st Standing Conference on Organizational Symbolism—Cretive De-Construction*, Warsaw, Poland.

Evans, Martin. 2003. "The Relational Oxymoron and Personalisation Pragmatism." *Journal of Consumer Marketing* 20 (7). MCB UP Ltd: 665–85. doi:10.1108/07363760310506193.

Filiciak, Miroslaw. 2003. "Hyperidentities: Postmodern Identity Patterns in Massively Multiplayer Online Role-Playing Games." In *The Video Game Theory Reader*, edited by Mark J. P. Wolf and Bernard Perron. New York: Routledge. 87–102.

Fournier, Susan. 1998. "Consumers and Their Brands: Developing Relationship Theory in Consumer Research." *Journal of Consumer Research* 24: 343–53. doi:10.1086/209515.

Foxman, Maxwell. 2014. "How to Win Foursquare: Body and Space in a Gamified World." In *Rethinking Gamification*, edited by Mathias Fuchs, Sonia Fizek, Paolo Ruffino, and Niklas Schrape. Hybrid Publishing Lab, Leuphana University of Lüneburg, Germany: Meson Press. 71–90.

Frasca, Gonzalo. 2001. "SIMULATION 101: Simulation Versus Representation." www.ludology.org. http://www.ludology.org/articles/sim1/simulation101.html.

———. 2003. "Simulation vs. Narrative: Introduction to Ludology." In *The Video Game Theory Reader*, edited by Mark J P Wolf and Bernard Perron. New York: Routledge. 221–236.

Geertz, Clifford. 1973. *The Interpretation of Cultures: Selected Essays*. New York: Basic Books.

Genette, Gérard. 1980. *Narrative Discourse: An Essay in Method*. New York: Cornell University Press.

Grönroos, C. 1994. "From Marketing Mix to Relationship Marketing: Towards a Paradigm Shift in Marketing." *Management Decision* 32 (2): 4–20. http://www.emeraldinsight.com/doi/abs/10.1108/00251749410054774.

Grunig, James E. 1992. *Excellence in Public Relations and Communication Management*.Hillsdale, NJ: Erlbaum.

———. 2009. "Paradigms of Global Public Relations in an Age of Digitalisation." *PRism* 6 (2). 1–19.

Hunt, Shelby D. 2007. "A Responsibilities Framework for Marketing as a Professional Discipline." *Journal of Public Policy & Marketing* 26 (2). American Marketing Association: 277–83. doi:10.1509/jppm.26.2.277.

Juul, Jesper. 2004. "The Definitive History of Games and Stories, Ludology and Narratology." *The Ludologist*. http://www.jesperjuul.net/ludologist/index.php?p=66.

———. 2005. *Half-Real: Video Games between Real Rules and Fictional Worlds*. Cambridge, MA: MIT Press.

Katz, H.E. 2014. *The Media Handbook: A Complete Guide to Advertising Media Selection, Planning, Research, and Buying*. Fifth ed. London: Routledge.

Kotler, Philip. 1988. *Marketing Management: Analysis, Planning, Implementation, and Control*. Englewood Cliffs, NJ: Prentice-Hall.

———. 2000. *Marketing Management*. Upper Saddle River, NJ: Prentice-Hall.

Kotler, Philip J., and Gary Armstrong. 2010. *Principles of Marketing*. Upper Saddle River, NJ: Prentice-Hall.

Kress, Gunther R., and Theo van Leeuwen. 2001. *Multimodal Discourse: The Modes and Media of Contemporary Communication*. London: Hodder Arnold.

Landow, George P. 1994. *Hyper/Text/Theory*. Baltimore: Johns Hopkins University Press.

Laurel, Brenda. 1993. *Computers as Theatre*. Reading, MA: Addison Wesley.

Mark, M., and C.S. Pearson. 2001. *The Hero and the Outlaw: Building Extraordinary Brands through the Power of Archetypes*. New York: McGraw Hill Professional.

McGonigal, Jane. 2010. "Gaming Can Make a Better World." *TED Conference*. https://www.ted.com/talks/jane_mcgonigal_gaming_can_make_a_better_world.

Muniz Jr., Albert M., and Thomas C. O'Guinn. 2001. "Brand Community." *Journal of Consumer Research* 27 (4): 412–32.

Murray, Janet. 1997. *Hamlet on the Holodeck: The Future of Narrative in Cyberspace*. Cambridge, MA: MIT Press.

O'Brien, L., and C. Jones. 1995. "Do Rewards Really Create Loyalty?" *Harvard Business Review* 73 (3): 75–82. doi:10.1016/0024-6301(95)94312-M.

Öhrvall, Sara, and Megan Miller. 2012. "Reflections from SXSW Interactive 2011: Bonnier R&D's Insights and Observations from the Great Austin Geek-a-Palooza." *Bonnier R&D*. http://www.bonnier.com/Growth-Media-/rd/blog/2011/March/Reflections-from-SXSW-Interactive-2011/.

Pincas, Stéphane, and Marc Loiseau. 2008. *A History of Advertising*. Köln: Taschen.

Propp, Vladimir. 1968. *Morphology of the Folktale. Publication / Indiana University Research Center in Anthropology, Folklore and Linguistics, 10*. 2. ed. Austin, TX: University of Texas Press.

Rey, P.J. 2012. "Gamification, Playbor & Exploitation." *The Society Pages*. https://thesocietypages.org/cyborgology/2012/10/15/gamification-playbor-exploitation-2/.

Rheingold, Howard. 1995. *Virtual Community: Finding Connection in a Computerised World*. New ed. London: Minerva.

Ritzer, G., and N. Jurgenson. 2010. "Production, Consumption, Prosumption the Nature of Capitalism in the Age of the Digital 'Prosumer'." *Journal of Consumer Culture* 10 (1): 13–36.

Roper, Juliet. 2005. "Symmetrical Communication: Excellent Public Relations or a Strategy for Hegemony?" *Journal of Public Relations Research* 17 (1): 69–86. doi:10.1207/s1532754xjprr1701_6.

Ryan, Marie-Laure. 2001. *Narrative as Virtual Reality: Immersion and Interactivity in Literature and Electronic Media: Parallax (Baltimore)*. Baltimore: Johns Hopkins University Press.

Shannon, C., and W. Weaver. 1969. *The Mathematical Theory of Communication*. Urbana: University of Illinois Press.

Smythe, Dallas Walker. 1977. "Communications: Blindspot of Western Marxism." *Canadian Journal of Political and Social Theory / Revue Canadienne de Theorie Politique Etsociale* 1 (3). 1–27.

Stavrakakis, Y. 2006. "Objects of Consumption, Causes of Desire: Consumerism and Advertising in Societies of Commanded Enjoyment." *Gramma: Journal of Theory and Criticism* 14: 83–106.

Tapp, Alan. 2008. *Principles of Direct and Database Marketing: A Digital Orientation*. Harlow, UK: Financial Times/Prentice Hall.

Urbanski, Al. 2014. "Is Swarm the De-Gamification of Foursquare?" *Direct Marketing*. http://www.dmnews.com/mobile-marketing/is-swarm-the-de-gamification-of-foursquare/article/355853/.

Varey, Richard. 2002. *Marketing Communication: A Critical Introduction*. London: Routledge.

Vargo, S.L., and R.F. Lusch. 2004. "Evolving to a New Dominant Logic for Marketing." *Journal of Marketing* 68 (1): 1–17.

Zackariasson, Peter. 2007. *World Builders: A Study on the Development of a Massively Multiplayer Online Role-Playing Game*. PhD diss., Umeå University, Umeå School of Business, Umeå, Sweden.

Zichermann, Gabe. 2011. "How Games Make Kids Smarter." *TEDxKids@Brussels*. https://www.ted.com/talks/gabe_zichermann_how_games_make_kids_smarter.

Zichermann, Gabe, and Joselin Linder. 2010. *Game-Based Marketing: Inspire Customer Loyalty Through Rewards, Challenges, and Contests*. Hoboken, NJ: John Wiley & Sons.

7 Samsung Nation
A Gamified Experience
Tracy Harwood and Tony Garry

Introduction

Through gamification, customers and firms purportedly cocreate value with outcomes suggested to enhance customer brand loyalty (Bitner & Shipper, 2014). Gamification is the use of game mechanics within non-ludic contexts to encourage a more fun-based experience that motivates engagement behaviors (Zichermann & Cunningham, 2011). We examine the interrelationships between the game mechanics devised by a game developer, customer motivations for participating in a gamified context and cocreated outcomes, particularly in relation to customer loyalty. The research context is Samsung Nation's gamified brand web-based experience. The research design uses the qualitative approach of netnography and participant observation to draw out key themes in data. Datasets reported on comprise daily leaderboard analyses, website and social media posts related to the Samsung Nation experience.

Whilst Samsung Nation has been pitched as a particularly successful gamified experience by commentators, our analysis highlights some interesting findings related to design and execution of the game mechanics, dynamic gameplay, depth of emotional engagement, interest/boredom thresholds, celebrity status and connection between the leaderboards and branded website, linking to loyalty-based outcomes. We present our analysis using quotes and images from the datasets. The findings are related to theory with managerial implications drawn. Finally further areas for investigation are highlighted.

Literature Review

Gamification

Gamification is the use of game mechanics in nongame environments (Deterding et al., 2011). In a marketing context, mechanics are used to support or enhance dynamic customer involvement with the brand and influence behavioural responses by reinforcing brand values through exposure, thereby increasing opportunities to purchase (Zichermann & Linder, 2011). Importantly, drawing on ludic principals of playfulness, interaction with the brand becomes more fun (Robson et al., 2014). Robson et al. (2014) propose a framework that interrelates *mechanics* of the gameplay context (i.e., the goals, rules, challenges and rewards [badges] of the game) (see e.g., Sicart, 2008), with the *dynamics* of playful interaction with the game, and the consequential *emotional* engagement of the consumer resulting from participation. This perspective draws on service-dominant logic (Vargo & Lusch, 2004), wherein the firm provides the operant resources (mechanism) and the customer derives value (gamefulness) from the interaction experience (Huotari & Hamari, 2012; Hamari, 2013). In effect, the experience of the brand through gamification consumption becomes more hedonic than utilitarian. Research has found influence in utilitarian contexts relating to hedonic consumption to be low (Hamari, 2013). Hilderband et al. (2014) found commitment as a consequence of involvement with branded game mechanics to increase.

Pre-Formed Customer Loyalty

Commitment, from the firm's perspective, is a desirable state, leading to loyalty and repurchase behaviour, which gamification appears to be well designed to achieve. For example, the goal of most B2C/consumer-oriented organisations is to develop and maintain brand-consumer relationships manifesting in consumer loyalty (e.g., Reicheld & Sasser, 1990; Oliver, 1999; Davis et al., 2000): loyal consumers are considered to be more cost effective to keep and valuable to the organisation than new customers (Reicheld & Sasser, 1990). A key antecedent of successful relationships is a positive brand experience (Şahin et al., 2011), which gamification may contribute towards by guiding interactive experiences. However, much of the literature in this area concentrates on post-purchase behaviours posited as reflective of such positive experiences and ultimately, of consumer loyalty (e.g., Dick & Basu, 1994; Pritchard et al., 1999). To this end, consumer loyalty has generally been defined in terms of repurchasing behaviour (e.g., Assael, 1992) and/or propensity to switch to competing brands (e.g., Keller, 1993). In particular, confirmation/disconfirmation mechanisms (e.g., Bitner, 1990) are frequently used to explain the "nexus" of variables identified within the relational marketing literature that encapsulate positive ongoing relationships (Hong & Wang, 2011).

This approach does not, however, consider the "manipulability" of customer loyalty prior to experiencing the actual product or service (Hong & Wang, 2011), and "pre-formed loyalty"' is increasingly being recognized as a mechanism by which firms may shape consumer attitudes in the absence of actually experiencing the firm's product offering. This in turn may manifest itself in a positive predisposition to the firm's offering. Indeed, given the absence of any monetary investment by consumers prepurchase, they may be potentially more susceptible to positive attitudinal development. Reminiscent of Muñiz and O'Guinn's (2001) "community triangle", interactions between brand-customer, customer-customer and customer-noncustomer provide opportunities for not only reinforcing brand loyalty among existing customers, but also engendering positive attitudinal developments among non-customers. Through interaction experiences, a noncustomer may "attach themselves emotionally to a firm" and its brands with consequential affective loyalty (Brakus et al., 2009). The resultant affective loyalty may be developed through the personal involvement that a potential customer has with a brand (Gabarino & Johnson, 1999). In such circumstances, Hong and Wang (2011) define loyalty as "the emotional attachment to and the desire to prolong a relationship with a firm . . . without an evaluation process of the actual [product] performance of the firm" (p. 195). Hence, gamification may be seen as a resource for supporting prepurchase relational development, as well as service support beyond purchase by providing a stimulus for prolonged interaction and affective involvement.

Intrinsic and Extrinsic Rewards

The nature of value generated by customers in a gamified context may relate to playfulness, evoking emotional responses such as a sense of fun. Drawing on self-determination theory, this enables customers to derive intrinsic rewards from participation, such as self-gratification (Ryan & Deci, 2000). This differs from extrinsic motivations for engaging in loyalty programmes that typically proffer economic rewards such as financial incentives (Meyer-Waarden, 2015) that have been found to influence higher levels of loyalty and intent behaviour when involvement is high and rewards are delivered immediately (Yi & Jeon, 2003; Meyer-Waarden, 2015). Therefore the immediacy of receiving rewards delivered through web-based gamified mechanisms that involve high levels of participation through mechanics and result in play-related rewards, such as badges and peer recognition, suggest value is also extrinsically motivated, leading to loyalty and associated behaviours.

Furthermore, there is an increasing recognition among firms that the product is not an end in itself, but an enabler of interactive consumer-brand experiences together with relationships with other like-minded individuals who may or not be existing customers. Kuo and Feng's (2013) meta-analysis of the literature on interactive consumer experiences identifies four principal categories of benefits of such interactions: first, utilitarian benefits encompassing cognitive, functional and problem solving benefits (e.g., Dholakia et al., 2004; Nambisan & Baron, 2009); second, hedonic benefits encompassing entertainment values (e.g., Dholakia et al., 2004; Tynan et al., 2014); third, benefits to self-esteem such as self-enhancement (e.g., Yen et al., 2011); and finally, social benefits (e.g., Muñiz & O'Guinn, 2001).

Specifically, relationships help to build trust that diminishes perceptions of risk of opportunistic behavior, resulting in a sense of loyalty (e.g.,

Bhattacherjee, 2002; Goldenberg et al., 2002) where, in the event of no direct experience, social indicators may be used to evaluate brands (Deephouse & Carter, 2005). The challenge for firms is to develop game mechanisms that enable meaningful brand-related interactions and experiences both pre- and post-product consumption whilst engendering brand trust and ultimately, brand loyalty (Fisher & Smith, 2011).

Value Cocreation

Mechanics in gamified experiences often tie together fun and enjoyable experiences (intrinsic reward) with extrinsic rewards (e.g., digital badges) through the design of challenges. Game developers create rule-based structures that challenge players to pursue goals (Deterding et al. 2011; Deterding, 2015). There is, however, an important difference in the design of gamified experiences: within games development, a design problem is in persuading players to engage in economic exchanges beyond free-to-play components or those prepurchased with the game (e.g., Hamari & Lehdonvirta, 2010). Player resistance is often triggered because of a perception of inconsistency of value in exchange benefits (i.e., between playfulness and economic exchanges) (Hamari & Lehdonvirta, 2010). Within brand gamified contexts, economic exchange is congruent with expectations of interactions with a brand, and thus resistance to such value exchanges, motivated instead by challenges and achievement of associated rewards (badges), should be low. Furthermore, as Hamari (2015) found albeit in a games-development environment, the social and peer achievement context of gamesplay may be expected to increase purchase intent.

Building on this from a service dominant logic perspective, value production and creation are rapidly evolving away from product- and firm-centric processes towards a more experiential orientation (e.g., Belk, 1988; Grönroos, 2008; Vargo & Lusch, 2008). The discursive power model advocating cocreativity between consumer and firm has emerged (e.g., Holt, 2002), largely facilitated by new technologies and servicescapes. The implication of this has been the traditional and distinct roles of value creation that consumer and firm fulfill is converging (Prahalad & Ramaswamy, 2004) and increasingly cocreating value (Lusch & Vargo, 2006) within the context of an "experience environment" (Pine & Gilmore, 1998). Cocreativity between consumer and firm implies value is uniquely and contextually interpreted by the beneficiary (e.g., Denegri-Knott et al., 2006; Vargo & Lusch, 2008; Pongsakornrungslip & Schroeder, 2011). Cocreated experiences are differentiated from "consumer involvement" and "co-production" processes insofar as it is active and demanding consumers that determine value (Bonsu & Darmody, 2008) by choosing to willingly interact with the experience environment to "create their own unique personalised consumption experience" (Prahalad & Ramaswamy, 2004: 9).

Increasingly, cocreation processes take place within web-based consumption communities (Cova et al., 2007; Rowley et al., 2007), where norms and codes of conduct are established through an iterative and coevolving process between consumer and firm (Denegri-Knott et al., 2006), yet facilitated by the firm (e.g., Rowley et al., 2007). Linkages between value cocreation and value capture, however, remain ambiguous and are variously cited as requiring a deeper and more comprehensive understanding (cf. Gummesson, 2008; Payne et al., 2008; Cova & Dalli, 2009; Cova et al., 2011). Foundations comprise of skills, information and knowledge that are transformed through value-generating processes encompassing physical activities, mental effort and socio-psychological procedures into value-in-use or "value-in-context" experiences (Ballantyne & Varey, 2008; Chandler & Vargo, 2011). Gamification may therefore offer insight into the capture of cocreated value by the firm within an experience environment.

In framing our empirical investigation, we draw on these concepts to explore the interrelationships between the game mechanics devised by a game developer, customer motivations for participating in a gamified context and cocreated outcomes, particularly in relation to loyalty.

Methodology

Participants' lived experiences were expressed in this research through the web sphere associated with the Samsung Nation brand community (Schneider & Foot, 2004, 2005), including a website and social media fora. To address the research aims of following the community, a netnographic approach was selected to enable an examination of the lived experiences of participants in the Samsung Nation game (Miles & Huberman, 1994; Kozinets, 2002). Previous investigations into web-based phenomena suggest it is an approach that is useful for "confirming, contrasting and contributing to" academic literature (Garver, 2003) and to capturing contextual richness embodied within such environments (Strauss & Corbin, 1990). Our research attempted to establish the critical relations and trace the boundaries of the social phenomenon in cyberspace (Guimaraes, 2005; Bouellstorff et al., 2012). Netnography is a qualitative methodology that adapts ethnographic research techniques "to study cultures and communities that are emerging through computer-mediated communications" (Kozinets, 2002: 62) by reflecting on the Internet context as a site of cultural and sociological interest (Hine, 2009; Kozinets, 2010). Thus, netnography is increasingly used in contemporary market-related research contexts (e.g., Catterall & Maclaran, 2002; de Valck et al., 2009) with particular benefits noted such as it can be less time consuming, is flexible for observation and analysis (Law & Urry, 2004), is potentially less obtrusive than other techniques and is consequently cheaper (Langer & Beckman, 2005; Xun & Reynolds, 2010). Furthermore, online communities offer the potential to study the social and economic behavior of large numbers of participants (Yuan et al., 2007). Drawing on previous web-based studies (e.g., Kozinets, 2002, 2010;

Rokka, 2010), a five-stage process was adopted for this research comprising: entrée; data collection; analysis and interpretation; research ethics; and membership.

Entrée was achieved by one of the researchers joining the Samsung Nation community website, registering as a user and participating in the game experience challenges across the levels of the game during a three-month data collection period. Participation in the game involved registering products (which had been previously bought), searching online for relevant information using key words identified by the game, using social media to "like", "tweet" and post comments on the fora in relation to the key words, thereby earning reward points. Data was collected using multiple techniques (Cova & Pace, 2006) comprising "content grabs" from repeated online browsing of the Samsung Nation environment; "screen grabs" of leader-boards and participant observer achievements; field notes from participant observation of the Samsung Nation website; offline and online compilation of information on Samsung and Samsung Nation; and online compilation of social network and fora postings (all postings were in English). Data collection was undertaken systematically throughout the period of active engagement by the researchers in the game. Three hundred posted contributions (by other game players) were identified, accounting for 70 printed pages of text. The authors' progressively analysed data collected during the study. Data was identified and coded relating to the key processes and outcomes of the gamified experience using a qualitative content analytic approach to identify key themes within the data (Krippendorff, 1980). Data was coded by two researchers independently, subsequently compared and differences of opinion discussed and agreed upon to determine the final outputs of analysis. The analytic process adhered to the constant comparative method (Glaser & Strauss, 1967) whereby new data was compared with previous interpretations. This process was continued until data saturation was reached, which determined the length of the study data collection period.

Participant observation enabled screen captures of achievements to be collected and analyzed for the study, including details of badges, awards and rewards; number and types of activities involved; points achievement, leaderboard rankings and follow-up activities. Some activities related directly to website postings whilst others merely required participants to follow links embedded within the game context (e.g., to "like" or "share") whilst others were "hidden" and related merely to clicking on a page link a number of times during a visit or over a period of time, or being a member for a number of hours or days. The data (postings) were extracted across the breadth of product categories supported and where possible were attributed to observed leaderboard members followed during the period of study. Following guidelines on the use of data that exists within the public domain (Frankel & Sang, 1999; Langer & Beckman, 2005), there has been no attempt to contact or seek the permissions of Samsung Nation participants whose postings and rankings have been collected, analyzed and reported on for this chapter. However, to ensure anonymity, call signs (identities) have been removed in the presentation of our findings.

Background of Samsung Nation

Samsung Nation was the first gamified experience using a high-profile brand in conjunction with its moderated consumer electronics website (Samsung, 2012). The organization stated that its gamified proposition had over 1.2M players with 4M unique visitors every month. According to published information (website), Samsung Nation described itself as a "social loyalty program" that attempts to "recognise and empower our most passionate fans" (Contreras, 2011a). Described as a "fusion of social media and gamification" (Lopez, 2011), Samsung Nation launched in October 2011 with the aim of harnessing its community of followers through game mechanics and social experiences (Lopez, 2011). It was targeted at early adopters, socialisers and collectors and visitors to "sign up" by incentivizing them to explore and engage with website content. In return, game participants could "unlock" badges and progress up a leaderboard as they explored the website. Contreras, Samsung's social media manager, suggested Samsung's aim was "to increase engagement and advocacy by enhancing the overall experience of our customers and fans on Samsung.com" (Contreras, 2012).

Contreras (2012) proposed the objectives of Samsung Nation were to reward interaction, facilitate discovery and "create a sense of interconnectedness among passionate advocates". In essence, it was an attempt to reward consumers' seeking behavior that may lead to "increased brand loyalty, not to mention increased profits" (Singer, 2012). Samsung defined the success of its gamified environment as increased engagement throughout the entire website. Engagement is defined as the posting of "user generated content like comments, [product] reviews, as well as interactions with Samsung content and increased sharing to social networks" (Contreras, 2011b). Competition between participants was encouraged through the promise of peer and organizational recognition: "For those of you who crave a little competition and want those bragging rights, rack up more points than other fans, and you'll be highlighted on our Samsung Nation leader board" (Samsung Nation website). Point and badge accumulation enabled participants to qualify for a monthly sweepstake of Samsung's products, with the provision of links to a range of social media that facilitated progression through the game.

Findings

Samsung Nation Game Mechanics

Samsung Nation is based on the Badgeville™ gamification platform. The experience focuses primarily on generating engagement with the electronics manufacturer's website and associated social media using a range of tasks and activities, some related to branded product purchases and others related to brand community. Samsung has positioned the experience as a "social loyalty programme" aimed at their most loyal customers. Its stated goal is to "increase engagement and advocacy by enhancing the overall experience of our customers and fans on Samsung.com" (Contreras, 2012), rewarding customers and simultaneously growing profits. There is a high level of engagement with the website, evidenced through numbers of comments and "likes", yet the first part of the process for participating in the game is clearly designed for data capture. By asking customers to sign up to the experience, customers provide their personal information, including name and contact information. This phase is where customers select an identity for their gameplay and agree to abide to the "rules" of play.

Once registered, the game offers a short tour and tutorial related to how the experience develops, including "unlocking" badges by completing tasks and moving up the leaderboard based on points accumulation. Early rewards achieved are points that contribute towards achieving levels of play related to simply logging into the account created and navigating through a few pages of the website. Points are awarded, for example, for registering products = 500 points; reading and commenting on articles = 300 points; watching videos = 200 points; providing a Facebook "Like" = 200 points; Twitter "share" = 100 points; providing a question in a Q&A forum = 100 points; providing an answer in a Q&A forum = 300 points. Badges also enable players opportunities to win monthly sweepstake competitions for Samsung-branded products.

Using ludic descriptions of game mechanics (e.g., Sicart, 2008), components of game complexity were identified and summarized in Table 7.1. These appear to progress through two layers of play: the first being overt

Table 7.1 List of game mechanics identified in Samsung Nation

Game mechanic	Samsung Nation
Goal: aim of the game	Leading position on the leaderboard
Turn: a portion or round of the game during which some key action takes place	Process of completing tasks associated with navigating the website—posting a product-related comment; liking another person's comment; registering a product purchase; etc.
Resource management: retaining, using, exchanging points acquired	Achievement of certain points gives access to restricted areas of the website and competitions; some tasks require collaborative completion in order to achieve points
Challenge: quest or task that must be completed to earn rewards	Defined or guided tasks and "hidden" tasks
Awards: rewards	Badges; points; leaderboard position

challenges, guided by the game rules, which are shared with customers; the second is covert and hidden within gameplay, where customers appear to "discover" rewards through some action related to clicking on a particular web page or link within a web page, albeit the actions that result in consistent rewards are also hidden. This aligns with Contreras' (2011b) claim that the process of earning badges and rewards is a combination of clear "pathways" and serendipitous exploration of the website. Furthermore "rare rewards" are reserved for "advanced" or "rare behavior" such as visiting the site between midnight and 4:00 a.m. and visiting and interacting with the site on national holidays or Samsung-specified dates (Contreras, 2011b).

In analyzing the game mechanics, notable omissions from gamesplay contexts were identified. More specifically:

- there is no "capture" or directly competitive component, wherein players claim the resources of others participating in the game;
- play "turns" of all players are equal (including "rare behavior" turns). For example, there is no "catch-up" component often seen in games, whereby experienced players at the top of the leaderboard are assigned more difficult "turns" than less-experienced players, say at the beginning of the game. That said, a number of the challenges are only achieved through a process of discovery, which undoubtedly requires allocating time and developing navigational skill to uncover.
- achievement of the winning condition is not a necessity for play continuation, given that participation is dynamic as positions shift along the leaderboard with each task completed. As such, there is no end to the gameplay.

Importantly, the overarching goal of the game appears to be secondary for most customers, primarily because achievement of the leading position does not generate special reward beyond peer recognition (i.e., position on the board), which is posted to players' Samsung Nation page. The information provided about position on the leaderboard is limited to a snapshot suggesting the possibilities for social exchanges with those in positions higher or lower on the board is also limited. Moreover, once an award (badge) is achieved (task completed and points awarded), these are not time delimited, exchangeable or directly redeemable against product purchases.

Customer Perspectives of the Game Mechanics

From the customer perspective, there is a gap between achievement and reward insofar as the challenges to attain a particular award are neither explicit nor transparent. One participant states:

> Samsung Nation seems like a fun way to get people to interact with the company. problem is, there is little to no direction on how to interact.

> Your general blurb and little pop-ups do not direct a person as to exactly what to do to earn badges and get involved in the community:
>
> (blog, 9 March)

A persistent theme in posts on the website is frustration with game "turns" and reward allocation: "Some of these badges just wont unlock, i have been visiting several times late [at night] and it still does not give me the owl badge. Hmmoh" (blog, 1 May). Reflective of the serendipitous nature of accumulating rewards highlighted by Contreras (2011b), this appears to be part of a deliberate strategy by Samsung to "evoke suspense" in terms of earning badges: "We don't want to give too much away, but let's just say that there will be surprises along the way" (Samsung website).

Comments suggested norms have emerged in relation to gameplay and achievement of intrinsic rewards:

> This makes learning about products fun! And with the wide range of quality products, I'll be visiting here a lot.
>
> (Blog, 6 December)

This kind of dynamic interaction indicates a key attribute of the community's participation in the game relates to the social exchanges and intrinsic reward. Whilst the challenge is evident in the process of gameplay, skills are rarely shared, and calls for assistance largely go unanswered by either Samsung or other customers. Since achievements evidenced through leaderboards provide a cue to customers about engagement levels of others within the community, such attempts to interact without success could damage any camaraderie among customers. Thus dynamic exchange is somewhat limited to turn taking, as evidenced through the leaderboard. This is perhaps not because customers do not want to share but rather more because the game mechanics are unclear:

> You get letters by visiting certain pages on the site. I have 2 of them but do not remember what pages I got them on.
>
> (blog, 1 January)

Information and knowledge appear to add limited value to the product related level of exchange. The firm states (Contreras, 2011a): "we won't reward you for submitting a 5-star review, but we will reward you for submitting any kind of product review. We want to make our site more engaging and that requires us to allow customers to speak their minds". There is little data suggesting it has encouraged more than superficial contributions, which ultimately resulted in a badge for the poster rather than insight for the firm or other customers.

Loyalty and Rewards

Additionally, customer achievement through the acquisition of points and badges, and relative positions on the leaderboard went unrecognised by fellow participants: there was a distinct lack of congratulatory messages, likes or shares as might be expected, indicating a limited level of exchange perhaps moderated by the brand. In addition, a number of customers made insightful comments about the sustainability of the site based purely on extrinsic rewards: "Depending on what they decide to give away based on one's points will determine if it lasts longer than 6 months" (blog, 16 November), intimating a level of communication that did not require direct response albeit this contributes to community presence. Rewards of the nature intimated, however, do not appear to have been offered.

The apparent failure in the game mechanics to realize dynamic exchange between customers, whether synchronous or asynchronous, also highlights difficulties in achieving some of the awards. For example, one customer requests information: "Anybody have an idea as to how to unlock any of the Teams badges/achievements?" (blog, 17 December) but does not receive a reply.

Customers voiced frustration at how their participation was being treated:

> It would be a good thing if Samsung recognized the 3D TV, Blu-ray and Receiver I registered earlier this year toward my various badges. You have both my loyalty and my money; a little quid pro quo?
>
> (blog, 30 December)

This appears to implicitly compromise the cocreated value derived from participation. Despite this, one commentator has subsequently claimed that it has been successful because it increased anonymous to registered users by 47 percent and increased the number of answers to frequently asked questions (Davey, 2015), intimating success for the firm is measured by traffic flow rather than quality of contributions.

The leaderboard plays a central role in communicating dynamic gameplay by exhibiting customers' relative progress to others. In gamesplay contexts, this in turn results in leaders becoming community celebrities where their technical prowess and achievements may be appreciated by likeminded others. However, a number of customers of Samsung Nation have posted negative comments linked to their pursuit of a higher rank on the leaderboard:

> I am unable to see my SAMSUNG NATION results . . . Where did they go? I haven't been able to see it in almost a month? You got me addicted and took it away! I can see when I earn new badges (it comes on the bottom of the screen) but can't see which badges and points I've earned overall. . . . I'd love to know where I rank . . . PLEASE HELP!!!!!!!!!!!!
>
> (blog, 21 February)

For example, a snapshot taken during the data collection period of August 20 highlighted the leading customer held some 17,187,150 (all time) points. This score is astonishing considering the relative point value for actions, albeit the identities of high scorers were not observed on the website or related fora demonstrating their contributions to point-accumulating activities.

There is evidence of directedness of attentional enjoyment towards the game and its environs, extending across the Samsung Nation website and fora. Motivation appears to be primarily intrinsic—a fun way to engage with the brand. Findings highlight the apparently random nature of how badges are unlocked undermines the premise that the locus of causality is self-determined and frequently causes participants to post comments about their frustrations and anxieties with their experience. This, combined with the lack of clarity related to game challenges, appears to ultimately result in a level of diffidence towards the game:

> This is a great social exercise. The only problem is that the content on the website doesn't change regularly enough to keep up one's interest. After three or four days poking around the site hunting for badges, I'm pretty bored of this.
>
> (blog, 13 June)

As a result, the psychological immersion and enjoyment in the game that ultimately achieves a sense of flow in the experience is being continually interrupted through the evocation of negative emotions (diminishing enjoyment) and resultant behaviours.

Notwithstanding this finding, we could find no evidence that the lack of more positive emotional engagement impacts on purchase intention. Analysis of postings (and lack of postings), therefore, suggests emotions have an indirect role in engendering loyalty through the branded online community environment.

Cocreated Value

The lack of comments overall may, however, indicate the focus of engagement is with the brand and community beyond mere point accumulation associated with the game, or that the game itself had little material value in relation to brand consumption activities. Participation does incentivize social interaction, which in turn appears to drive indirect interaction with the products through dynamic gameplay, resulting in point accumulation: "I'm new to Samsung Nation. Heard about it from a friend. Looking forward to unlocking the badges!" (blog, 28 February).

Another outcome is identified in relation to the process of learning about products: "This makes learning about products fun! And with the wide range of quality products, I'll be visiting here a lot." (blog, 7 December). Postings highlight engagement with the game, implying a level of loyalty is being formed with the brand through play. As customers become more experienced with the game, issues related to the game mechanics that emerge indicate psychological lock-in (loyalty) to the game albeit evidenced in dissatisfaction. Numerous examples affirm customer intention to revisit the website, implying behavioural loyalty to both the brand and the game: "I hadn't been on this site very much previously but I'll definitely be visiting more often now. If only I knew how to unlock all the badges . . . :)" (blog, 29 November).

It is also evident that it is not essential that customers have direct experience of Samsung products in order to participate in the game. Contreras (2012) advocates that Samsung Nation is "sentiment agnostic" and Samsung will award badges to "our biggest critics", implying that non-customer opinions are equally sought, with an aim to make product engagement fun: participants are urged to "have fun . . . earn points, level up and unlock badges" as they navigate the website.

Whilst gameplay has therefore resulted in repeat visits and word-of-mouth communication resulting in customer franchise, it is difficult to judge the extent to which customers have been converted through play behaviour to (repeat) purchase behavior. Nonetheless, there is evidence that the firm benefits directly from the cocreated value derived within the experience environment: value provides a stickiness resulting in a transient form of customer retention for the purposes of gameplay and also attracts new customers. This suggests dynamic gameplay and emotional engagement contribute towards loyalty, most notably through the social context by building the sense of community presence.

Discussion

The aim of this chapter was to explore the interrelationships between game mechanics, gameplay dynamics and customer motivations, considering how value is cocreated in a gamified context. Gamification has been described as a means to provide pleasurable participant experiences through an amalgamation of "content, community and commerce" reminiscent of brand communities and gamesplay (Zichermann & Cunningham, 2011; Zichermann & Linder, 2011). From a firm perspective, the primary driver of gamification is to capture the value cocreated with customers to enhance opportunities for engaging them ultimately in outcomes that enhance brand experiences, brand loyalty and (repeat) purchase behaviour.

Gamification

As a process that draws on ludic principals of playfulness, evidence supports the notion that the mechanics incorporated into the Samsung Nation game are helpful in generating a level of engagement. The components used, however, appear to be incomplete in communicating the full sense of a game, such as that evoked through goals, rules, challenges and rewards (Robson et al., 2014). In particular, the case highlights that clarity is required for goals and rules of engagement in order to address the interactive feedback provided by customers in relation to the value they generate from their experience (Huotari & Hamari, 2012; Hamari, 2013).

Pre-Formed Customer Loyalty

In evaluating the extent to which customer loyalty is achieved through gamesplay, there is evidence that the game mechanics reinforce brand community and drive engagement with the brand through the series of activities (Gabarino & Johnson, 1999; Brakus et al., 2009). The rewards provide intrinsic and extrinsic motivation for dynamic gamesplay, supporting ongoing emotional involvement. This results in a level of loyalty to the branded environment, manifesting in the mechanistic collecting of points and badges. Where the rules of play are tied to existing modes of engagement with the brand through its website (e.g., viewing reviews, etc.) then this may result in increased traffic through the website. That said, direct interaction between customers is limited in the example we analyzed, albeit there is recognition among customers that others are present within the environment and have potential to engage in dynamic exchange.

The dynamic exchange observed encompasses both customers and noncustomers, suggesting that it may be possible to support attitudinal development particularly in noncustomers through gamified mechanisms (Brakus et al., 2009; Zichermann & Linder, 2011). There is, however, little evidence to suggest the gamified platform analyzed directly generates and reinforces outcomes such as purchase or repeat purchase. Moreover, the evidence we have considered suggests that, overall, loyalty associated with the brand has *pre-formed* as "engagement loyalty" with the community environment in which the game is played—at this level, we hesitate to position this as a pathological addiction (see e.g., Gopaladesikan, 2013; Saliceti, 2015) but the consideration of online behavior in relation to gamified brand experiences is presently little understood and worthy of further investigation. That said, whilst expectations of the game appear to have been *moderated* by the brand, the lack of loyalty evidenced as a consequence of the apparent incomplete (or poor) game design does not appear to have *mediated* brand outcomes.

Intrinsic and Extrinsic Rewards

Our analysis of the gamified experience suggests there is a fundamental disconnect in the iterative nature of Liu et al's (2011) gamified loop (goal, challenge, task completion, reward, engagement), which negates the intrinsic motivators frequently evoked by gamification (e.g., Man, 2011; Witt et al., 2011). Key to this is a number of mechanism flaws that intimate why gamified outcomes remain unfulfilled insofar as customers are concerned.

That said, the identified deep-level engagement that borders on obsessive behavior intimates immersion in gameplay has been achieved. It is perhaps one reason why content posted and aligned with play is relatively superficial. For example, there is no incentive (extrinsic reward) to spend time reading articles or viewing products beyond a "click on a page". Participant comprehension and experiential mastery of the challenges and the accompanying positive sensation of competence through endeavour and labour that this engenders are therefore absent (Csikszentmihalyi, 1975). This undermines one of the key goals of gamification in building community. On the other hand, the process of engagement with the website may be sufficient reward and intrinsic motivation in itself (Saliceti, 2015). Either way, our findings imply there may be a fifth category of benefit for customers from such interactions, extending Kuo and Feng's (2013) current framework (utilitarian, hedonic, self-esteem and social).

For others, the lack of guidance with achieving goals, either from community members or the firm, ultimately resulting in disengagement from the branded environment, intimates that there needs to be a clear engagement/disengagement strategy in the game design to maintain relationships with customers beyond the immediate completion of challenges. Genuine engagement that the website may naturally engender may be compromised by the frustrations with acquiring badges highlighted in the findings (e.g., Abuhamdeh & Csikszentmihalyi, 2012). As a result, *softer* activities such as sustaining membership, reaffirming and strengthening the underlying values of the community and providing a platform to bring together and bond individual members maybe absent (Cova & Cova, 2002).

Value Cocreation

From a firm perspective, the nature of cocreation with customers is interesting. There is a lack of corporate engagement with the customer beyond the game mechanics and the provision of an online proposition of content. There is limited space for task completion and content creation. This is flawed insofar as the relationship between achievement and reward is neither transparent nor explicit. It is, however, effective in achieving a populated environment in which customers may experience the presence of community, albeit indirectly through leaderboards and asynchronous communications. Previous research in the area of brand communities and gamesplay suggests a primary motivator of social exchange within such contexts is the genuine endeavour of customers to seek and proffer assistance, advice and opinions to and from other participants through online dialogical exchange (e.g., Brodie et al., 2011). There is no evidence that this exists in the Samsung Nation gamified context. Paradoxically, the introduction of game mechanics may, therefore, erode the engagement that already exists with the brand community (e.g., Muñiz & O'Guinn, 2001).

Whilst there may be a case for increasing serendipitous brand interaction and knowledge among customers through the exploration of the website in a quest to accumulate points, such engagement may be only cursory (e.g., Ouwersloot & Oderkerken-Schröder, 2008) and may ultimately lead to brand disillusionment (Thom et al., 2012). In the process of capturing the cocreated value, therefore, the challenge for the firm is that the negative experience is also visibly captured, and this has potential to damage relational outcomes.

Samsung is effectively facilitating its customers' desires for recognition and self-fulfilment through engagement with its gamified environment whilst carefully appropriating their output: "with every click . . . every comment or status. . . . a user contributes toward co-creating value" (Man, 2011:6). However, there is evidence to suggest some participants are recognizing an exploitative element to Samsung Nation, resulting in some customers participating in deviant behaviours (e.g., Cova et al., 2008). Reflective of the cultural industry's "work as play mantra" (Bonsu & Darmody, 2008), immaterial labour in the form of creativity, communication, emotion, cooperation and values may be "put to work" by firms (e.g., Lazzarato, 1996; Terronava, 2000). Within this context, the boundaries between play and content provision subtly dissolve, and the outputs of participants' immaterial labour produced through performing various tasks in an attempt to achieve points and badges becomes commercially advantageous.

Conclusion

Whilst undoubtedly driving website traffic and supporting corporate analytics through initial *cognitive lock-in* (Mollen & Hugh, 2010; Davey, 2015), there is little evidence to suggest that the game mechanics reviewed here generate and reinforce high-quality customer behavior. This contradicts much of the rhetoric surrounding gamification that advocates increased levels of engagement. However, there needs be a recognition that it is game content and not just game mechanics that contribute to successful gamified experiences and ultimately engagement. Gamification focuses primarily on removing ludic forms of gamesplay from the experience and replacing it with mechanics imposed on branded content. Whilst this may encourage gamefulness, it is evidently not gameplay per se. The issue with such content is that it is both expensive to produce and to maintain and may therefore be beyond the resource base and focus of most commercial entities. Thus, the challenge for firms is to take existing brand content and develop game mechanics that fulfill expectations and optimize appropriate engagement. Marketers must therefore be aware that well-designed game mechanics that integrate seamlessly with the main functionalities and structure of an existing system are essential for the successful implementation of gamified engagement platforms. Merely transposing points systems, badges and leaderboards may lead to superficial engagement.

At a practical level the study provides insight into the outcomes of gamification, based on the analysis of one gamified experience: Samsung

Nation. Whilst this research has limitations for generalizing findings to other servicescapes adapting to this mode of customer engagement, there are some important managerial implications that we have highlighted. These relate not just to the game design that should consider the gamified loop through which customers will interact but also the range of emergent engagement behaviours and the ways in which these will be rewarded. Whilst some may be planned and desirable (seeking of extrinsic and intrinsic rewards), others we have observed may have the impact of *corrupting* the game and *bastardising* the brand community.

Future research may explore the specific roles game mechanics and types of dynamic gameplay within a range of servicescape contexts in order to evaluate the depth of emotional engagement using a more structured and quantifiable approach.

References

Abuhamdeh, Sami and Mihaly Csikszentmihalyi. 2012. "Attentional involvement and intrinsic motivation," *Motivation & Emotion*, 36: 257–267.
Assael, Henry. 1992. *Consumer behaviour and marketing action* (4th ed), Boston: PWA-Kent.
Ballantyne, David and Richard Varey. 2008. "The service-dominant logic and the future of marketing," *Journal of the Academy of Marketing Science*, 36: 11–14.
Belk, Russell. 1988. "Possessions and the extended self," *Journal of Consumer Research*, 15(2): 139–168.
Bhattacherjee, A. 2002. "Individual trust in online firms: Scale development and initial test," *Journal of Management Information Systems*, 19(1): 211–241.
Bitner, Jenny V. and Jeffrey Shipper. 2014. "Motivational effects and age differences of gamification in product advertising," *Journal of Consumer Marketing*, 31(5): 391–400.
Bitner, Mary-Jo. 1990. "Evaluating service encounters: The effects of physical surroundings and employee responses," *Journal of Marketing*, 54(April): 69–82.
Bonsu, Samuel and Aron Darmody. 2008. "Co-creating second life: Market-consumer cooperation in contemporary economy," *Journal of Macromarketing*, 28: 355–368.
Bouellstorff, Tom, Bonnie Nardi, Celia Pearce and T.L. Taylor. 2012. *Ethnography and virtual worlds: A handbook of method*, Oxford: Princeton University Press.
Brakus, Josko, Bernd Schmitt and Lia Zarantonello. 2009. "Brand experience: What is it? How is it measured? Does it affect loyalty?," *Journal of Marketing*, 73(39): 52–68.
Brodie, Roderick, Linda Hollebeek, Biljana Jurić and Ana Ilić. 2011. "Customer engagement: Conceptual domain, fundamental proposition, and implications for research," *Journal of Service Research*, 14(3): 252–271.
Catterall, Miriam and Pauline Maclaran. 2002. "Researching consumers in virtual worlds: A cyberspace odyssey," *Journal of Consumer Behaviour*, 1(3): 228–237.
Chandler, Jennifer and Stephen Vargo. 2011. "Contextualisation and value-in-context: How context frames exchange," *Marketing Theory*, 11(1): 35–49.
Contreras, Esteban. 2011a. "Samsung nation: Join the fun," accessed 15 June 2014, http://www.samsung.com/us/article/samsung-nation-join-the-fun

Contreras, Esteban. 2011b. "How samsung is unlocking loyalty with game mechanics," Bazaarvoice, interview Ian Greenleigh, blog posted November 4, accessed 10 June 2014, http://www.bazaarvoice.com/blog/2011/11/04/how-samsung-is-unlocking-loyalty-with-game-mechanics/

Contreras, Esteban. 2012. "Badgeville: Our blog", NY Times Features Badgeville Customer Samsung Nation; blog posted February 20 by Adena DeMonte, accessed 1 June 2014, http://blog.badgeville.com/2012/02/20/ny-times-features-badgeville-customer-samsung-nation/

Cova, Bernard and Daniele Dalli. 2009. "Working consumers: The next step in marketing theory?," *Marketing Theory*, 9: 315–339.

Cova, Bernard, Daniele Dalli and Detlev Zwick. 2011. "Critical perspectives on consumers' role as 'producers': Broadening the debate on value co-creation in marketing processes," *Marketing Theory*, 11(3): 231–241.

Cova, Bernard, Robert V. Kozinets and Avi Shankar. 2008. *Consumer tribes*, London: Butterworth Heineman.

Cova, Bernard and Stefano Pace. 2006. "Brand community of convenience products: New forms of customer empowerment—the case 'my Nutella the community'," *European Journal of Marketing*, 40(9/10): 1087–1105.

Cova, Bernard, Stefano Pace, and David J. Park. 2007. Global brand communities across borders: The warhammer case. *International Marketing Review* 24 (3): 313–29.

Cova, Bernard, and Véronique Cova. 2002. Tribal marketing. *European Journal of Marketing* 36(5/6): 595–620.

Csikszentmihalyi, Mihaly (1975). *Beyond Boredom and Anxiety: Experiencing Flow in Work and Play*, San Francisco: Jossey-Bass.

Davey, Neil. 2015. "Why it's not game over for gamification, MyCustomer", 9 March 2015, accessed 27 March http://www.mycustomer.com/feature/experience-social-crm/why-its-not-game-over-gamification/169360?src=0f7a2a6b

Davis, Robert, M. Buchanan Oliver and Roderick Brodie. 2000. "Retail service branding in electronic-commerce environments," *Journal of Service Research*, 3(2): 178–186.

De Valck, Kristine, Gerrit H. van Bruggen and Berend Wierenga. 2009. "Virtual communities: A marketing perspective," *Decision Support Systems*, 47(3): 185–203.

Deephouse, David and Susanne Carter. 2005. "An examination of differences between organizational legitimacy and organizational reputation," *Journal of Management Studies*, 42(2): 329–360.

Denegri-Knott, Janice, Detlev Zwick and Jim Schroeder. 2006. "Mapping consumer power: An integrative framework for marketing and consumer research," *European Journal of Marketing*, 40(9/10): 950–971.

Deterding, Sebastian. 2015. "The lens of intrinsic skill atoms: A method of gameful design," *Human-Computer Interaction*, 30(3/4): 294.

Deterding, Sebatian, Dan Dixon, Rilla Khaled and Lennart Nacke. 2011. "From game design elements to gamefulness: Defining 'gamification'," Paper presented at MindTrek Conference, New York, NY: ACM Press.

Dholakia, Uptal, Richard Bagozzi and Lisa Klein Pearo. 2004. "A social influence model of consumer participation in network- and small- group-based virtual communities," *International Journal of Research in Marketing*, 21: 241–263.

Dick, Alan and Kunal Basu. 1994. "Customer loyalty: Toward and integrated conceptual framework," *Journal of the Academy of Marketing Science*, 22(2): 99–113.

Fisher, Dan, and Scott Smith. 2011. Cocreation is chaotic: What it means for marketing when no one has control. *Marketing Theory* 11 (3): 325–50.

Frankel, M.S. and S. Sang. 1999. "Ethical and legal aspects of human subjects research on the internet," Report, American Association for the Advancement of Science. Available online at http://www.aaas.org/sites/default/files/migrate/uploads/report2.pdf

Gabarino, Ellen and M.S. Johnson. 1999. "The different roles of satisfaction, trust, and commitment in customer relationships," *Journal of Marketing*, 63(2): 70–87.

Garver, M.S. 2003. "Customer-driven improvement model: Best practices in identifying improvement opportunities," *Industrial Marketing Management*, 32(6): 455–466.

Glaser, Barney G. and Anselm Strauss. 1967. *The discovery of grounded theory: Strategies for qualitative research*, London: Wiederfield and Nicholson.

Goldenberg, Jacob, Barak Libai and E. Muller. 2002. "Riding the saddle: How cross-market communications can create a major slump in sales," *Journal of Marketing*, 66(2): 1–16.

Gopaladesikan, Sudarshan. 2013. "Where does gambling fit in gamification: Legal issues and a success story," 3 April, accessed 29 Mar 2015, www.gamification.co/2013/04/03/gambling-and-gamification/

Grönroos, Christian. 2008. "Service logic revisited: Who creates value? and who co-creates?," *European Business Review*, 20(4): 298–314.

Guimaraes, M. 2005. "Doing anthropology in cyberspace: Fieldwork boundaries in social environments," in C. Hine (ed), *Virtual methods: Issues in social research on the internet* (pp. 141–156), New York: Berg.

Gummesson, Evert. 2008. "Quality, service-dominant logic and many-to-many marketing," *The TQM Journal*, 20(2): 143–153.

Hamari, Juho. 2013. "Transforming homo economicus into homo ludens: A field experiment on gamification in a utilitarian peer-to-peer trading service," *Electronic Commerce Research and Applications*, 12(4): 236.

Hamari, Juho. 2015. "Why do people buy virtual goods? Attitude toward virtual good purchases versus game enjoyment," *International Journal of Information Management*, 35(3): 299–308.

Hilderbrand, Christian, Tobias Schlager, Andreas Hermann and Gerald Haubl. 2014. "Product gamification," *Advances in Consumer Research*, 42: 664–665.

Hine, Christine. 2009. "Defining project boundaries," in A.N. Markham and N.K. Baym (eds), *Internet inquiry: Conversations about method* (pp. 1–20), London: Sage.

Holt, Douglas B. 2002. "Why do brands cause trouble? A dialectical theory of consumer culture and branding," *Journal of Consumer Research*, 29(1): 70–90.

Hong, Soonkwan and Yong J. Wang. 2011. "Invested loyalty: The impact of ubiquitous technology on current loyalty paradigm and the potential revolution," *Journal of Strategic Marketing*, 19(2): 187–204.

Huotari, K. and Johu Hamari. 2012. "Defining gamification: A service marketing perspective" Paper presented at the 16th International Academic MindTrek Conference, Tampere, Finland, October 3–5, New York, NY: ACM Press.

Keller, Lane Kevin. 1993. "Conceptualizing, measuring and managing customer-based brand equity," *Journal of Marketing Research*, 29: 1–22.

Kozinets, Robert V. 2002. "The field behind the screen: Using netnography for marketing research in online communities," *Journal of Marketing Research*, 39(February): 61–72.

Kozinets, Robert V. 2010. *Netnography: Doing ethnographic research online*, London: Sage Publications Ltd.
Krippendorff, Klaus. 1980. *Content analysis: An introduction to its methodology*, London: Sage Publications.
Kuo, Ying-Feng and L. Feng. 2013. "Relationships among community interaction characteristics, perceived benefits, community commitment, and oppositional brand loyalty in online brand communities," *International Journal of Information Management*, 33: 948–962.
Langer, R. and S.C. Beckman. 2005. "Sensitive research topics: Netnography revisited," *Qualitative Market Research: An International Journal*, 8(2): 189–203.
Law, John and John Urry. 2004. "Enacting the social," *Economy & Society*, 33(3): 390–410.
Lazzarato, Maurizio. 1996. "Immaterial labor," in trans. P. Colilli and E. Emery, in M. Hardt and P. Virno (eds), *Radical thought in Italy: A potential politics* (pp. 133–147), Minneapolis and London: University of Minnesota Press.
Lehdonvirta, V., and J. Hamari. 2010. Game design as marketing: How game mechanics create demand for virtual goods. *International Journal of Business Science and Applied Management* 5 (1): 14–29.
Liu, Y., Alexandrova, T. and Nakajima, T. (2011a), "Gamifying intelligent environments", Ubi-MUI'11 Proceedings of the 2011 International ACM Workshop on Ubiquitous Meta user Interfaces, New York, NY, pp. 7–12.
Lopez, Jeff. 2011. "Samsung among the first to innovate with Badgeville's behavior platform," accessed 10 November 2014, http://www.gamification.co/2011/11/08/samsung-among-the-first-to-innovate-with-badgevilles-behavior-platform/
Lusch, Robert F., and Stephen L. Vargo. 2006. Service-dominant logic: Reactions, reflections and refinements. *Marketing Theory* 6 (3): 281–8.
Man, P. 2011. *Playing the real life: The ludification of social ties in social media*, New Media Studies, University of Amsterdam. http://www.scribd.com/doc/53189712/Man-Playing-the-Real-Life
Meyer-Waarden, Lars. 2015. "Effects of loyalty program rewards on store loyalty," *Journal of Retailing and Consumer Service*, 24: 22–32.
Miles, Matthew B. and A. Michael Huberman. 1994. *Qualitative data analysis: An expanded sourcebook*, Thousand Oaks, CA: Sage.
Mollen, Anne and Wilson Hugh. 2010. "Engagement, telepresence and interactivity in online consumer experience: Reconciling scholastic and managerial perspectives," *Journal of Business Research*, 63: 919–925.
Muñiz, Albert and Thomas C. O'Guinn. 2001. "Brand community," *Journal of Consumer Research*, 27(4): 412–431.
Nambisan, S. and R.A. Baron. 2009. "Virtual customer environments: Testing a model of voluntary participation in value co-creation activities," *Journal of Product Innovation Management*, 25(4): 388–406.
Oliver, Richard L. 1999. "Whence consumer loyalty?," *Journal of Marketing*, 63(4): 33–44.
Ouwersloot, H. and Gaby Oderkerken-Schröder. 2008. "Who's who in brand communities-and why?," *European Journal of Marketing*, 42(5/6): 571–585.
Payne, A., Storbacka, K. and Frow, P. (2008), "Managing the co-creation of value", *Journal of the Academy of Marketing Science*, Vol. 36 No. 1, pp. 83–96.
Pine, 2nd, B J, and J. H. Gilmore. 1998. *Welcome to the experience economy*. Vol. 76. UNITED STATES: Harvard Business School Press.

Pongsakornrungslip, Siwarit and Jonathan Schroeder. 2011. "Understanding value co-creation in a co-consuming brand community," *Marketing Theory*, 11(3): 303–324.

Prahalad, C.K. and Venkat Ramaswamy. 2004. "Co-creation experiences: The next practice in value creation," *Journal of Interactive Marketing*, 18(3): 5–14.

Pritchard, M.P., Mark E. Havitz and D.R. Howard. 1999. "Analyzing the commitment–loyalty link in service contexts," *Journal of the Academy of Marketing Science*, 27: 333–348.

Reicheld, Frederick F. and W. Earl Sasser. 1990. "Zero defections: Quality comes to services," *Harvard Business Review*, September-October: 105–111.

Robson, Karen, Kirk Plangger, Jan H. Kietzman, Ian McCarthy and Leyland Pitt. 2014. "Understanding gamfication of consumer experiences," *Advances in Consumer Research*, 42: 352–356.

Rokka, Joonas. 2010. "Netnographic inquiry and new translocal sites of the social," *International Journal of Consumer Studies*, 34(4): 381–387.

Rowley, J., B. Kupiec-Teahan and E. Leeming. 2007. "Customer community and co-creation: A case study," *Marketing Intelligence & Planning*, 25(2): 136–146.

Ryan, Richard and Edward Deci. 2000. "Self-determination theory and the facilitation of intrinsic motivation, social development, and well-being," *American Psychologist*, 55: 68–78.

Şahin, Azize, Cemal Zehir and Hakan Kitapçi. 2011. "The effects of bran experiences, trust and satisfaction on building brand loyalty: An empirical research on global brands," *Procedia-Social and Behavioral Sciences*, 24: 1288–1301.

Saliceti, Francesa. 2015. "Internet addiction disorder (IAD)," *Procedia—Social and Behavioral Sciences*, 191: 1372–1376.

Samsung. 2012. "SAMSUNG adds social media cachet to ENERGY STAR by featuring it on SAMSUNG nation, the industry's first gamified corporate website", accessed 10 November 2013, http://www.samsung.com/us/news/20290

Schneider, Steven M., and Kirsten A. Foot. 2004. "The web as an object of study." *New Media & Society* 6 (1): 114–22.

Schneider, Steven M. and K.A. Foot. 2005. "Web sphere analysis: An approach to studying online action," in C. Hine (ed), *Virtual methods: Issues in social research on the internet* (pp. 157–170), Oxford: Berg.

Sicart, Miguel. 2008. "Defining game mechanics", *International Journal of Computer Game Research*, 8(2). Available online at http://gamestudies.org/0802/articles/sicart.

Singer, N. (2012), "You've W won a badge (and now we know all about you)", *New York Times*, available at: www.nytimes.com/2012/02/05/business/employers-and-brands-use-gaming-to-gauge-engagement.html?_r=0 (accessed 24 September 2014).

Strauss, Anselm and Juliet Corbin. 1990. *Basics of qualitative research*, London: Sage.

Terronava, Tiziana. 2000. "Free labor: Producing culture for the digital economy," *Social Text*, 63/18/2: 35–58.

Thom, Jennifer, David R. Millen and Joan DiMicco. 2012. "Removing gamification from an enterprise SNS," Paper at the ACM Conference on Computer Supported Cooperative Work, Seattle, WA, February.

Tynan, Caroline, Susan McKechnie and S. Hartley. 2014. "Interpreting value in the customer service experience using customer-dominant logic," *Journal of Marketing Management*, 30(9/10): 1058–1081.

Vargo, Stephen L., and Robert F. Lusch. 2004. "Evolving to a new dominant logic for marketing." *Journal Of Marketing* 68, 1: 1–17.

Vargo, Stephen and Robert Lusch. 2008. "Service-dominant logic: Continuing the evolution," *Journal of the Academy of Marketing Science*, 36: 1–10.

Witt, Maximilian, Christian Scheiner and Susanne Robra-Bissantz. 2011. "Gamification of online idea competitions: Insights from an explorative case," Informatik Schaft Communities, Jahrestagung der Gesellschaft für Informatik, 4.-7.10.2011, Berlin.

Xun, Jiyao and Jonathan Reynolds. 2010. "Applying netnography to market research: The case of the online forum," *Journal of Targeting, Measurement and Analysis for Marketing*, 18: 17–31.

Yen, H. , Hsu, S. and Huang, C. (2011), "Good soldiers on the web: understanding the drivers of participation in online communities of consumption", *International Journal of Electronic Commerce* , 15 (4): 89–120.

Yi, Youjae, and Hoseong Jeon. 2003. "Effects of loyalty programs on value perception, program loyalty, and brand loyalty." *Journal of the Academy of Marketing Science* 31 (3): 229–40.

Yuan, Ruixi, Li Zhao and Wenyu Wang. 2007. "Cooperation and competition dynamics in an online game community," In D. Schuler (ed.) *Online Communities and Social Computing*, Second International Conference July 22-27, 2007 (pp. 475–84). Beijing, China.

Zichermann, Gabe and Christopher Cunningham. 2011. *Gamification by design*, Cambridge: O'Reilly.

Zichermann, Gabe and Joselin Linder. 2011. *Game-based marketing*, New Jersey: John Wiley & Sons.

8 Play a Game, Save the Planet! Gamification as a Way to Promote Green Consumption

Christian Fuentes

Introduction

Gamification is in vogue (Richter, Raban, and Rafaeli 2014). Gamification as a strategy for improving and enhancing/changing user engagement and behaviour has been a much-discussed topic within academia and industry (Hamari, Koivisto, and Sarsa 2014). The core idea is to improve user experience and change user behaviour by adding game design elements (in a nongame context) to services or applications, making them more engaging, fun, meaningful and persuasive (Deterding et al. 2011, Nicholson 2012, Cugelman 2013). Some have seen this design strategy as the next generation digital marketing technique and argued that gamification can be used to market and promote everything from new technology to sustainable consumption (Hamari and Lehdonvirta 2010, Richter, Raban, and Rafaeli 2014, Robson et al. 2015). And indeed, as a review of the field shows, gamification has already been used in a variety of different contexts, such as education, health, innovation, online retail and sustainable consumption (Domínguez et al. 2013, Hamari, Koivisto, and Sarsa 2014, Insley and Nunan 2014, Lieberoth 2015, see also, Hamari 2013).

The promise of gamification is that by including elements from games an application, service or practice is changed, made more fun and engaging (Deterding et al. 2011). It is easy to understand the allure of gamification. But does it work? What does research tell us?

Given that this is a fairly new phenomenon and even newer field of academic inquiry, it comes as no surprise that research on gamification is somewhat limited. However, although the field is new, it has grown at a rapid pace (Deterding et al. 2011, Hamari, Koivisto, and Sarsa 2014). Two questions seem to be central to the emergent field of gamification: What is gamification? And: Does it work? To answer these questions, many of the papers addressing gamification do two things. First they launch various definitions and discuss how to break down gamification into elements that can be used to define, differentiate and measure gamification (Deterding et al. 2011, see, e.g., Cugelman 2013). Second, following the definition, they examine the psychological and behavioural effects of gamification, using both quantitative and qualitative methods (although qualitative studies are in minority, see Hamari, Koivisto, and Sarsa 2014).

These studies show that there is a great deal of agreement on what constitutes gamification (although the issue is somewhat contested, see e.g., Deterding et al. 2011, Domínguez et al. 2013, Hamari 2013, Hamari, Koivisto, and Sarsa 2014) and that gamification does work, at least to some extent and under some conditions (Hamari 2013, Hamari, Koivisto, and Sarsa 2014). Consequently, taken together, these studies give a fairly comprehensive and cohesive picture of what gamification is and its effect.

However, what this field of research has been less interest in is *how* game elements are made part of an application or service and *what* happens as they are. That is to say, there are few studies that examine in detail how game elements are integrated with a specific application and connected to a specific theme and how the incorporation of these elements transforms the application, the message and/or the issue at stake.

There is a need, I contend, to go beyond merely determining if gamification works (has the expected effect) and examine what is does, how it changes the services, contexts and phenomenon to which it is applied. What I am suggesting is that we need more critical studies of gamification. If gamification is quickly becoming a widespread design and marketing technique and a part of contemporary business practices, as it has been suggested, then we must critically examine what it is that this marketing technique performs (on critical approaches within marketing see, Tadajewski and Maclaran 2009).

In this chapter I set out to take a first step in this direction by examining how gamification is used to promote green consumption and what happens as green consumption is gamified. The aim of this chapter is to develop and illustrate an analytic approach that allows us to trace and critically examine the performance of gamification *and* its performative effects.

In what follows I analyse how "game mechanics" are built into a smartphone app—the Green Guide—to make this application more engaging and enjoyable for its users, promoting, in the process, the greening of consumption practices. I discuss how gamification becomes part of the socio-material script (Akrich 2000, Jelsma 2003) of the app and what it in turn performs as it is put to use by consumers in their efforts to engage in green consumption. The argument is that gamifying green consumption not only promotes green consumption but also transforms this form of consumption.

The analysis builds on an ethnographic study of the Green Guide app. The material used in this chapter was collected as part of larger study of ethical consumption apps—that is, smartphone applications intended to assist consumers in their ethical consumption—conducted during 2014 and 2015. The Green Guide was one of three apps studied (the others were the Swedish Fairtrade app and the Shopgun app). The study examined the developers of the apps, the apps themselves and the users and uses of the apps.

More specifically, the empirical material was generated through four research practices. First, we interviewed the "designers" of the apps to get an understanding of the ideas and process behind the making of the apps (seven interviews with both software developers and the organizations behind the apps; interviews were digitally recorded and transcribed in full). Second, digital observations of the apps were conducted (this involved the careful mapping and documenting of all the pages of the apps documented through screen shots and screen video). Third, we also conducted interviews with consumers who had tried out the apps for a period of two weeks (18 interviews, consumers had different occupations and educational background and ranged from their 20s to their 50s, digitally recorded and transcribed in full). We asked these consumers of their experiences with the apps and how they were actually used in practice. Forth and finally, we conducted digital observations online to find out how consumers—in general—talked about these apps. We searched blogs, social media, product reviews and online communities for open/public posts and comments regarding the apps (documented using screen shots). Although all the material collected informs this chapter, focus is on the digital observations of the green guide app.

Theoretically, the analysis will make use of a set of concepts borrowed from Actor Network Theory (ANT) (Law 1991, Law and Hassard 1999) to conceptualize apps (or in this case the Green Guide application) as a socio-material, active and scripted "gamified technology" (Cugelman 2013). Smartphone applications are a form of technology, and like all technology they come with a set of prescriptions, they come with scripts that enable, encourage and sometimes even force some types of actions while making others difficult or impossible (Akrich 2000, Latour 2000a, b). Scripts are thus materialized plans of action (Akrich 2000). They are "texts" inscribed in the materiality of an object (or in this case an application software) that tell the user how to use that object.

In this framework, designers inscribe their visions in objects (Ingram, Shove, and Watson 2007). In the process of designing an object, ideas of the world, values, and images of who the users are become parts of the product, materialized. Therefore, designers—here used in the broadest sense of the word to mean simply anyone who creates objects—not only make objects, but they also enact specific ways of understanding the world.

However, and this is important, scripted objects are not deterministic. A socio-material script is always described by the user and is in the process translated (Latour 1991, Akrich 2000). To deal with this the concept of de-scription is often used. A script is then always de-scribed, and in the act of de-scription the initial script is not always followed.

Applying these concepts, the smartphone app Green Guide is approached as a scripted device. It has been inscribed by various designers and comes with a set of consumer prescriptions. These prescriptions, I will show, can be "read" by closely examining the digital artefact.

The Green Guide and Its Gameful Prescriptions

The Green Guide app has been developed, distributed and marketed by the Swedish Society for Nature Conservation (hereafter referred to as SSNC). The SSNC is a charitable environmental organisation, founded more than hundred years ago and today Sweden's largest NGO and most influential environmental organization with over 221,000 members (www.naturskyddsforeningen,.se, 2015). It works to "pressure politicians, influence legislation, and inform and organize seminars, debates, and conferences" (www.naturskyddsforeningen.se, 2015). Its priority areas are climate change, seas and fishing, forests, agriculture and environmental toxins. The SSNC also publishes a magazine (which it distributes to its members), books and reports on a range of environmental topics.

For the SSNC developing, marketing and managing the Green Guide is another way to promote green consumption, a way to assist consumers to make "responsible" choices and "green" their everyday consumption practices. They see the app, alongside books and reports, but also Facebook and their website, as a tool to drive environmental politics by promoting more environmentally sustainable consumption. The Green Guide app is then designed to enlist consumers and support and encourage green consumption.

Although the designers and developers of the app talk in terms of making the app "fun", "encouraging" and "useful", what is used when developing this app are a series of game elements. Game mechanisms are thus here used a way encourage consumers to use of the app and to engage in green consumption.

What is then the "game" inscribed in the Green Guide? How are gaming elements introduced into this nongame context? What gaming prescription does this app come with? And what else is it prescribing in the process?

Below I discuss the various gameful prescriptions found in the Green Guide app and the gaming mechanics involved in them.

Read Green! Prepare for the Challenge

Consumers embarking on this app-enabled quest to become green consumer heroes begin by reading. While this may not sound all that heroic, it is a crucial first step. It is by reading that the "players" are here introduced to the challenges that lie ahead.

The Green Guide encourages and enables consumers to get informed and use this acquired knowledge to change their practices. The Green Guide provides consumers with a database of sustainability information that aims to assist consumers in making their everyday consumption more sustainable. The type of green consumption promoted by this app goes beyond the narrower green consumerism versions that are commonly reproduced through (commercial) marketing (see, e.g., Fuentes 2011, 2015). It encourages consumers to consume less, to change practices (and not merely purchase "green" products) and even to get "political" and work to persuade others to consume green.

The Green Guide app has organized the information it provides into a variety of green consumption themes: the home, food, children, travel, clothes, work and the garden. The aim is to influence and enable consumers to shift to more sustainable consumption practices by making available a database of "green advices", as they refer to them. The information is practical in nature and presented in an accessible format. The Green advice is formulated as imperatives and consumers are told to, for example, "Make eco nr 1!", "Love vintage and second hand!", "Eat less meat!", "Watch out for plastic toys!", "Recycle" and "Fly less!"

The prescription built into this app is thus to "read up!" and get informed. The Green Guide prescribes consumers to be knowledgeable. By reading through the green advice provided by the Green Guide, consumers are made aware of the challenges involved in becoming a green consumer while simultaneously preparing for them. There is a balance to be achieved between presenting these "green" changes as easy enough to be feasible but difficult enough to be a challenge. As previous research on gamification has shown, if the "challenge" is too easy, users do not feel motivated (Richter, Raban, and Rafaeli 2014). If it is too difficult, the risk is that it will deter consumers from enlisting in the activities. Tasks, or series of tasks, have to be well balanced to encourage players engagement (Domínguez et al. 2013).

Pledge Green! Challenged Accepted, Challenge Completed

The Green Guide app does not only invite consumers to read about various green consumption practices. Through the *pledge function,* they also encourage and enable them to commit to these practices. For every green advice given, there is also the possibility to "pledge green"—that is, tick the box beside the advice, promising to carry out that practice or marking that you already do perform this practice. Pledging, in this context, has a double function. On the one hand it is a way to promise that you will engage in this practice in the future, a way to commit to being greener. But it also seems to be presented and used by consumers as a way to keep score of what you already do or have done, a way to visualize and account for your achievements. This also seems to produce satisfaction among consumers, a sense of accomplishment:

> The Green Guide has this . . . it's this thing that's said to hit the spot . . . That you can click. And you feel personal satisfaction. You just go yes, yes. And then you see how clever you are.
>
> Kristina

Pledging is then presented and used as a scorecard, a way of keeping track of what consumers have done in order to green their everyday practices. The app visualizes what you have done but also what activities are left to do, accomplishments and future challenges.

Here we see how achievements, one of the more central and motivating game mechanisms (Hamari and Eranti 2011, Richter, Raban, and Rafaeli 2014), is inscribed into the app. According to Hamari and Eranti (2011) "achievements are goals in an achievement/reward system (different system than the core game) whose fulfilment is defined through activities and events in other systems (commonly in the core game)". The pledging function in the Green Guide app transforms the green advice into green achievements. The green advice, describing what should be done in order to green that practice (for example detoxing your kitchen by removing a number of toxic and semitoxic products) becomes a description of what is referred to in games as "operational rules"—that is the rules that describe what players have to do to complete the achievement and earn a badge or points (Hamari and Eranti 2011, 6).

However, while a game achievement would (usually) also require players to complete a task within the game (or in a parallel game system), here the "green players" are expected to complete the tasks in their own lives. Here the "game" is stretched beyond the app and into parts of the user's life, becoming a type of pervasive game (Deterding et al. 2011). By ticking the box "Yes, I got this!" consumers are binding themselves to perform this action in their everyday lives.

Interestingly, the ticking of the box is also taken as proof of the completion of the green practice. Thus, by "ticking" a series of green advices, consumers are slowly increasing their points as green consumers. As they promise to "detox their kitchens", "make ecological nr 1", "switch to eco-milk", "avoid toxic sportswear", "recycle right", "eat less meat" and many other green practices, they are awarded points (a point for each advise). Taken together the various green advices become a series of achievements organized under different themes; they form a sort of achievement system where points are accumulated (and as I will discuss below, also produce hierarchical statuses or levels). According to game studies, points, as a feedback mechanism, encourage mastery of the game and also work to stimulate competition (more on this below) (Richter, Raban, and Rafaeli 2014).

Check Your Green Status! The Becoming of a Green Action Hero

A third prescription built into the app is "check your status!" Making use here of another common game element often used to motivate players—status achievement (Richter, Raban, and Rafaeli 2014)—the Green Guide: a) assigns users a status (rank or level according to number of green advices ticked) and b) enables and encourages them to check that status.

As you pledge to perform certain green practices, you get positive feedback from the app. To take one example, when pledging to buy ecological food you get a message saying:

> Congratulations, you are now an eco-nerd! You are contributing to a healthier planet, consuming fewer pesticides and in addition eating tastier food.

In this brief message consumers are provided with a label for the commitment (eco-nerd, which is meant to be something positive in this context) and are also reminded of the positive health, environmental and taste consequences of consuming ecological foods. The positive feedback they receive is designed both to frame green consumption as a meaningful activity and to support users' construction of green identity. It also, and simultaneously, accentuates that this is an achievement.

In addition, pledges are also recorded on individual users' green status profiles according to levels of commitment to and engagement in green consumption as suggested by the Green Guide achievement system. As you earn "points", the app assigns you a status. You go from "Greenhorn" to "Eco-fighter" to finally "Planet saver" (with numerous positions in between). In total, the apps green status hierarchy consist of seven "levels", each corresponding to an interval of points:

Greenhorn 11/79
Eco-rookie 22/79
Everyday-warrior 33/79
Eco-fighter 45/79
Globe-defender 56/79
Eco-champion 66/79
Planet-saver 79/79

The display shows consumers their status and how many "points" they have earned. It also visualizes where in the hierarchy consumers are and how many accomplishments that remain and within which theme/are of consumption. Consumers are encouraged to keep track of the progress and also analyse their own green consumption.

The app then both evaluates and gives value to consumers' green practices. It puts labels on consumer achievements, supporting green consumers' identity projects.

Communicate Green! Getting the Game Going

Finally, consumers are also enabled and encouraged to communicate their pledges and scores through Twitter and Facebook. When pushing the pledge button for prioritized actions or when they achieve a new green status, they are given the option to "boast to your friends". There are two buttons, one for Twitter and one for Facebook, and with a single click the users' private actions and environmental status goes from private to public.

One of the ideas behind gamification has been to draw on the "persuasive power that emerges when people compare their badges amongst each other" (Hamari 2013, 237). Social comparison has thus been acknowledged as one of the driving forces behind both gaming and gamification (Domínguez et al. 2013). Game achievements have also in other contexts been shown to produce communal status (Richter, Raban, and Rafaeli 2014). In the case of the Green Guide, the idea is that by sharing their green pledges and status, consumers are both making their friends and followers aware of the existence of the app (and green consumption) and simultaneously, prompting them to use the app and engage in green consumption. The idea is then to share in order to "get the game going"—getting the game going both in the sense of encouraging further use of the app and also by encouraging comparison among green consumers.

Few of the consumers we interviewed found this function interesting, however. For many consumers, bragging about their green consumption seemed "ridiculous" or simply "unnecessary". While some talked about the potential of this function for others, they did not see it as a useful function in their own practices:

> ... once you've clicked on "Yes, I'm on it" then you get [the message] "Boast to your friends". And then you can choose to boast on Facebook or Twitter, I think. ... it doesn't feel like this is what you want to do. You see, I think it would be completely ridiculous to just go: "Ok, I'll clear out my broom cupboard".
>
> Jenny

"Bragging" was pointless, these consumers argued. Even more, they found bragging about sustainable consumption socially unacceptable. Sustainable consumption was a private act—an act worth doing but one that you keep to yourself, or at least not one to be communicated on social media.

However, while our informants did not find this function useful, the online observations show a different picture. On Instagram users posted images under the hashtags "grönguide", "miljövänligt", "naturskyddsföreningen" bragging about their green consumption status as well as about specific acts of sustainable consumption linked to the Green Guide app. The communicated to their followers the green changes they made to their everyday consumption practices with the assistance of the Green Guide app. Consumers showed for example how they cooked ecological food, recycled and dried clothes outdoors instead of using a (energy consuming) dryer. In these cases, the de-scription of the apps did indeed align with the script.

Although there is no way of knowing to what extent this function was used to "brag", it is clear that it was used by some and with the intent to spread the green message while simultaneously positioning themselves as green consumers. Reading the comments that these Instagram posts generated, there seemed to be evidence that this also "got the game going" to some extent. The posting of one's green status was often followed by positive feedback from "followers" as well as comments by users intended to show that also they were engaged in green consumption.

The Green Consumption Game

Informed by ANT and more specifically the concepts of script, prescription and description, I have offered a reading of the Green Guide app's gameful prescriptions. I have argued that this app, aimed at promoting green consumption, is scripted to encourage and enable a series of consumer actions/tasks that link together, forming a game of sorts. The Green Guide apps prescribes that consumers prepare for green challenges (Read Green), accept and complete green challenges (Pledge Green), monitor and keep score of their green development (Check Your Green Status) and communicate their green achievements to peers (Communicate Green). The Green Guide app enables a series of potentially "gameful" (Deterding et al. 2011) green consumer actions while simultaneously providing users with positive feedback when they engage in these actions.

Game elements are thus introduced into the Green Guide to encourage participation and engagement with the app and green consumption. This device is an example of a "gamified technology" scripted to encourage consumers to engage with the app and in green consumption.

The gamification of the Green Guide, I argue, has the potential to address a number of problems commonly associated with green consumption. Research on green and ethical consumption has shown that this form of consumption is very knowledge demanding (Moisander 2007, Fuentes 2014b). Green consumers have to be able to recognize and evaluate a plethora of environmental and social labels (Pedersen and Neergaard 2006) and also need to keep themselves informed about the latest sustainability issues. Many experience this task as overwhelming.

Green consumption can also be emotionally demanding. Consumers engaging in green or ethical consumption often have to deal with the ambiguity and uncertainty that often comes with making difficult ethical decisions. This in turn can at times lead to consumer anxiety (Connolly and Prothero 2008).

In addition, green consumption research has also shown that green consumption is often used a way to build and communicate a green or alternative identity (Moisander and Pesonen 2002). Green consumption is often framed as a form of self-development where becoming a more moral consumer is the aim (Cherrier and Murray 2007, Connolly and Prothero 2008). Green consumption becomes then a form of communication, a way to fashion a self-narrative.

Because of this, many now argue that for efforts to promote green consumption to be successful, one must take into account and utilize its symbolic dimension and make green consumption meaningful (Prothero and Fitchett 2000, Prothero, McDonagh, and Dobscha 2010). How to accomplish this is, however, not always clear.

All these "problems" can potentially be "solved" by introducing game elements to the Green Guide App and framing green consumption as a game. First, by turning green consumption into a game meaning is ascribed to green consumption, framing it as a fun experience and a manageable project. The complex project of becoming a green consumer in a consumer society is broken down to a series of challenges to be accomplished. One can say that it translates the long-term and abstract goal of achieving sustainability into a series of specific, practical and achievable short-term goals (a better strategy according to some studies, Richter, Raban, and Rafaeli 2014). Thus what can seem as an overwhelming problem (being a sustainable consumer in consumer culture) is divided into a number of smaller manageable tasks (e.g., buy ecological foods).

Second, in the "Green Consumption Game" consumers need not to engage in angst-producing ethical reasoning; the game tells them what the right course of action is and also rewards them as they take that action. Ambiguity is taken out of the picture and replaced with certainty and purpose.

Finally, the Green Consumption Game scripted by the Green Guide app is a status and identity game. It is designed to enact a green status game where consumers compete to be the most green. This builds on the social mechanisms that lead people not only to compare themselves and their achievements to "similar others" but also to seek improve their position in relation to this group (Richter, Raban, and Rafaeli 2014).

In addition, this gamified technology makes it easier for consumers to convince both themselves and others of their green identity. As part of the "green game" consumers receive continuous feedback, supporting their green actions and building up their confidence as green consumers. Like other games and gamified experiences (Richter, Raban, and Rafaeli 2014), the functions of the Green Guide are designed to produce a sense of accomplishment and progress. It is designed to provide consumers with a sense of agency and a feeling of progress.

It is also a game that provides consumers with green labels that consumers can use to construct themselves as green and also communicate their green status/identity to other consumers. Through the use of these labels this app is also connecting to the widespread and powerful discourse of green consumers as "heroes" (Gabriel and Lang 2006, Autio, Heiskanen, and Heinonen 2009).

The gamification of the Green Guide has thus the potential to contribute to the promotion of green consumption by enlisting consumers and encouraging them to engage in a series of green consumption activities. By introducing game design elements into this smartphone application, both the use of the app and the performance of green consumption actions is (potentially) made more enjoyable, easier and meaningful.

The Dark Side of the Game: Unsustainable Mechanism in Play

However, and this is important, the same mechanisms that make the Green Guide a potential promoter of green consumption can also have a number of negative consequences for the promotion of green consumption. This piece of gamified technology does not merely promote green consumption; it *performs* green consumption and enacts a specific version of green consumption.

Adding game elements to an app does not mean that a game is automatically created or that the gamified experience is meaningful to consumers (Nicholson 2012). As ANT tells us, prescriptions have to be de-scribed (Akrich 2000). And as consumption studies have so convincingly shown, consumers do not merely follow instructions and messages but actively recreate meanings and use objects and devices in unexpected (unscripted) ways (Arnould and Thompson 2005). Or phrased in game terms, just because you design a game does not mean that a game experience is created; this is coproduced by the players (Huotari and Hamari 2012), and it can be produced differently by different consumers (Nicholson 2012, Insley and Nunan 2014).

There is, however, still some value, I argue, in critically discussing the prescriptions built into this app—to critically discuss what it is that this piece of gamified technology is trying to get us to think and do. The consequences of following the script of the Green Guide app are not clear-cut. On the one hand, the app seems well designed to get consumers motivated about green consumption. On the other, the same aspects that may drive consumer engagement can also have negative consequences for how green consumption is approached and performed. One way to approach this critical analysis is to examine more closely the type of green consumer enacted by these gameful prescription (for a simlar approach see, Fuentes 2014a); to pose the question: What kind of green consumer is the app designed to produce? What kind of green player does the Green Guide work to enact?

The green player inscribed into the app is a fun-looking consumer who wishes to be sustainable but does not want to deal with the complexities involved in environmental problems. That is to say, the green consumer model built into the app is a consumer who is preoccupied with sustainability issues but also with the fashioning of her/his identity as an alternative, political or environmental consumer.

The app is designed to cater to and also enact a consumer who sees her or his move to more sustainable living as a life project, a way to improve and be a more moral individual. Finally, the green player inscribed into this gamified technology is a consumer who cares about the environment but also cares about her or his standing vis-à-vis other green consumers. That is, this green player is also in the status game.

In designing the Green Consumption Game, SSNC and the app developers are clearly drawing on and reproducing a specific image of green consumers as social and cultural beings, experience-oriented identity makers and status-seekers.

This image is not without support. Studies have argued that the experiential aspects play a vital role in driving green consumption (Soper 2007, Thompson and Coskuner-Balli 2007). Soper (2007) talks about "alternative hedonism" and "the sensual pleasures of consuming differently" (p. 211). The pleasurable and the moral are integrated in the producing of green experiences, Soper argues. Alternative hedonism, she stipulates, is a self-reflexive practice leading to the search for alternative pleasures. Partly driving green consumption then is "a distinctively moral form of self-pleasuring or a self-interested form of altruism: that which takes pleasure in committing to a more socially accountable mode of consuming" (Soper 2007, 217).

There are also now numerous studies that explore and illustrate the identity-making processes of green and ethical consumers (see, e.g., Moisander and Pesonen 2002, Cherrier 2006, Cherrier and Murray 2007, Connolly and Prothero 2008). These studies show that green consumption is often linked to the formation of identity. Studies demonstrate how consumers construct identities for themselves as environmentally conscious subjects through ordinary consumption practices, by consuming ordinary consumption objects or through acts of nonconsumption (see, e.g., Cherrier 2006, Connolly and Prothero 2008). Green consumption is, at least sometimes, driven by a desire to construct and communicate identities as good/responsible/consciously/ethical consumers.

And finally, studies have also shown that status can be an important driver of green consumption (Elliott 2013, Carfagna et al. 2014) and that green consumption practices are more prominent in areas where consumption is more visible (Pedersen 2000). Here green consumption becomes a way to produce social status, a way to "enact a set of ecologically oriented high-status tastes" and a strategy for "claiming status and distinction" (Carfagna et al. 2014, 160). In other words rather than being merely a way to enact an "environmentalist ethos", green consumption "acts as a vehicle for signaling social status, and it appeals to people for this reason" (Elliott 2013, 295).

The Green Guide app has then potential to be successful by connecting to socio-cultural mechanisms driving green consumption. However, and herein lies the paradox, by doing so the Green Guide app and the SSNC are also reproducing three central consumer culture mechanisms driving escalating and unsustainable levels of consumption (Warde and Shove 1998). Players of the Green Guide Game are instructed: 1) that it is through consumption (and not other fields) that we are to forge and communicate our identities, 2) that consumption is an appropriate field for status production and 3) that consumption is and should primarily be fun (and not about restraint or responsibility or any other meanings it can be ascribed). The promotion of green consumption becomes also the promotion of an unsustainable consumer culture.

Conclusions

The aim of this chapter has been to develop and illustrate an analytic approach that allows us to trace and critically examine the performance of gamification and its performative effects. Applying the concepts of script, prescription and de-scription and drawing on a digital ethnography of the Green Guide app, this chapter has shown how and with what effects game design elements were made part of the app.

The Green Guide app, the analysis shows, enables and encourages a series of potentially "gameful" green consumer actions and connects these to the production of green experiences, green identities and green status. As I made clear in the previous section, while the Green Guide Game certainly has the potential to encourage consumers to use the app and engage in green consumption, it also potentially serves to reproduce many of the mechanisms associated with contemporary consumer culture and unsustainable consumption. There is then potentially a dark side to the Green Consumption Game enacted by this app.

This analysis has also been an effort to contribute, in some small way, to the development of more critical studies of gamification. As this analysis illustrates, there is something to be gained from not only studying if gamification has the desired and expected results of engaging consumers and driving use but also how gamification is performed and what the performative effects of this in turn may be. As I have tried to show, while the app has the potential to "work" in the sense that it may achieve the goal of promotion green consumption, this may come with unexpected effects. Looking beyond narrow goal achievement and considering the performative effects of this gameful technology can thus be a possible avenue for more critical examinations of gamification.

To conclude, I would agree with Deterding et al. (2011, 5) in that "gamified applications present emerging phenomena that warrant new concepts and research". Although the integration of gameful elements into applications or service may not be completely new (see Hagberg and Cochoy, this volume), it seems nowadays to be conducted with more intensity and with new (technological) means. Against this background, the concept of gamification is productive in the sense that it allows us to capture and analyse an aspect of design and marketing technique that is gaining popularity. Gamification in this context is above all useful as an analytical concept. It is a term that allows us to bring to fore and discuss this specific design and marketing technique and its consequences. What I have tried to do in this chapter is thus to answer the call made by Deterding and colleagues for "new concepts" to understand gamification by offering a socio-material and critically oriented way of analysing the performance and performative effects of gamification.

References

Akrich, Madeleine. 2000. "The De-Scription of Technical Objects." In *Shaping Technology/ Building Society—Studies in Sociotechnical Change*, edited by Wiebe E. Bijker and John Law, 205–224. London, England and Cambridge, MA: The MIT Press.

Arnould, Eric J., and Craig J. Thompson. 2005. "Consumer Culture Theory (CCT): Twenty Years of Research." *Journal of Consumer Research* 31 (March): 868–882.

Autio, Minna, Eva Heiskanen, and Visa Heinonen. 2009. "Narratives of 'Green' Consumers—the Antihero, the Environmental Hero and the Anarchist." *Journal of Consumer Behaviour* 8 (1): 40–53.

Carfagna, Lindsey B., Emilie A. Dubois, Connor Fitzmaurice, Monique Y. Ouimette, Juliet B. Schor, Margaret Willis, and Thomas Laidley. 2014. "An Emerging Eco-Habitus: The Reconfiguration of High Cultural Capital Practices Among Ethical Consumers." *Journal of Consumer Culture* 14 (2): 158–178.

Cherrier, Hélène. 2006. "Consumer Identity and Moral Obligations in Non-Plastic Bag Consumption: A Dialectical Perspective." *International Journal of Consumer Studies* 30 (5): 515–523.

Cherrier, Hélène, and Jeff B. Murray. 2007. "Reflexive Dispossession and the Self: Constructing a Processual Theory of Identity." *Consumption, Markets and Culture* 10 (1): 1–29.

Connolly, John, and Andrea Prothero. 2008. "Green Consumption—Life-Politics, Risk and Contradictions." *Journal of Consumer Culture* 8 (1): 117–145.

Cugelman, Brian. 2013. "Gamification: What It Is and Why It Matters to Digital Health Behavior Change Developers." *JMIR Serious Games* 1 (1): 1–6.

Deterding, Sebastian, Dan Dixon, Rilla Khaled, and Lennart Nacke. 2011. "From Game Design Elements to Gamefulness: Defining 'Gamification'." MindTrek'11, September 28–30, 2011, Tampere, Finland.

Domínguez, Adrián, Joseba Saenz-de-Navarrete, Luis de-Marcos, Luis Fernández-Sanz, Carmen Pagés, and José-Javier Martínez-Herráiz. 2013. "Gamifying Learning Experiences: Practical Implications and Outcomes." *Computers & Education* 63: 380–392.

Elliott, Rebecca. 2013. "The Taste for Green: The Possibilities and Dynamics of Status Differentiation Through 'Green' Consumption." *Poetics* 41: 294–322.

Fuentes, Christian. 2011. "Green Retailing: A Socio-Material Analysis." PhD Thesis, Department of Service Management, Lund university, Lund, Sweden.

Fuentes, Christian. 2014a. "Enacting Green Consumers: The Case of the Scandinavian Preppies." *Culture Unbound: Journal of Current Cultural Research* 6: 963–977.

Fuentes, Christian. 2014b. "Managing Green Complexities: Consumers' Strategies and Techniques for Greener Shopping." *International Journal of Consumer Studies* 38 (5): 485–492.

Fuentes, Christian. 2015. "How Green Marketing Works: Practices, Materialities and Images." *Scandinavian Journal of Management* 31 (2): 192–205.

Gabriel, Yiannis, and Tim Lang. 2006. *The Unmanageable Consumer*. Los Angeles—London—New Delhi—Singapore: Sage.

Hamari, Juho. 2013. "Transforming Homo Economicus Into Homo Ludens: A Field Experiment on Gamification in a Utilitarian Peer-to-Peer Trading Service." *Electronic Commerce Research and Applications* 12: 236–245.

Hamari, Juho, and Veikko Eranti. 2011. "Framework for Designing and Evaluating Game Achievements." Proceedings of DiGRA 2011 Conference: Think Design Play., Hilversum, Netherlands, September 14–17, 2011.

Hamari, Juho, Jonna Koivisto, and Harri Sarsa. 2014. "Does Gamification Work?—A Literature Review of Empirical Studies on Gamification." 47th International Conference on System Science, Hawaii.

Hamari, Juho, and Vili Lehdonvirta. 2010. "Game Design as Marketing: How Game Mechanics Create Demand for Virtual Goods." *International Journal of Business Science and Applied Management* 5 (1): 14–29.

Huotari, Kai, and Juho Hamari. 2012. "Defining Gamification—A Service Marketing Perspective." The 16th International Academic Mindtrek Conference, Tampere, Finland, October 3–5, 2012.

Ingram, Jack, Elizabeth Shove, and Matthew Watson. 2007. "Products and Practices: Selected Concepts from Science and Technology Studies and from Social Theories of Consumption and Practice." *Design Issues* 23 (2): 3–16.

Insley, Victoria, and Daniel Nunan. 2014. "Gamification and the Online Retail Experience." *International Journal of Retail & Distribution Management* 42 (5): 340–351.

Jelsma, Jaap. 2003. "Innovating for Sustainability: Involving Users, Politics and Technology." *Innovation* 16 (2): 103–116.

Latour, Bruno. 1991. "Technology Is Society Made Durable." In *A Sociology of Monsters: Essays on Power, Technology and Domination*, edited by John Law, 103–131. London: Routledge.

Latour, Bruno. 2000a. "When Things Strike Back: A Possible Contribution of 'Science Studies' to the Social Sciences." *British Journal of Sociology* 5 (1): 107–123.

Latour, Bruno. 2000b. "Where Are the Missing Masses?—The Sociology of a Few Mundane Artifacts." In *Shaping Technology/ Building Society—Studies in Sociotechnical Change*, edited by Wiebe E. Bijker and John Law, 225–258. Cambridge, MA: The MIT Press.

Law, John, ed. 1991. *A Sociology of Monsters: Essays on Power, Technology and Domination*. London and New York: Routledge.

Law, John, and John Hassard, eds. 1999. *Actor Network Theory and after*. Oxford: Blackwell Publishing.

Lieberoth, Andreas. 2015. "Shallow Gamification: Testing Psychological Effects of Framing an Activity as a Game." *Games and Culture* 10 (3): 229–248.

Moisander, Johanna. 2007. "Motivational Complexity of Green Consumerism." *International Journal of Consumer Studies* 31: 404–409.

Moisander, Johanna, and Sinikka Pesonen. 2002. "Narratives of Sustainable Ways of Living: Constructing the Self and the Other as a Green Consumer." *Management Decision* 40 (4): 329–342.

Nicholson, Scott. 2012. "A User-Centered Theoretical Framework for Meaningful Gamification." Paper Presented at Games+Learning+Society 8.0, Madison, WI.

Pedersen, Esben Rahbek, and Peter Neergaard. 2006. "Caveat Emptor—Let the Buyer Beware! Environmental Labelling and the Limitations of 'Green' Consumerism." *Business Strategy and the Environment* 15 (1): 15–29.

Pedersen, Lene Holm. 2000. "The Dynamics of Green Consumption: A Matter of Visibility?" *Journal of Environmental Policy & Planning* 2: 193–210.

Prothero, Andrea, and James A. Fitchett. 2000. "Greening Capitalism: Opportunities for a Green Commodity." *Journal of Macromarketing* 20 (1): 46–55.

Prothero, Andrea, Pierre McDonagh, and Susan Dobscha. 2010. "Is Green the New Black? Reflections on a Green Commodity Discourse." *Journal of Macromarketing* 30 (2): 147–159.

Richter, Ganit, Daphne R. Raban, and Sheizaf Rafaeli. 2014. "Studying Gamification: The Effect of Rewards and Incentives on Motivation." In *Gamification in Education and Business*, edited by Torsten Reiners and Lincoln Wood, 21–46. New York–London: Springer.

Robson, Karen, Kirk Plangger, Jan H. Kietzmann, Ian McCarthy, and Leyland Pitt. 2015. "Is It All a Game? Understanding the Principles of Gamification." *Business Horizons* 58 (4): 411–420.

Soper, Kate. 2007. "Re-Thinking the "Good Life"—The Citizenship Dimension of Consumer Disaffection with Consumerism." *Journal of Consumer Culture* 7 (2): 205–229.

Tadajewski, Mark, and Pauline Maclaran. 2009. "Critical Marketing Studies: Introduction and Overview." In *Critical Marketing Studies*, edited by Mark Tadajewski and Pauline Maclaran. (Vol. I, pp. xvii–xlvii). London: Sage.

Thompson, Craig J., and Gocken Coskuner-Balli. 2007. "Enchanting Ethical Consumerism—The Case of Community Supported Agriculture." *Journal of Consumer Culture* 7 (3): 275–303.

Warde, Alan, and Elizabeth Shove. 1998. "Inconspicuous Consumption: The Sociology of Consumption and the Environment" Published by the Department of Sociology, Lancaster University, UK at http://www.comp.lancs.ac.uk/sociology/papers/Shove-Ward-Insconspicous-Consumption.pdf.

Part III
Conceptual Perspectives

9 Gamification for Sustainability
Beyond the Ludo-Aesthetical Approach

Per Fors and Thomas Taro Lennerfors

Introduction

In recent years, using elements from game design in nongaming contexts, gamification, has become a major trend within the industry (Deterding et al. 2011). If we put our trust in Jane McGonigal, consultant and author of the book *Reality is Broken: Why Games Make Us Better and How They Can Change the World* (2011), gamification has the power to save the world due to its potential to promote desirable behaviors. Al Gore, former vice president of the U.S. and environmentalist, argues that gamification can be effective not least within the area of environmental sustainability, where saving the world is the ultimate goal. By gamifying ordinary life practices, such as recycling, energy saving and sustainable consumption, games could be "the new normal" (Gore 2011). Although gamified solutions have not been developed to a great extent within the area of sustainability yet, applications that promote energy-efficient behavior, make recycling fun and help us travel more eco-friendly do exist on the market today.

In this chapter, we aim to describe gamification for sustainability and its challenges for developers and researchers. Furthermore, we will situate it in relation to other ways of promoting sustainable consumption, such as through raising awareness and visualization. In contrast to these two methods, we argue that the main difference is that within gamification, positive, enjoyable and fun affects are mobilized in order to promote the desirable behavior. Although we tie in to the idea of using affects for the promotion of sustainable behavior, we believe that only focusing on positive affects may not be the right way for sustainable gamification. By turning to theories of the Danish philosopher Søren Kierkegaard (1813–1855), we are able to introduce new ways of conceptualizing affects in the gamification discourse. We argue that in addition to fun and enjoyment, negative or neutral affects, such as anxiety, could prove productive for gamification for sustainability. As video games should be seen not as a completely new phenomenon, but as an extension of traditional media such as books or movies (Murray 1995), we further suggest that most gamified applications fail to include important aspects of video games that could prove useful for provoking these productive affects. By drawing on narratological game theory and combining these ideas of games with our philosophical backdrop, we develop a model for conceptualizing approaches to gamification for sustainability. We propose that developers and businesses should seek alternative vistas among a plethora of opportunities presented in this chapter, rather than the most prevalent approach at present (which we call the ludo-aesthetical approach) when developing gamified applications for sustainability.

Gamification for Sustainability

As sustainability is a hot topic as well as gamification, businesses have demonstrably jumped on the gamification for sustainability bandwagon already. *The Fun Theory* (2009), which includes *World's Deepest Bin* and *Bottlebank Arcade*, is a Volkswagen initiative that has received much publicity, not least at YouTube, where the commercials have received several million views each. The idea is to promote their environmentally friendly cars as innovative and fun to drive. The application *A Glass of Water* from Toyota (2012) and *Commute Greener* from Volvo (2012) build upon the very same idea, a green image and innovative strategies to reach sustainable targets, applicable to consumers and professional drivers alike. *Vampire Hunter* (SAP 2013) is a game in which employees of an organization can hunt down "energy vampires" (e.g., old light bulbs and devices in standby) at work and post them on social networks. In applications such as *Opower* (2007), the user can track its energy consumption and compete with neighbors on lowering it. *Greenify* (Lee et al. 2013) is a real-life action game designed to teach its users about climate change. *Oroeco* (2013) is tracking the environmental impact of the daily lives of its users. In order to become more sustainable, the user must take "actions", such as changing energy providers or buying a new, more efficient car. According to our review of existing applications, there is certainly a market for gamification for sustainability.

In the literature on gamification, there are those who claim that gamification for marketing purposes, which is one of the main applications for the concept even within the area of sustainability, and gamification for meaningful purposes are inherently different (Nicholson 2012, 2015). In contrast to BLAP gamification (abbreviation for badges, leaderboards, achievements and points), where game elements simply add some more fun to the task, meaningful gamification aims to intrinsically motivate its user long-term. Here, rewarding in-game points or badges is not enough (ibid.). While external rewards can be effective in certain contexts, they can also demotivate in contexts where intrinsic motivation is essential. Helping people to make their own, conscious decisions without extrinsic motivation is often more effective, since as soon as the external rewards are removed, the motivation for performing a certain task will diminish (Kohn 1999).

As gamified applications for meaningful purposes such as for sustainable behavior require long-term behavioral change, extrinsic motivators will only do for a limited amount of time. Michael Wu (2011) argues that "no single gamification strategy can bring long-term sustainable values, because no games can last forever". He maintains that after a while, every game based on extrinsic motivators like badges, points and even tangible rewards such as discounts will become dull and demotivating. This is what Wu calls the gamification backlash, and it is caused by the overjustification effect, which means that the extrinsic motivators fail to keep up with the accelerated expectations of the user. When the user has become familiar with the content of the gamified application, he or she will require more and alternating rewards and challenges in order to keep playing. Because of the fact that no gamification strategy seems to work forever, the most challenging aspect of designing gamified solutions within the area of meaningful gamification is to generate intrinsic motivation for the gamified task in order to be effective long-term (Nicholson 2012, 2014; Wu 2011).

There is, however, a chance that the gamified activities focused on extrinsic motivation will trigger intrinsic motivation. When a runner using *Zombies, Run! 3* (Six to Start 2014)—a fitness application where the user is running from zombies, gathering supplies and building up an anti-zombie squad—realizes the intrinsic value of exercising, he or she will no longer require the game or its in-game rewards to work out. A gamification strategy therefore does not have to be long-term if the initial extrinsic motivation and rewards, detached from the actual goal of the game, is able to trigger intrinsic motivation. However, in order to find intrinsic motivation the user must often be able to see or feel the actual real-life benefits of its efforts. In gamification for fitness, the results are often measurable; you gain or lose weight, you can run longer and faster, etc. In education, you learn more and will be able to perform better in school. When the gamified activities instead aim toward ecological sustainability, you will probably not be able to see any visible results. Even though saving energy will save you money, many other choices you will have to make in order to live and consume more sustainable, such as choosing eco-friendly food and clothes, will cost you money.

Another problematic issue raised by Robertson (2010) is that gamified solutions do not offer meaningful choices. Even though there are win conditions, there are no fail conditions, meaning that if you perform badly you will not be punished for it. Gamified applications are always tempting with the carrot instead of threatening with the stick. This is not how games work. In *BioShock* (2K Games 2007) the player can choose between harvesting the power of the corrupted Little Sisters in order to gain the full potential of the ADAM points or to free them and only gain a fraction of the points. Harvesting the Little Sisters will make you more powerful, but you will end up evil in the end. Freeing them will instead give you certain rewards later on and results in a more positive ending. These kinds of ethical dilemmas are rarely seen in gamified applications but are inherent to most games. The gamification movement is instead trying to tell us that "change should be fun, social and easy" (Kuntz et al. 2012, 127), but change is not always easy, and in video games, it does not have to be all about fun and enjoyment in order to motivate the user to keep playing.

Drawing on existing literature, we can conclude that the gaming aspects in gamified applications are often limited to badges, leaderboards, achievements and points (Lee 2013; Owen 2013) and that the effect of the application is diminishing with time (Hamari et al. 2014; Zichermann and Cunningham 2011). While these applications might be effective for marketing purposes, they are not designed to help the user find intrinsic motivation for most meaningful tasks. In addition to that, most gamified applications reward even the smallest effort, while the user is never punished for not trying. Even though gamification "works" (Hamari et al. 2014), it is very context dependent. Furthermore, Froehlich (2015) argues that while gamification could prove useful for behavioral change, broad change on a societal level—which is required for ecological sustainability—can only be done efficiently if social, structural and regulatory policy support these changes. Tang and Kay (2014) also recognize the long-term challenges for the concept but do not bring any radically new ideas to the table.

While Froehlich (2015) and Tang and Kay (2014) among others do not offer any practical solutions to how gamification could be able to tackle these challenges, other authors do. Nicholson (2012) argues that there needs to be more variety and options in the application as motivation is individual and applications for meaningful purposes is not a "one-size-fits-all". Al Marshedi et al. (2014) argue that a focus on flow, relatedness, purpose, autonomy and mastery in the design of gamified applications could improve the sustainability of these applications. Even though we are generally sympathetic towards these suggestions, we believe that rethinking the concept completely might be necessary in order to work long-term for meaningful purposes.

In the next section, we will present other methods of invoking sustainable behavior, in order to understand how gamification has become a popular concept for business within the sustainability discourse.

The Pursuit of Sustainability: Information, Visualization, Gamification

For pursuing environmental sustainability, there are according to Ehrhardt-Martinez two major approaches: the techno-economic approach and the people-centered approach (2010). The techno-economic approach in the case of reducing energy consumption is to replace old, inefficient electronic equipment with new, more efficient and "smarter" technology (ibid.). There are many proponents of smart systems, where the autonomous intelligence of the system takes over where human attention and motivation wane. However, it is hardly enough to create a sustainable society (cf. Lennerfors 2013, 2014). For instance, it is rarely justifiable to switch from old, inefficient equipment, from a life-cycle perspective (Lennerfors et al. 2014,

2015). Furthermore, Huesemann (2003) argues that technology by itself will not be able to solve any environmental problems, because developing and producing technology is inherently unsustainable. Even though we can see environmental benefits where the technology is used, the environmental degradation will take place elsewhere within the world-system (Hornborg 2001; Lennerfors et al. 2015). Studies have also shown that although we switch to more efficient technology, there is no direct environmental gain due to rebound effects (Murray 2011). One important direct rebound effect according to Murray is that when we use "green", more energy efficient technology, we tend to use it more frequently.

The people-centered approach focuses, as the name implies, on how people actually use energy. Thomas Dietz and his colleagues conducted a study in 2009 where they could see that a large amount of energy could be saved by simply using same old technology more efficiently. In some cases, reductions by between 25 to 30 percent could be achieved. But how can we promote this kind of sustainable behavior in the long term?

One commonly used method is to raise awareness of the consequences of certain actions. In 1981, Scott Geller, a well-known American professor in psychology, ran workshops in order to educate people how to use water and electricity more efficiently. After these workshops, tests showed that the students seemed more aware of water and energy issues and also knew how to change their behavior in order to use these resources more efficiently. In a follow-up study, however, they could observe that although these people were well aware of the environmental impact of their actions, they had not decreased their energy or water consumption. A study by Abrahamse et al. (2005) has also concluded that there is a low correlation between awareness and behavior in this respect. In a more recent study by Geller et al. (1983) on water consumption, aspects beyond awareness were studied. They also installed water-saving devices in the subjects' homes. In line with Murray's (2011) study on green technology, these devices did not decrease their water usage. It was, however, suggested that information in addition to social comments and feedback was more effective than just information (Geller et al. 1983).

Other researchers have been able to show that feedback on energy consumption, if done correctly, can affect the behavior of the user. Ellegård and Palm (2012), Fischer (2008) and Holmes (2007) have all shown that visualization of energy consumption and feedback on electricity use may lower the consumption, by on average between 5 and 12 percent (Fischer 2008). The most efficient way of providing this feedback is in real-time via a computer or smartphone screen. Gamification ties into visualization, since visualization might give the tools for the user to keep track of peak hours and compete with him or herself in order to lower the consumption. Adding more elements of competitiveness and gaming, such as rewarding badges and points for making progress and adding neighborhood leaderboards, seems to motivate the user to be more frugal with his or her energy usage.

Opower (2007), one of the most well known applications for this purpose, has helped people to lower their energy consumption by about 2 percent.

However, gamification, in contrast to information and visualization, more directly draws on affect to promote the desired behavior. The games for sustainability are expected to lead to feelings of fun, enjoyment, but also feelings of competitiveness when people are comparing their results with their peers. This is a significant shift from awareness and visualization, since awareness and visualization are intended to provide understanding to the subject rather than affect.

Game Theory and Existential Philosophy

So far we have argued that gamification is the latest trend in the pursuit of environmental sustainability and that it signifies a shift from the promotion of sustainability with a base in understanding, towards the promotion of sustainability with a base in affect. We therefore invoke theories from existential philosophy, especially from Søren Kierkegaard, who writes extensively about affect. Furthermore, we have seen indications of that developers of gamified applications for promoting sustainable consumption often draw inspiration from ludological aspects of games rather than narratological. By drawing on narratological approaches, where transformation of oneself is a key notion (Murray 1997), we suggest that some concerns with long-term effects of could potentially be solved. By combining these two bodies of literature, we aim to open up a range of alternative approaches for sustainable gamification and thereby propose new vistas for the area.

Ludology and Narratology

Within the area of video game research, there are two major discourses: the narratological and the ludological (Dymek 2010). While the two have similarities, they differ in a number of important aspects on how researchers and practitioners should approach the area of video games. The main difference is how the narrative of the game is situated. According to the ludological research stream, the narrative could be of importance in certain video games, although the narrative is not what constitutes the game. The rules, mechanics and gameplay are often more important for the experience of the game than the characters and the story line, which is the main focus of the narratologists (Frasca 2003). Even though a play-through of a single-player game seems similar to watching a movie from an external observer's point of view, the experience of the actual player is completely different. Hailing from the ludological perspective, John Carmack, former CEO of Id Software, argues that "[the] story in a video game is like story in a porno. Everyone expects it to be there, but it's not really important" (Kushner 2004 120). Some researchers also argue that there are aspects of video games that could be described as either ludic or narrative elements of games, even though they are often intertwined (Newman 2004; Thon 2007, 2011). While some researchers argue that narrative elements are often cut scenes, while the ludic elements are "play scenes" (Nietzel 2014), we distinguish between the two as follows: The narratological or narrative elements include aspects in which the narrative is central. This means that events driving the narrative forward or in some way is developing the character is defined as a narratological element.

While the ludological perspective holds that the narrative is secondary, the narratologists beg to differ. Janet Murray, probably the most prominent proponent of the narratological perspective of video games, writes: "Storytelling can be a powerful agent of personal transformation. The right stories can open our hearts and change who we are. Digital narratives add another powerful element to this potential by offering the opportunity to enact stories rather than to merely witness them. Enacted events have a transformative power that exceeds both narrated and conventionally dramatized events because we assimilate them as personal experiences" (Murray 1997, 170).

The narratological approach implies that video games could be described as an extension of more traditional media such as movies and books, as they are all built around a narrative in order to be interesting. In *Video Games—A Popular Culture Phenomenon* (2002), Berger applies Propp's 31 Narratemes (Propp 1968) to the video game *Riven* (1997) and concludes that all vital elements of the one hundred folk tales analysed by Vladimir Propp could also be identified in *Riven* (1997) in some modernized form. According to Murray, even games like *Tetris* (1984) can be analyzed from a narratological perspective: "The game is a perfect enactment of the over-tasked lives of Americans in the 1990s—of the constant bombardment of tasks that demand our attention and that we must somehow fit into our overcrowded schedules and clear off our desks in order to make room for the next onslaught" (Murray 1997, 144). Even though one might argue that she is pulling the narratological standpoint over the top with this argument, the point is clear; all games are essentially interactive narratives.

There are three crucial points in Murray's narratologist approach: immersion, agency, and transformation. Immersion is when the player of a video game or the reader of the book is experiencing deep involvement with the narrative of the medium, according to Murray, "the experience of being transported to an elaborately simulated place" (1997, 98). According to some researchers, immersion is only applicable when there is no interactivity between the media and the reader or player (e.g., Bolter and Grusin 2000), but others argue that immersion and interaction can be reconciled "in one unified domain" (Albæk et al. 2011, 39), a view that we also share. However, immersion is not only connected to the narratological aspects of the game. In a study conducted by Brown and Cairns (2004), the researchers developed a framework for immersion with three levels of player immersion: engagement, engrossment and total immersion. In order to reach the highest level of immersion, total immersion, factors such as "graphics, plot, and sounds in addition to emergent gameplay" were considered most crucial (Nacke and Lindley 2010, 2). This means that immersion is not exclusive for story-based games but that most games require a well-developed narrative in order to immerse the player.

Agency is the second crucial aspect of the narratologist view. Because of the nature of the media, users are able to create their own story by making meaningful choices inside the game. In single-player games, these choices will affect for example the difficulty of the game, who your friends (and enemies) are and how the game ends. Even though this gives the player a sense of freedom, there are only so many truly meaningful alternatives that have implications for the story. However, as the player is aware that actions within the game will have certain consequences, ethical decisions are key to in order get the right gaming experience.

Transformation, the third central notion of Murray's narratologist approach to video games is the most problematic according to Mateas (2005). He interprets the concept in three distinct ways: transformation as masquerade, transformation as variety and personal transformation. The first distinction implies that the player can transform him or herself to something else within the game, the second that the game itself is transforming as it is played, and the third that the player changes while playing the game. For meaningful gamification, we argue that the third way of transforming through play should be the very core of the concept.

As previously mentioned, agency is absent from most gamified applications (Robertson 2010). Games offer fail conditions as well as win conditions, and meaningful choices within the game will decide whether you succeed or fail. According to our examination of gamified applications for sustainability, none of them will punish you if you fail, and the choices you make will not decide your very fate. As the narratives in many of these applications are either absent or very shallow, the absorbing feeling of immersion will not be there to keep the user playing. Even platforms claimed to be "narrative based" (e.g., *GamEffective*, *SuperBetter*) fail in these two crucial respects of what constitutes a game from a narratological point of view. As transformation of oneself is dependent on aspects such as immersion and agency, they will probably not prove helpful for long-term behavioral change either.

Apart from the apparent lack of proper narratological approaches to gamification, which obstructs personal transformation through play, another dimension seems to be missing. Video games, but also movies and books, exploit a great number of affects to get our full attention. Fun and enjoyment are two important affects used in gamified applications, but other affects, such as anxiety and fear, are used to a much lesser extent. Turning to Søren Kierkegaard, we argue that such affects should be exploited as well in applications for meaningful gamification to promote ethical behavior such as a sustainable lifestyle.

Søren Kierkegaard's Modes of Existence

To throw light on affect, we invoke a certain strand of ethical theory—the phenomenological tradition. We argue that gamification promotes the emotional state and affects of fun, joy and enjoyment, and we aim to, by reading selected works of Kierkegaard, highlight other important affects for ethical action, in order to expand the vistas for research and practice of gamification. In a number of Kierkegaard's works, he is contrasting two modes of existence, the aesthetical and the ethical. We have suggested that the prevalent approach to gamification is the paradigmatic example of an aesthetical mode of existence and wanted to see what could be achieved by drawing on the complete opposite mode, namely the ethical.

Also anxiety is a central concept in Kierkegaard's works. According to him, anxiety is an affect that should be embraced, because the lack of anxiousness is a sign of spiritlessness. Without anxiety the freedom of the human being is not possible, and without freedom we are unable to change. According to Rollo May's reading of Kierkegaard: "One would have no anxiety if there were no possibility whatever. Now creating, actualizing one's possibilities, always involves negative as well as positive aspects. It always involves destroying the status quo, destroying old patterns within oneself, progressively destroying what one has clung to from childhood on, and creating new and original forms and ways of living" (2015, 40).

The Aesthetical

With aesthetical, Kierkegaard means that a person lives a life guided by her senses, since aisthesis is the Ancient Greek term for perception or sensation. Most of Kierkegaard's work is written in pseudonyms and the book *Either-Or* concerns two different persons, A and B. A is an aesthete, while B is leading an ethical life. A's writings consist of a number of essays and a collection of aphorisms. The aphorism in itself is a sign of what guides the aesthete in his life—ephemeral encounters, short-lived passions, the flux of desire. What is in focus for the aesthete is enjoyment: "There are, as is known, insects that die in the moment of fertilization. So it is with all joy: life's highest, most splendid moment of enjoyment is accompanied by death" (Kierkegaard 2004, 20).

One might suppose that the aesthetic person is happy and truly enjoying life, but that is not the case. Rather, A's writings show deep tendencies of depression and cynicism: "In addition to my other numerous acquaintances, I have one more intimate confidant-my depression. In the midst of my joy, in the midst of my work, he beckons to me, calls me aside, even though physically I remain on the spot. My depression is the most faithful mistress I have known—no wonder, then, that I return the love." (Kierkegaard 2004, 20)

A particularly interesting essay for our cause in *Either-Or* is *Rotation of Crops*, where the aesthete recommends not entering into any relationships of friendship nor marriage. The freedom to be able to metaphorically rotate crops is key. The aesthetic person says that: "I for my part am not looking for stories—I certainly have enough of them; I am seeking immediacy" (Kierkegaard 2004, 381). He is always in action and states: "I am constantly on the go and say, like Figaro: One, two, three, four schemes at a time" (Kierkegaard 2004, 341). While the aesthete searches for short-term love and engagement, and thus seem the most flexible and unconstrained of all, he explains that he "feel[s] as a chessman must feel when the opponent says of it: That piece cannot be moved" (Kierkegaard 2004, 22).

Apart from the aphorisms, the aesthete writes about Don Juan in a wonderful piece called the *Seducer's Diary*, which concerns a person who becomes obsessed with seducing a woman, finally succeeds but loses interest in her. What seems to be left in the very core of the aesthete's life, peeking beneath the activity of new loves, new projects, new things to do, is depression.

How is this relevant for gamification? Visualization can be seen from a logico-analytical perspective: it is giving us the correct information in order for us to take reasoned decisions regarding our energy consumption, and we thus suggest that visualization is also influenced by the aesthete's point of view. In a picture promoting the visualization tool *Energywatch* from *Vattenfall* (Vattenfall 2010, 10), we see a woman monitoring her energy consumption, while enjoying a cup of coffee. It is obvious from reading the expression on her face that she is not only concerned with learning and understanding but also with pleasure and joy. It seems to be the case that it is not about understanding one's energy consumption, nor becoming horrified by it, but rather to watch the energy consumption as if it was entertainment.

With such kind of philosophical backdrop to visualization, which could be a means for transforming into a caring and sustainable individual but rather have become a way to enjoy oneself, the shift of attention to gamification is not surprising. Gamification is currently mobilizing enjoyment and fun to create a sustainable society and is thus the paradigmatic example of the aesthetic way of life: be sustainable for as long as it is fun, then quickly move onto the next fun thing.

The Ethical

In *Seducer's Diary*, the seducer mentions how "the ethical is as boring in science as in life . . . Under the aesthetic sky everything is buoyant, beautiful, transient; when ethics arrives on the scene, everything becomes harsh, angular, infinitely langweiligt [boring]" (Kierkegaard 2004, 367). From the point of view of the aesthete, the ethical person is boredom personified. In *Either-Or*, the ethical person writes long letters to the aesthete, explaining the aesthetical and ethical validity of marriage. For the ethical person, marriage is a perfect example of the ethical way of life, being committed long-term to a project, constantly having to handle the ups and downs.

In *Concept of Anxiety* (Kierkegaard 1980), it is explained that ethics is an ideal science, in the sense that it wants to bring ideality into the everyday. Ethics shows ideality as a task and presupposes that human beings have the capacity of the attributes for moving into the ideal. Thereby, ethics develops a contradiction, since it manifests difficulties and impossibilities. Ethics is thus quite the contrary from aesthetics, which is a matter of showing the infinite possibilities of the human being, encouraging her to enjoy as much and multifariously as possible. In the understanding of the ethical that Kierkegaard has, ethics only judges; it does not give birth.

The ethical person takes full responsibilities of her life. She feels the weight of responsibility and understands the infinity of ethical demands. She feels that she constantly fails, because of the infinity of demands and because of the intrusion of the ideal into reality. The ethical judges and according to it, might never be able to fulfill its demands. You cannot bargain with ethics, and therefore ethics never really gets close to reality (Kierkegaard 1980, 17). We interpret the affect of ethics to be commitment, the feeling of working for a good cause, the feeling of courage, and sometimes a feeling of impossibility, the feeling of not really reaching what you strive for.

The ethical stage is also concerned with anxiety. Anxiety for Kierkegaard is the anxiety for the spirit, anxiety for being oneself (Kierkegaard 1980). As opposed to fear, anxiety does not have an external cause: "I must point out that [anxiety] is altogether different from fear and similar concepts that refer to something definite, whereas anxiety is freedom's actuality as the possibility of possibility" (Kierkegaard 1980, 42). Anxiety is an affect that shows that the human being contains more than she is aware of and that there are possibilities both frightening and tempting. In the aesthetic mode of life, the fear of losing the sources of enjoyment is answered by constantly rotating crops in order to find the next source of satisfaction. But at least in our reading, there is no fundamental turn inwards towards the potential of possibility in the aesthetic mode of life. A complete absence of anxiety, which is inherent in the aesthetic mode of life, therefore precludes the possibilities of human beings becoming what they really are, namely something more than themselves. According to Kierkegaard, anxiety is the feeling that like no other feeling can impose responsibility; "one cannot look to others, to the crowd . . . to measure [the] progress [of] becoming a full human being" (Marino 2012).

In order to reach a sustainable society, it is easy to blame others such as other consumers, companies or countries, but according to Kierkegaard anxiety imposes a feeling of responsibility, which we believe is necessary for this kind of long-term behavioral change that sustainability inherently requires. Anxiety, for Kierkegaard, is thus essentially a productive feeling. Then the question is: How to we respond to anxiety? How do we deal with our anxiety? For Kierkegaard, anxiety is not the final stage but something that could be surpassed. However, the possibility to overcome anxiety is only granted the human being who admits that anxiety has nothing to do with the external world. The free human being does not blame other people but admits that the reason for the world being as it is, is a consequence of oneself. If we hold "the external" responsible, it is because we do not want to be ourselves, and this is inherently spiritless for Kierkegaard (1980).

Beyond the Ludo-Aesthetical Approach to Gamification

To sum up, Kierkegaard describes two fundamentally different modes of relating to life, the aesthetical and the ethical, with different inherent affects present. For gamification, the aesthetical affects are currently central, while ethical affects are not drawn on to the same extent. Because the ethical way of life is about long-term commitment, which is key to a sustainable lifestyle, we argue that affects such as the feeling of impossibility and anxiety should be taken into consideration. In this section, we combine these modes with the ludological and the narrative approaches to game theory. Although narratological approaches to gamification are rare, they seem appropriate when trying to achieve long-term goals and behavioral change, not least because of the narratological notion of transformation. Games and other narrative-driven media, such as movies and books, do not only evoke positive affects but all kinds of affects, to immerse the player or reader. In this section, we have combined these two dimensions in an attempt to outline a model for unexplored possibilities for gamification.

Ludo-Aesthetical Gamification

Among the investigated gamified applications for sustainable behavior, the majority of them focus on ludo-aesthetical approaches to motivation; "change should be fun, social and easy" (Kuntz et al. 2012, 127). This means that these applications promote an aesthetical way of life, where the anxiety of the user is dealt with by constantly exposing him or her to positive affects. When the application can no longer keep up with the increased need of extrinsic rewards and new, fun things to indulge in, the application can no longer deal with the anxiety of the user. This means that these kinds of applications will probably not be sufficient to promote the long-term behavioral change. Moreoever, all transformational aspects of video games are lacking; the character development is nonexistent, the game environment is static and the personal transformation, crucial for meaningful gamification, is absent due to the lack of narratological aspects. While ludo-aesthetical approaches to gamification are suitable in certain contexts, such as marketing, there is a need to go beyond them within the area of gamification for sustainability and other meaningful aspects in order to enhance motivation.

Ludo-Ethical Gamification

While ludological aspects such as leaderboards, points and other competitive aspects are exploited in order to create fun and enjoyment in ludo-aesthetic gamification, negative and neutral affects, such as anxiety and feeling of obligation, are availed. Ludo-ethical gamification could utilize ludic elements, but to produce anxiety. Obviously, an application that only aimed to produce the feeling of anxiety and inadequacy would not be used. However, these aspects are ludo-ethical aspects are used in many games to encourage the player to keep playing.

In *World of Warcraft* (Blizzard 2004), the players can take daily quests, "dailies", which can be repeated every day in order to gain a reputation within a certain faction or for other in-game rewards. While most players consider these dailies boring and repetitive, they feel obliged to carry them out because they will otherwise miss out on important in-game content. The same system is used in other games in order to keep the players active, often in the end-game stage of MMORPGs. In *Counter-Strike: Global Offensive* (Valve 2012) players will lose their rank if they are inactive for a couple of weeks. For players who have achieved the highest rank possible, The Global Elite, this loss could be devastating. This feature will keep the player in a constantly anxious state, worrying about his or her rank. The ludo-ethical approaches to gamification could thus motivate players to keep carrying out boring quests or play even though they are not in the mood. Even though exploiting these affects proves useful within games, the method is still to be seen within meaningful gamification. If a player misses out on quests in a gamified application for sustainability, he or she can always come back another day to carry them out, without punishment.

Narrato-Aesthetical Gamification

Even though many gamification platforms are claimed by their developers to be narrative-driven, no application today can match the narratives of *Warcraft* (Blizzard 1994), *The Elder Scrolls* (Bethesda 1994) or *Half-Life* (Valve 1998), which means that the transformational power of the media is absent (Mateas 2005). Narrato-aesthetical gamification would mean to create a narrative that satisfies the needs of the aesthetical person, namely the needs for fun, enjoyment, and crop rotation. One could imagine a narrative world with a plethora of activities to be pursued, none of them providing negative feedback or requiring hard decisions. The narrato-aesthetical gamification would thus be quite similar to the BLAP gamification but with paidic elements rather than ludic, in a form that resembles storytelling. As the game will never force or persuade you to do anything, no new behavior or values will be imposed on the user. As these applications will only obscure the anxiety within the user by the means of games, the use will never be able to evoke this anxiety in some productive manner. We argue that while this approach is unproductive for meaningful purposes, it could be valuable for marketing purposes, as commercial products or services could be placed within the virtual world of the application.

Narrato-Ethical Gamification

This approach includes narrative-driven applications aimed at producing a sense of responsibility and productive anxiety, a sense of long-term projects. Since the narrative structure is temporal per se, similarly to the ethical structure of Kierkegaard, the narrative and the ethical could be a good fit. An archetype from the game world of this kind of application is *Everybody's Gone to the Rapture* (The Chinese Room and SCE Santa Monica Studio 2015). Here, the player is walking around as an unknown being in an empty village where an accident has recently occurred. The player can listen to certain radio recordings, but apart from that, the player cannot interact with anyone or anything; all ludological elements are stripped off. Another narrato-ethical example from the game world is *Life is Strange* (Dotnod Entertainment 2015). In *Life is Strange*, the player is controlling Max, an art student, who has the power to reverse time. The player is not merely a spectator as in *Everybody's Gone to the Rapture* but able to make decisions with important consequences. For example, you have to comfort a friend, Kate, using the correct words in order to prevent her from committing suicide, and in order to save your village, you will have to sacrifice your childhood friend, Chloe. Depending on what you value, there are different paths to choose from. Many times, the choice that seems most fun and the most morally correct thing to do differs, and in order to experience the perfect narrative, the user must make boring or really hard choices, which distinguishes narrato-ethical aspects from the narrato-aesthetical ditto.

As demonstrated, games with narrato-ethical aspects do exist today and have become increasingly popular in recent years. Some even argue that the concept of story-driven games where meaningful decisions are central is the new norm. However, gamified applications built upon narrato-ethical aspects remain to be developed. One might however question their fit for the market. If the present world is guided by the aesthetical mode of existence, gamified application built purely on the narrato-ethical approach might not be of interest. Still, drawing on narrato-ethical aspects for promoting a desired effect, in this case commitment for a sustainable lifestyle not only as long as it is fun but also because the user feels obliged to, could prove effective.

Concluding Discussion

In this chapter we have discussed how gamification is currently used for promoting a sustainable lifestyle. We have positioned the concept and contrasted it to other approaches, such as the techno-economical and people-centered approach, of which previous examples of methods are information and visualization. In contrast to earlier approaches, gamification draws on affect for promoting sustainability, but it draws on a limited palette of affects. In gamified applications only the aesthetical affects are present, but in games, we can see ethical and aesthetical affects effectively combined. For example, the ethically correct choice and the most enjoyable choice are sometimes separated. The player realizes that in order to achieve the perfect gaming experience, he or she must sometimes resist tempting but unethical decisions, or make ethical decisions even though they seem really boring or hard. If these complex aspects could be implemented in gamified applications, they could be much more effective in creating long-term value for the user, for business and for society. Therefore, we have developed a framework for gamification for sustainability, combining game theory and existential philosophy. In contrast to other authors (e.g., Al Marshedi et al. 2014; Nicholson 2012, 2014; Tang and Kay 2014) who have recognized the difficulty of gamification to handle long-time change, we have in this chapter turned back to the roots of gamification in order to find completely new ways of perceiving what the concept could contain. This discussion will concern two issues, one practical and one academic. First, to the practical implications.

Our critique of concurrent approaches to gamification (the ludo-aesthetical) has mainly concerned the in-game world, but one might suggest that these approaches could be efficient to promote initiatives for ecological sustainability outside the applications. In other words, even though people stop using the gamified applications after a while, they might still become more and more sustainable subjects in the real world. Our basic approach in relation to this is that ludo-aesthetical approaches to gamification are not suitable for promoting a feeling for long-term commitment of the playing subject, since the aesthetic approaches are by nature short-term and do not create intrinsic motivations for sustainability in itself. This does not mean that the approach has no value but that the ludo-ethical approach might be more effective for producing an incentive to be more sustainable outside the game, irrespective of whether the person continues to play the game or not. The reason is that the ludo-ethical games create a feeling of lack in the subject playing them, a lack that might be present although the subject is no longer playing the game. The narratological approaches are expected to keep the subject playing the game for a long time, since the narrative structure of the game keeps the subject interested, whether it is by aesthetical or ethical means. However, we have not found any gamified applications inspired by some of these views. If we go back to games, we have seen that very story-driven games such as *Everybody's Gone to the Rapture* and *Life is Strange* do indeed exploit neutral and negative affects such as anxiety, which creates a feeling of responsibility for what happens in-game. As it is hard to compare this responsibility with responsibility for real-life issues such as sustainability, the practical implications of narrato-ethical gamification are absent from this chapter but could be interesting to investigate further in forthcoming studies.

The second issue relates to the academic viability of the suggested approach. It might seem odd in our hyper-modern era to be inspired by a 19th century philosopher. However, we subscribe to Poltronieri's claim that "one can see that there is a great effort on the part of academics in making this field of knowledge [i.e., gamification] be dealt with by newer approaches, when there are already disciplines, such as philosophy, which have observed the issue of games for many centuries" (Poltronieri 2014, 183). Other gamification scholars have also been inspired by philosophy, such as Ruffino (2014) and Schrape (2014). Our chapter should therefore be situated within the stream of research that is conducted using philosophy to understand IT trends such as gamification. Our contribution to the research on gamification is to use Kierkegaard's philosophical ideas to throw light on the various possible affects that can be promoted by means of games. We believe that the chapter has shown that it can be of value to draw on philosophy from earlier periods to understand a contemporary phenomenon such as gamification, and also invite further research that corroborates this tradition.

References

Abrahamse, Wokje, Steg, Linda, Vlek Charles and Talib Rothengatter 2005. "A review of intervention studies aimed at household energy conservation." *Journal of Environmental Psychology*, 25: 273–91.

Albæk, Katarina R. et al. 2011. "The Influence of Interactivity on Immersion Within Digital Interactive Narratives". Aalborg University Copenhagen. Accessed February 28. http://www.academia.edu/1074744/The_Influence_of_Interactivity_on_Immersion_Within_Digital_Interactive_Narratives

Al Marshedi, Alaa, Wills, Gary B., Wanick, Vanissa and Ashok Ranchhod 2014. "Towards a sustainable gamification impact". Presented at 2014 International Conference on Information Society (i-Society), London, November 10–12.

Berger, Arthur A. 2002. *Video Games: A Popular Culture Phenomenon*. New Brunswick: Transaction Publishers.

Bolter, Jay D. and Richard Grusin. 2000. *Remediation: Understanding New Media*. Cambridge: MIT Press.

Brown, Emily and Paul Cairns. 2004. A grounded investigation of game immersion. Presented at CHI 2004. Vienna, April 24–9.

Deterding, Sebastian. 2014. "Eudaimonic Design, or: Six Invitations to Rethink Gamification." In *Rethinking Gamification*, edited by Mathias Fuchs, Fizek, Sonia, Ruffino, Paolo and Niklas Schrape, 305–31. Hybrid Publishing Lab, Leuphana University of Lüneburg, Meson Press.

Deterding, Sebastian, Dixon, Dan, Khaled, Rilla and Lennart Nacke 2011. "From game design elements to gamefulness: Defining gamification." Presented at the 15th International Academic MindTrek Conference: Envisioning Future Media Environments. Tampere, September 28–39.

Dymek, Mikolaj. 2010. "Industrial phantasmagoria: Subcultural interactive cinema meets mass-cultural media of simulation." PhD diss., Royal Institute of Technology, Stockholm, Sweden.

Ehrhardt-Martinez, Karen, Kat A. Donnelly and John A. "Skip" Laitner. 2010. *Advanced Metering Initiatives and Residential Feedback Programs: A Meta-Review for Household Electricity-Saving Opportunities*. Washington, DC: American Council for an Energy-Efficient Economy. Accessed February 27th, 2016. http://www.energie2007.com/images/upload/aceee_etude_juin_2010_advanced_metering_initiatives.pdf

Ellegård, Kajsa and Jenny Palm. 2012. Are you an individual or a household? Consequences for energy policy from concept confusion. Energy Policy, 38:2858-64.
Fischer, Corinna. 2008. "Feedback on household electricity consumption: A tool for saving energy?" *Energy efficiency*, 1: 79–104.
Frasca, Gonzalo. 2003. "Simulation versus Narrative." In *The Video Game Theory Reader*, edited by Mark J. Wolf and Bernad Perron, 221–35. New York: Routledge.
Froehlich, Jon. 2015. "Gamifying Green: Gamification and Environmental Sustainability." In *The Gameful World*, edited by Steffen Walz and Sebastian Deterding, 563–96. Cambridge: MIT Press.
Geller, E. Scott, Jeff B. Erickson and Brenda A. Buttram. 1983. "Attempts to promote residential water conservation with educational, behavioral and engineering strategies." *Population and Environment*, 6: 96–112.
Gore, Albert A. 2011. "Pre-Festival Summit Keynote." Presented at the 8th Annual Games for Change Festival, New York, June 20.
Hamari, Juho, Jonna Koivisto and Harri Sarsa. 2014. "Does gamification work? A literature review of empirical studies on gamification." Presented at 47th Hawaii International Conference on System Sciences. Waikolola, January 6–9.
Holmes, Tiffany G. 2007. "Eco-visualization: Combining art and technology to reduce energy consumption." Presented at the 6th ACM SIGCHI conference on Creativity & cognition, 153–162. New York, June 14–15.
Hornborg, Alf. 2001. *The Power of the Machine: Global Inequalities of Economy, Technology, and Environment*. New York: Rowman Altamira.
Huesemann, Michael H. 2003. "The Limits of Technological Solutions to Sustainable Development." *Clean Technologies and Environmental Policy*, 5: 21–34.
Kierkegaard, Søren. 1980. *The Concept of Anxiety*. Princeton: Princeton University Press.
Kierkegaard, Søren. 2004. *Either/or: A Fragment of Life*. Westminster: Penguin Classics.
Kohn, Alfie. 1999. *Punished By Rewards: The Trouble with Gold Stars, Incentive Plans, A's, Praise, and Other Bribes*. Boston: Houghton Mifflin.
Kuntz, Kathy, Rajan Shukla and Ingo Bensch. 2012. "How many points for that? A game-based approach to environmental sustainability." Presented at the American Council for an Energy-Efficient Economy Summer Study on Energy Efficiency in Buildings, 126–137. Pacific Grove, August 12–17.
Kushner, David. 2004. *Masters of Doom: How Two Guys Created an Empire and Transformed Pop Culture*. New York: Random House Incorporated.
Lee, Joey , Matamoros, Eduard, Kern, Rafael, Marks, Jenna, de Luna, Christian and William Jordan-Cooley 2013. "Greenify: Fostering sustainable communities via gamification." Presented at CHI'13 Extended Abstracts on Human Factors in Computing Systems, 1497–502. Paris, April 27-May 2.
Lennerfors, Thomas T. 2013. "Smart Ethics. in ICT-Ethics: Sweden and Japan." In *Studies in Applied Ethics*, edited by Elin Palm, 31–42. Linköping: LiU Tryck.
Lennerfors, Thomas T. 2014. "Sustainable and Fast ICT: Lessons from Dromology." *Journal of Information, Communication and Ethics in Society*, 12: 284–97.
Lennerfors, Thomas T., Per Fors and Jolanda van Rooijen. 2014. "Sustainable ICT: A Critique from World Systems Theory." In *ICT and Society*, edited by Kimppa, , Kai, Whitehouse, Diane, Kuusela, Tiina and Jackie Phahlamohlaka, 57–68. Berlin, Heidelberg: Springer.
Lennerfors, Thomas T., Per Fors and Jolanda van Rooijen. 2015. "ICT and Environmental Sustainability in a Changing Society: The View of Ecological World Systems Theory." *Information Technology & People*, 28: 758–74.

Marino, Gordon. 2012. "The Danish doctor of dread." *The New York Times*. Accessed February 28. http://opinionator.blogs.nytimes.com/2012/03/17/the-danish-doctor-of-dread/?_r=0

Mateas, Michael. 2005. "Build it to understand it: Ludology meets narratology in game design space." Presented at Changing Views: Worlds in Play. Vancouver, June 16–20.

May, Rollo. 2015. *The Meaning of Anxiety*. New York: W. W. Norton & Company.

McGonigal, Jane. 2011. *Reality Is Broken: Why Games Make Us Better and How They Can Change the World*. New York: Penguin.

Murray, Cameron K. 2011. "Income dependent direct and indirect rebound effects from 'green' consumption choices in Australia." Munich Personal RePEc Archive. Accessed February 27, 2016. https://mpra.ub.uni-muenchen.de/34973/3/MPRA_paper_34973.pdf

Murray, Janet H. 1997. *Hamlet On the Holodeck: The Future of Narrative in Cyberspace*. Cambridge: MIT Press.

Nacke, Lennart, and Craig A. Lindley. 2008. "Flow and immersion in first-person shooters: Measuring the player's gameplay experience." Presented at the 2008 Conference on Future Play: Research, Play, Share. Toronto, November 3–5.

Newman, James. 2004. *Videogames*. London: Routledge.

Nicholson, Scott. 2012. "A user-centered theoretical framework for meaningful gamification." Presented at Games+Learning+Society 8.0, Madison, June 13–15.

Nicholson, Scott. 2014. "Exploring the Endgame of Gamification" In *Rethinking Gamification*, edited by Mathias Fuchs, Fizek, Sonia, Ruffino, Paolo and Niklas Schrape, 289–304. Hybrid Publishing Lab, Leuphana University of Lüneburg, Meson Press.

Nietzel, Britta. 2014. "Revision of Narrativity of Computer Games." In *The Living Handbook of Narratology*, edited by Peter Hühn, Jan Christoph Meister, John Pier, and Wolf Schmid Accessed February 28. http://webcache.googleusercontent.com/search?q=cache:OnRK_juqPZ4J:www.lhn.uni-hamburg.de/users/britta-neitzel+&cd=2&hl=sv&ct=clnk&gl=se

Owen, Paula. 2013. *How Gamification Can Help Your Business Engage in Sustainability*. Oxford: Do Sustainability.

Poltronieri, Fabrizio. 2014. "Communicology, Apparatus, and Post-History: Vilém Flusser's Concepts Applied to Videogames and Gamification." In *Rethinking Gamification*, edited by Mathias Fuchs, Fizek, Sonia, Ruffino, Paolo and Niklas Schrape, 165–86. Hybrid Publishing Lab, Leuphana University of Lüneburg, Meson Press.

Propp, Vladimir I. 1958. *Morphology of the Folktale (Vol. 9): American Folklore Society*. Austin: University of Texas Press.

Robertson, Margaret. 2010. "Can't play, won't play." Hide & Seek: Inventing New Kinds of Play, October 6. Accessed 19 March 2015. http://www.hideandseek.net/2010/10/06/cant-play-wont-play/.

Ruffino, Paulo. 2014. "From Engagement to Life, or: How to Do Things with Gamification?" In *Rethinking Gamification*, edited by Mathias Fuchs, Fizek, Sonia, Ruffino, Paolo and Niklas Schrape, 47–70. Hybrid Publishing Lab, Leuphana University of Lüneburg, Meson Press.

Schrape, Niklas. 2014. "Gamification and Governmentality." In *Rethinking Gamification*, edited by Mathias Fuchs, Fizek, Sonia, Ruffino, Paolo and Niklas Schrape, 21–46. Hybrid Publishing Lab, Leuphana University of Lüneburg, Meson Press.

Tang, Lie M. and Judy Kay. 2014. "Gamification: Metacognitive scaffolding towards long term goals?" Presented at 4th International Workshop on Personalization Approaches in Learning Environments, 63–68. Aalborg, July 11.

Thon, Jan-Noël. 2007. "Unendliche Weiten? Schauplätze, fiktionale Welten und soziale Räume heutiger Computerspiele". In *Computer/Spiel/Räume. Materialien zur Einführung in die Computer Game Studies*, edited by Klaus Barteles and Jan-Noël Thon, 29–60. Hamburg: Universität Hamburg.

Thon, Jan-Noël. 2011. "Zu Formen und Funktionen narrativer Elemente in neueren Computerspielen". In *Erzählformen des Computerspiels. Zur Medienmorphologie digitaler Spiele*, edited by Jürgen Sorg and Jochen Venus. Bielfeldt: Transcript 2012/In press.

Vattenfall. 2014. "EnergyWatch." Accessed March 31 2015. https://www.vattenfall.se/sv/file/Installationsmanual-EnergyWatch_30593622.pdf.

Wu, Michael. 2011. "The Gamification Backlash + Two Long Term Business Strategies." Lithium. Accessed at March 19, 2015. http://community.lithium.com/t5/Science-of-Social-blog/The-Gamification-Backlash-Two-Long-Term-Business-Strategies/ba-p/30891

Zichermann, Gabe and Christopher Cunningham. 2011. *Gamification By Design: Implementing Game Mechanics in Web and Mobile Apps*. Sebastopol: O'Reilly Media, Inc.

Ludography

A Glass of Water, 2012. Developed by Toyota Motor. Iphone. Toyota Motor.

BioShock, 2007. Developed by Irrational Games, Digital Extremes and Feral Interactive. Windows, OS X, Playstation and Xbox 360. 2K Games.

Bottlebank Arcade, 2009. Developed by The Fun Theory. Arcade. Volkswagen.

Commute Greener, 2012. Developed by Volvo IT. Iphone, Android and browser. Volvo Group.

Counter Strike: Global Offensive. Developed by Valve Corporation. Playstation 3, Xbox 360, Microsoft Windows, Linux, Mac OS. Valve Corporation.

Everybody's Gone to the Rapture. Developed by The Chinese Room and SCE Santa Monica Studio. Playstation 4. Sony Computer Entertainment.

Half-Life, 1998–2004. Developed by Valve Corporation, Gearbox Software and Taito Corpration. Mac OS X, Playstation, Windows, Xbox, Linux. Valve Corporation, EA Games and Sierra Entertainment.

Life is Strange. 2015. Developed by Dotnod Enternainment. Playstation 4, Xbox One, Playstation 3, Xbox 360, Windows. Square Enix.

Oroeco, 2013. Developed by Oroeco Inc. Browser. Oroeco Inc.

Riven 1997. Developed by Cyan, Inc. Macintosh, Windows, Playstation, Saturn, Pocket PC, Iphone.

Tetris, 1984. Developed by Aleksej Leonídovitj Pázjitnov. Multi platform.

The Elder Scrolls, 1994–2014. Developed by Bethesda Game Studios, ZeniMax Online Studios and Vir2L Studios. Bethesda Softworks.

The World's Deepest Bin, 2009. Developed by The Fun Theory. Volkswagen.

Vampire Hunter, 2013. Developed by SAP. Browser and Iphone.

World of Warcraft, 2004. Developed by Blizzard Entertainment. Windows and OS X. Blizzard Entertainment.

Zombies, Run! 3, 2014. Developed by Six to Start. Android and Iphone. Six to Start.

10 Designing for the Play Instinct
Gamification, Collective Voodoo and Mumbo Jumbo

Stephen Webley and Karen Cham

Introduction

In its simplest sense, "gamification" is a recently established engagement method that aims to accelerate performance by implementing game-style incentivisation mechanics into nongame environments, such as businesses and services. Currently, it is most often applied as a "user experience design" (UXD) method, the contemporary convergence of human-computer interaction (HCI), user-centred design (UCD) and marketing that aims to increase user engagement, closing the "semantic gap" in the user experience (UX) by providing a higher level of engagement for people using machines—through call centre interfaces, for example. Quantifiable returns are indeed demonstrated when more engaging elements are designed into any communications touchpoint, a long-established tradition in both media and advertising and HCI. However, the recent evangelization of both gamification methodologies and "gurus" demonstrates a fundamental, and startlingly absolute, absence of understanding of the paradigms of computing, design practice and game studies in the gamification world.

As a result, the use of the term has expanded to engulf many types of codified behaviour and engagement techniques and is now almost entirely detached from any recognizable rigorous anchor in any discipline—not least UXD, which drives most digital engagement today and modern game studies, arguably originating in a contemporary sense with the work of Johan Huizinga (1938). Gamification experts now patent, licence and sell complicated and often spurious models and techniques that promise the magic bullet of exponential growth, and it is argued here it has become the ultimate "humpty dumpty" term. This paper aims to reverse this trend, demonstrating that gamification has gamified itself to become an ideology in its own right and that it is paradoxically this in itself that will hinder growth of the technique and models of good practice, motivating adherents to "gamify" only as an end in itself. The authors redefine gamification as a design mechanic, contextualize it in user experience design (UXD) practice and anchor it in established theoretical and philosophical concepts from game theory, then define a model of good practice to underpin ethical gamified engineering of behaviour long term as we move close to "the Singularity," the theoretical event horizon, or "point of no return" when human/machine interaction becomes symbiosis.

To this end, this chapter undertakes a number of gamification case studies; sets out how UXD, not gamification, is the design process focused on human motivation in digital systems and explains how that evolved from a convergence of human computer interaction (HCI) and user centered design (UCD) in the early 1970s, detailing how and why it converges with marketing to address designing for persuasion through the construction of ideologies. Gamification as social engineering is then explored through the optics of psychoanalysis, with its roots in the continental philosophical traditions, and massively multiplayer online games (MMOGs), unpacking our contemporary understanding of what play actually is and what it involves, from a theoretical and philosophical perspective. Finally, the authors argue that play and motivation converge in the production and function of ideology. Thus it is only ever through a model of the mind that can accommodate ideology that one can begin to "master motivation and engagement" at all, and only then—*by design*.

This chapter posits that gamification for business growth does not need to be complicated, evangelical or mystified, utilising Huizinga's "collective mumbo-jumbo" of aesthetic idioms to obfuscate the ideological nature of play. What is provided here is a rigorous theoretical framework to observe, establish or monitor the dialectical construction of motivation, jeopardy and reward in any ideological context to underpin an ethical manifesto for gamification as part of the Singularity.

Gamification

> *"When I use a word," Humpty Dumpty said in rather a scornful tone, "it means just what I choose it to mean—neither more nor less."*

In June of 2012, Douglas Tarasconi Da Silveira, one of Professor Karen Cham's MA games design students, was approached by MJV from Brazil, well-known pioneers in the field of technology implementation for banks and big corporations. One of their clients, one of the biggest banks in Brazil, had a huge call centre providing customer services support for insurance plans. MJV wanted to investigate using game mechanics to solve the problem of employee attendance and retention, as they were consistently suffering loss of trained staff. With a two- to three-month initial training period, these losses heavily influenced the company finances and meant that new employees never achieved fully qualified status, and increasing numbers of clients were unsatisfied with the service provided by the bank's call center.

Douglas took an established design lead approach to the problem and focused on defining the problem first. Research demonstrated that key factors in the poor employee experience (EX) were:

- The employees feel it is a very stressful environment.
- The employees feel pushed to their limits.
- The company pays one of the lowest salaries in Brazil.
- The employees work 8-hour shifts with two short breaks of 15 minutes, 1 hour after they start and 1 hour before they finish, and a 1-hour lunch break in the middle.
- The employees work 6 days in the week, varying one weekend day off.
- The employees are usually very poor.
- Some of them are students who work to pay for their studies, fitting their shifts around classes.
- As soon as the students find any other job slightly better, they leave.
- The employees who are not studying do not have much chance of a better job.
- Some of the female employees are already mothers with one or more children.
- The employees who stay are very unhappy.
- The employees feel they are "just a number" to the company.

These findings create an extremely poor EX manifest as a "lack of interest" from the company in their employees, and a corresponding lack of commitment from the employees. It is essentially a break in any psychological employer/employee contract. Douglas started thinking about ways of solving the company's problem by improving the EX by increasing employee engagement. Moreover, Douglas found the company was using a very complicated legacy of incompatible dashboard systems to manage the customer eservice provision, and some of the employees pointed out that the lack of unity across different software was frustrating and delayed their work processes.

This is a hugely common UXD scenario, legacy systems damaging user engagement, onboarding and conversion rates, such as sales on an ecommerce site, for example. As MJV had explicitly wanted to move into providing gamification services, Douglas adopted common game mechanics to solve the UX problems. For example, by integrating an information-based quiz into the Call Centre Intranet interface, he applied motivation, jeopardy and reward dynamics. The quiz had the preliminary aim of increasing an employee's factual knowledge of policy and processes with multiple-choice questions provided by the managers. For each right answer, the employee would receive a chocolate bonbon.

The outcomes were as expected, and the game mechanic changed the employees' behavior:

- Employees tried to answer more questions.
- Employees showed off their prizes and were proud of their achievements.

- Employees explicitly competed with each other to see who would be the best.
- Some employees were frustrated when incorrect but wanted to answer more successfully to win the prize.

A more advanced level of this quiz was an ongoing peer-to-peer FAQs competition. Previously, employees had to call their managers with any queries, a time-consuming method that often created a backlog and meant queries went unanswered within a reasonable period of time, which concurrently affected employees and their professional self-esteem. Douglas integrated a competitive element where the employees would write down their queries on Post-It Notes and deliver them to the managers' area manually. However, these questions were freely available for anyone to answer. For this test, Douglas used points, and the employee who answered most of the queries correctly using the company's standard operating procedures as a base of their answer would earn the points.

Outcomes
- There was some disagreement between the employees, but most of the time the questions were solved by peer-to-peer consultation.
- The manager checked some of their answers, and some were technically wrong.
- Employees were looking for more questions to answer.
- The employees found it a better and faster way to answer their queries
- The managers thought it was an improved system as they could focus on the most difficult questions, reducing backlog.

The third part of this prototype was the emergence of a champion. As soon as he showed the employees a ranking, people wanted to know what would be the prizes for those in first, second and third position. In summary, the results of this 240-minute paper prototype session were:

- 64 quizzes answered (with 76 percent of accuracy)
- 12 prioritization queries made (28.6 percent solved question by the employee)
- A decrease on the cue of waiting calls to be attended (from 9 on hold to 10 free employees in 30 minutes)
- Three compliments received in 30 minutes from clients.

This exercise was essential in order to provide quantitative data upon which to design a new gamified dashboard. The next stage saw the initiation of a prototype dashboard that would unify both previous systems utilized by the company and underpin greater employee engagement. UI dashboards are a necessary part of HCI experience and are often complex. However, how and to what extent complexities of a UI gamified system are necessary, including caveats and benefits of their design and function, is evident in the uptake of the last two generations of gaming consoles gamified UIs. These new-generation console dashboards go a long way to managing UI expectations and experience by operating a simple, and now standard, gamified system of avatars and rewards in a social media online context. Standardized gamified console dashboard mechanics were analyzed, modified and then utilized in the design for the gamified MJV dashboard to increase engagement. These gamified mechanics are:

- A personalized avatar.
- Feedback on a user's own performance in the context of his or her own trajectory and that of others.
- Optional hourly/daily/monthly challenges.
- Real-time updates on new rules and any other key changes.
- An internal "game-world" announcement feed and "friends" network.
- A dynamic call waiting queue and employees on calls.
- Real-time employee office rote-board featuring scheduled breaks; badges for achievement, attendance, punctuality, quality of work, client compliments.
- Rewards were also offered for employee retention, starting with one badge for the first day, first week, month, quarter and so on.

Douglas undertook a user-centered, design-led digital transformation of the employee experience by improving employee engagement by using incentivisation mechanics, currently enjoying a renaissance under the title "gamification". The elements that make this "gamified" are motivation, jeopardy, reward and the social status conveyed by the leaderboard, all anchored on a basic of user interaction design (UID) called "feedback". It is very much like supermarket loyalty schemes with an added public competitive element. In 2014 MJV registered the patent[1] to be the exclusive user of this gamification system in call centers in Brazil, with aims to expand to Europe.

Concurrently, the business of gamification is accelerating worldwide. There is a Gamification World Congress Awards and a "Gamification World Guru" who, for the last three years running, has been Yu-Kai Chou, an international economics graduate from UCLA. He has created a well-known gamification framework known as "Octalysis" and is the founder of "The Octalysis Group" and the self-published author of *Actionable Gamification, Beyond Points, Badges, and Leaderboards* (Chou, 2015) about the Octalysis method. He is described as a "behavioral scientist" at an Israel-based technology company that "helps websites increase retention, monetization, and loyalty".

Octalysis delivers quantifiable results, as do many incentivisation strategies in UX design. In his online materials, Yukai-Choi makes a number of key statements about design and game play that concern us here:

- *Gamification* is design that places the most emphasis on human motivation in the process.
- *Gamification* is what I call "human-focused design", that the gaming industry was the first to master.
- This is opposed to pure efficiency in "function-focused design"; most systems are designed to get the job done quickly.
- It is called gamification since games have spent decades (or even centuries depending on how you qualify a game) learning how to master motivation and engagement.

There are many inaccuracies in these statements above, which will be expounded in this chapter—inaccuracies about design, games, human motives and behavior. Moreover, in its delivery, the Octalysis framework obfuscates and mystifies ideology, narrative, archetypes and the like, all common to many aspects of design and game theory, rebranding them as its own cultural capital, which repositions the method as an ideology in and of itself. For example, the bastardisation of the long-established cognitive science principles of a "dual-process" approach, as "white hat" and "black hat" gamification, which is actually simply referring to addressing the conscious reflective self and what in psychoanalysis is referred to as the unconscious drives. Whilst all this is undeniably "epic" to use another Octalysis term, meaning ideological or a grand narrative (i.e., a narrative that gives meaning to all other narratives), it results in a cacophony of meaningless "hooks" that look suspiciously like another well-established technique—that of "pattern interruption" and "anchorage" from neuro linguistic programming (NLP).

Gamification "experts" now patent, licence and sell complicated and spurious models and techniques that promise the magic bullet of exponential growth, and there is also a growing corpus, arguably fueled by evangelism, that engages with the term across an entire spectrum of business, play and design practice. Simultaneously, any notion of "gamification" at all is still questionable, as there is still no concrete definition of what is, or is not, a gamified system. In this respect, gamification has become the ultimate "Humpty-Dumpty" term, having expanded to engulf many types of codified behaviour and engagement techniques. It is now almost entirely detached from any recognizable rigorous anchor in any discipline—not least game studies and/or user experience design (UXD), the contemporary convergence of HCI, user-centred design (UCD) and marketing that drives most digital engagement today. Additionally, Forbes recently stated, "Gamification is near the peak of the Gartner Hype Cycle and like most new trends and technologies, the initial hype surrounding the trend creates unrealistic expectations for success and many poor implementations follow.... We predict that by 2014, 80 percent of current gamified applications will fail to meet business objectives, primarily due to poor design" (*The Gamification of Business*, 2013).

This chapter aims to reverse the trend towards mythologised gamification lost in its own gamified collateral, suggesting that at worst, gamification has gamified itself as an ideology in its own right, and it is that, paradoxically, that will hinder growth of the technique and models of good practice. This chapter asks first, where our notions of design, play and gaming originate and converge, allowing the authors to define gamification as a design methodology, anchor it in established theoretical and philosophical concepts and contextualize it in user experience design (UXD) practice. They then define a model of good practice to underpin ethical gamified engineering of neuro and social plasticities long term.

Design

> *"The question is," said Alice, "whether you can make words mean so many different things."*

Design, as taught in British art schools, and practiced in the UK creative industries, finds its roots in the industrial design methodologies of the Bauhaus, a revolutionary art school founded in Weimar in 1919. The Bauhaus was distinguished by its internationalism, cosmopolitanism and artistic diversity (*Bauhaus Weimar*, 2016). It operated as an artists' collective, focused upon design practice in an industrial age and espoused the belief that *design could improve society*. All students were trained in a general approach to the basics of design in all contexts, with a concentration on industrial problems in their social context, mechanical tools and mass production. The original Bauhaus manifesto was aimed at building a design curriculum based on "a synthesis of art, science, and technology [and] the fulcrum . . . was the preliminary course," (Delle Monache and Rocchesso, 2014), a formalist approach to design process encapsulated in the Modernist ethos of "form follows function", "truth to materials" and "economy of design". The "Basics", as it came to be known, favoured an "economics" or "purity" of design that advocated that the designed object should function as well and as simply as possible, setting out the case for a basic usability and putting the user at the centre of the design process.

Additionally, the teaching of basic design was condensed into exercises with a focus on a research-based approach to problem solving, within the framework of specific constraints. MacLean et al. (1993) pointed out that the final output of a design also included what they called "design space"—a body of knowledge about the artefact, its environment, its intended use and the decisions that went into creating the design (Zhu, 2005). The "Point, Line & Plane" approach that was published much later (Kandinsky and Kandinsky, 1980) added a fundamental lexicon of geometric elements from which all other forms could be generated—a "constructivist" approach to design that clearly underpins parametrics and generative design methods today. In the Bauhaus, in 1919, we find the foundations of a user-centred, research-informed, usability-oriented, context-specific, analytical problem solving, industrial design practice that accounts for generative systems and is focused on social transformation.

It is fair to say that as a result of the sheer velocity of technological change, in recent years practice has led theory in all fields of digital design, not just those concerning gamification. Recent developments include mobile, ubiquitous, social and tangible applications, products, services and spaces that include but are not limited to websites, mobile phone apps, digital television, interactive artworks, computer games, software and "smart" products and environments, the "Internet of Things", "Internet of Place", virtual and augmented reality. Digital media design is often for interactive products and services, and it is that interactivity that has caused many some consternation (Cham, 2006). The term *interactive* is specifically used here to refer to "a machine system which reacts in the moment, by virtue of automated reasoning based on data from its sensory apparatus" (Penny, 1996).

Human computer interaction (HCI) was the practice to first address designing for the "human factors" in our interaction with machines. The term itself was first used in the mid-1970s and popularized in *The Psychology of Human-Computer Interaction* (Moran and Newell 1983). It is multidisciplinary, drawing upon computer science, cognitive psychology and ergonomics amongst other fields. Significantly, it established itself around 1980, concurrent to the advent of personal computing, when new and diverse non-specialist user groups started using computer systems. Whilst HCI, focusing upon the purely technical function and basic performative "usability", is often misunderstood, badly represented and sometimes poorly applied, it embodies the concept that working with an interactive computer system takes place in "a dialogue between the user and the computer" (Pérez-Quiñones and Sibert, 1996). Suffice it to say, through human computer interaction (HCI) computing has naturally been concerned with "Human Focussed Design" (Chou, 2015) practically since its inception.

In parallel, it is "interaction design" that refers to the shaping of products and services with a specific focus on the interaction between people and the designed object. Broadly speaking, there are two main uses of the concept, coming out of different intellectual traditions but "converging in practice and research" (Löwgren, Stolterman, and Lowgren, 2004). In their book, *Thoughtful interaction design: A design perspective on information technology* the authors first define the tradition of interaction design as it evolves out of user-centred product design. This perspective is manifest in the approach of the Royal College of Arts seminal design interactions MA, Donald Norman's book *The Design of Everyday Things* (Norman, 2002) and Durrell Bishops's legendary marble telephone answering machine (1992), a tangible interaction application that gamified the message leaving and retrieving process using marbles. It is therefore also user centred design (UCD), developing out of product, that pioneered "Human-Focused Design" (Chou, 2015), not the gaming industry, where user testing is often still very much about quality assurance.

In parallel to UCD is what is properly known as "*user* interaction design" (UID), a term used in the study, planning and design of the interaction between people and computers, which grew out of HCI. In what is considered by many to be the definitive textbook on UID, *Interaction Design, Beyond HCI* (Preece, Rogers, and Sharp, 2002), the authors importantly define UID as including many academic disciplines in addition to those associated with HCI, such as design, informatics, engineering and sociology. They also importantly defined an "affective" UID as design that aims to elicit positive responses such as "feeling at ease, being comfortable, and enjoying the experience or motivating users to learn, play, be creative, or be social". This is UID on steroids—a commercial practice that has taken on the name user experience design (UXD).

In her 1991 book *Computers As Theatre*, Brenda Laurel (Laurel, 1991) was the first to use the term *user experience* as a means to expound an embodied experience of interaction with machines.

> Thinking about interfaces is thinking too small. Designing human-computer experience isn't about building a better desktop. It's about creating imaginary worlds that have a special relationship to reality-worlds in which we can extend, amplify, and enrich our own capacities to think, feel, and act.
>
> (Laurel, 1991)

Two years later Don Norman, who was appointed as one of the first ever user experience architects at Apple, is quoted as saying:

> I thought Human Interface and usability were too narrow: I wanted to cover all aspects of the person's experience with a system, including industrial design, graphics, the interface, the physical interaction, and the manual.
>
> (Norman 1993)

User experience design is the currently defined as concerned with "experiences created and shaped through technology. . . . and how to deliberately design those" (Hassenzahl, 2013). UXD is a complex, new and evolving field. However, most digital media is experienced by an integration of peripheral devices such as a keyboard, console, screen and most often some form of a graphical user interface (GUI). As such, it is still "user interaction design" (UID) that is at the root of designing any user experience (UX). However, the International Organisation for Standardisation defines "user experience" as "a person's perceptions and responses that result from the use *or anticipated use* of a product, system or service".[2] Commercial UXD is therefore often defined as a subset of the broader fields of experiential marketing and customer and/or brand experience design and is most often focused upon CX, the customer experience.

In 2009 Eric Shaffer, founder and CEO at Human Factors International, and one of the first people to recognise that user studies would be a key issue for computing, stated that the interactive online environment offers "far more opportunities to influence customers' decision-making than traditional advertising or marketing channels do" and termed a new level of influential UXD as designing for "persuasion, emotion and trust" or "PET" (Shaffer, 2009). In terms of CX, designing for PET, using successful incentivisation techniques of any kind, leads to an increase in what is termed "conversion rates"—that is, quantifiable returns on how many users have undertaken the desired result (e.g., subscribed/purchased) and where, when and how that occurred. This data is then used to generate "predictive analytics", or more accurately, algorithmic patterns of user behaviours that provide actionable insights into how future users might behave in order to better inform UX designers how best to design for "conversion" in the future. It is therefore currently UXD that "places the most emphasis on human motivation in the process" (Chou, 2015), "gamification" being simply a particular set of low-level incentivisation mechanics, based on game design fundamentals, that are sometimes used as part of designing for the high levels of engagement required for PET.

Additionally, as Shaffer recognised, integrating a variety of low-level motivational devices such as loyalty schemes, premiums, special pricing, competitions, games, etc., as promotional incentives is long established in advertising and marketing. Furthermore, designing successfully for much higher levels of engagement that contextualise such mechanics have also a long-established pedigree in the same field with much greater degrees of success long term. For example, a successful brand is a designed (user) experience, where engendering persuasion, emotion and trust are core value mechanics; a brand is defined as "a perception that customers have about a product/company" (Boyle, 2007) with "branding [is] how the brand's promise is conveyed" (Adamson, 2008); *perception* and *promise* anchors branding squarely as a UXD practice, one that provides high levels of engagement such as those required for persuasion, emotion and trust. Here, "gamification" has existed for over a century as marketing incentives.

Providing a consistent branded experience across multiple evolving technical platforms is complex and has driven many commercial experts to describe an "evolving media eco-system" of "owned, bought and earned media"[3] thus, "branded UX" itself is a field of research. In 2011, a study undertaken by the branded UX consultant Raida Shakiry[4] found that the overall defining factor when trying to evaluate the multiplatform branded user experience was that of *emotion*. That is, without emotional engagement, the brand experience can be said to have failed, and where emotional responses are strong, the brand presence has succeeded. "Emotion" in this context was quantitively measured using biometric technologies such as eye tracking and EEG and is in fact more accurately defined in neuromarketing as cognitive sciences "system one" cognition, or precognitive responses;[5]

unmediated, visceral reactions from the "subconscious", addressed by Octalysis's "black hat" gamification and traditionally known as "affect".

In *Interaction Design; Beyond HCI*, Rogers, Sharp, and Preece (2002) explore the relationship between affect, UX and designing for PET quite comprehensively using McCarthy and Wright's "technology as experience framework" (2004), Patrick Jordan's "pleasure model for product design" (2000) and Donald Norman's "emotional design model" (2004). Predating Shaffer's PET definition, McCarthy and Wright argued that we must take into consideration the "emotional, intellectual, and sensual aspects of our interactions with technology" to offer an approach to understanding HCI through examining the "felt experience of technology". They draw on the work of Mikhail Bakhtin and John Dewey to define sensual/emotional/compositional and spatio-temporal modes of interaction; for example, Dewy's (1934) "Art As Experience" model that recognizes the role of aesthetics in experience. In *Designing Pleasurable Products: An Introduction to the New Human Factors* (Jordan, 2000) the author defines a parallel "pleasure model" for product design, defining pleasure as a result of interaction and building upon Lionel Tiger's (1992) definition of four hierarchical levels of pleasure in relation to using products "physio/socio/psycho" and most importantly, "ideo-pleasure", or "ideological" pleasure, a type of pleasure that concerns people's values. Octalysis uses the term "epic meaning and calling" to refer to the ideological level of user engagement, which of course, once emotionally engaged is far more motivating than badges and leaderboards in themselves.

For example, the "Tidy Street Project"[6] (2011), is an example of gamified ideo-pleasure that was overseen by Professor Yvonne Rogers, director of the University College London Interaction Centre. It was undertaken as part of "Change", an initiative funded by the Engineering and Physical Sciences Research Council (EPSRC) to explore how technology can be designed to change patterns of human behaviour. For this project, "participating residents were given feedback on how much electricity they were using compared to the average for their street, their town and for other UK regions". The results were displayed on the road surface outside the residents' homes. Tidy Street demonstrated the power of a well-established behaviour change mechanic in HCI, that of feedback, alongside gamification of residents' consumption of energy to engender a competitive edge, using the affordances of ideo-pleasure. The "Tidy Street" type of ideo-pleasure is that of "conscious consumerism", where one is encouraged to live out one's ideological concerns through purchasing patterns. Indeed, brands with a moral dimension, such as The Body Shop, American Apparel, or Ben & Jerry's have been defined as "ideological brands" (Floor, 2006) where the inclusion of moral values into a brand narrative is a special merit of branding ideology (Levy and Luedicke, 2012). However, such a definition of "ideological brands" fails to account for "the phenomenon of retail ideology from the broader perspective enabled by corporate sociology" (Borghini et al., 2009)—that is, the already ideological function of the corporation and its products and services. Ideo-pleasure is experienced not just via ethical mechanics but all one's tastes, aspirations and aesthetic judgements (Piller and Tseng, 2010), including one's choice of products as "brands exist as cultural, ideological, and sociological objects"(Schroeder, 2009). In *The Design of Everyday Things* Norman (1998) provides a useful hierarchical model of visceral, behavioral and reflective interaction that further enlightens the notion of ideo-pleasure residing in our consumption the object/experience; the *visceral* is the immediate physical aspects, the *behavioural* is the experience we have in use and the *reflective* is the pleasure, or attachment to the experience and, most importantly, *our attendant self image in using it*. Indeed, there is an "evident link between socio and ideo-pleasure in the construction of the self"(Piller and Tseng, 2010).

Once again, the common defining factor is high-level emotional engagement; as the author of *Buy.ology*, Martin Lindstrom, states, "Like religions, successful companies and successful brands have a clear and very powerful sense of mission" (Lindström and Lindstrom, 2008) and that a strong emotional relationship with a brand creates "brand loyalists, fans or evangelists" (Lindström and Lindstrom, 2008). In a research study he showed that similar emotions were experienced when participants were presented with strong brand icons to those experienced when users were presented with religious symbols. A brand is therefore an ideological *construct* that engenders persuasion, emotion and trust to engineer the ideo-pleasurable construction of the self, through the acquisition of the cultural capital that is associated with it. Gamification indeed. Lindstrom's framing of the user experience of a brand ideology as a religious one is useful in that it defines the human experience of the designed product as an emotional one. The "sense of mission" behind any brand is usually explicitly manifest in external-facing brand values, which are always qualitative and emotional, and we know from branded UX research that once the emotional engagement is broken, the brand value has gone. In terms of any gamified digital system, if it is to properly serve the value chain, it must be a model of the brand values at every level of interaction, that is for the employees, the customers and the shareholders or else we risk being bought and sold an ideology in and of itself—design voodoo.

One of the most ambitious gamified ideological systems to date is "Sesame Credit", a rating system of social behaviours recently introduced by the Chinese government to act as an omnipotent "social credit" tool by rating each citizen's trustworthiness in line with the government's Socialist value proposition. The proposal is that by 2020, everyone in China will be enrolled in a vast national database that compiles fiscal and government information and distils it into a single number ranking each citizen (Hatton, 2015). It has met with much horror in the Western press, despite being an expanded and explicit Socialist version of the implicit and long-established capitalist credit score system. Like credit scoring, sesame credit draws data from businesses and state institutions such as law courts and ratings agencies (Grigg, 2015), but in line with its socialist ideology, will pull in data from all Chinese social media, Alibaba online store and online gaming behavior. Additionally, as social media "friends" and online acquaintances with low scores function to lower the scores of those they are associated with, again in line with credit scoring, the system facilitates a gamified self-policing element to function (Creemers, 2015). Like most digital gamification systems, Sesame Credit is a gamified "coveillance" (Taylor, 2006) system that operates as an extrinsic MMORPG—massively multiplayer online role-play game.

Play

"The question is," said Humpty Dumpty, "which is to be master—that's all."

In terms of established design paradigms for gamification, it is sensible to identify market leaders and how they have affected end users psychosocially and ideologically. For this reason alone, the development of gaming console dashboards is of particular interest. The first online-gamified user interface was developed for Xbox Live, and integrated into the Xbox 360 on its release in Q4 2005. Xbox Live is an online multiplayer gaming and digital media delivery service that was first incorporated in the dashboard of the Xbox games console in 2002. The system was updated and fully gamified with the release of the Xbox 360 in 2005, and then further modified with the release of the Xbox One in 2013. It has also been extended to link the Xbox dashboard to other platforms, including handheld devices and Windows PCs.

"Gamertags" were the first gamified mechanic of the Xbox Live system, allowing users to identify themselves by a unique name, picture and avatar with an associated profile card detailing biographical and gaming information. The system then enabled users to modify their avatars by purchasing vanity items, such as clothing and pets, for example; prepurchasing games, purchasing apps, and purchasing downloadable content for games also rewarded players with additional vanity items. Gamer pictures can be purchased or won in competitions that associate the gamer to certain games or products, and personal pictures can be uploaded. Players' gamertags and profiles could be viewed using a number of online services and any player located, messaged and "friended" from within the Xbox Live service. There is also an avatar construction tool where animated avatars can be built and uploaded to appear in "friends" lists. The profile card serves as an online digital information panel that displays a summary of the user's profile on Xbox Live. A player's gamercard displays a summary of the following information about the player: gamertag—and whether they use the free or paid subscription service of Xbox Live, gamerscore—a score that registers how many games they play or complete, biographical details and location, duration of membership, the number of friends and followers and gamerpicture. The profile card also gives access a player's achievements list and social reputation.

Gamerscore, achievements and reputation are a system by which gaming skill, gaming time investment, game and app purchases, in-game and in-app purchases and consumption and player behavior can be compared, monitored and assessed in a social context. In its purest sense gamerscore is a point-accumulation system that reflects players' achievements in a score that is available for all Xbox users to see, and visualize, in comparative terms, how each individual earned these points. Points are awarded in games for completing achievements—these are various tasks and game "levels" and/or accruing victories against players in online challenges. Every commercially released game hosts up to one thousand points in available achievements, and DLC purchases for games increases the available amount of points for each game. However, digital media streaming apps and media provider services, available for download, also now award users with achievement points for their use.

The reputation system has become a tool for the Xbox Live community to police itself. Gamers can tag other users as "Preferred" and likely be grouped with them in future games (and if desired send them a friend request that works as social media and matchmaking friend list) or tag another player as somebody they wish to avoid. Choosing the latter then requires the player to say why they wish to avoid the other person, either for unsporting conduct and leaving online games early, or "trash talking" and abusive behavior, or generally being unskilled. On the Xbox 360 reputation is displayed as a five-star rating system, on Xbox One as a four-color rating of green through to red. Each gamer has the ability to see a breakdown of their reputation to see what type of behavior they are associated with, and friended players' behavior can be monitored.

The creation of this system quickly led to the emergence of a new market economy on the Internet and social media sites. Gaming websites and news services started to provide content that helped gamers strategize to quickly raise and "boost" their scores and their social standing. Boosting quickly became a transgressive method by which players could subvert matchmaking services to quickly unlock achievements. "Boosters" became infamous for undermining the gamified mechanics and learning to play the game in a way other than intended, and circumventing rules systems to increase scores became a new way to enjoy gaming. Interestingly this had no other function; boosting a score awarded nothing other than a perceived increase in social standing. This led to Microsoft issuing warnings and resetting boosters' gamerscores in a clampdown in 2008 (Grant, 2008). Perhaps more significantly, a gamified UI resulted in players taking on achievements and gamerscore as a primary goal and not necessarily playing games for the principle enjoyment of gaming. Playing games in a transgressive way was a direct result of a gamified system that could be "played" as extrinsic to the actual game being played, or purpose of the intrinsic exercise. Importantly this resulted in gamers playing games they would not have previously considered playing; players purchased, borrowed and pirated games as a way to increase their scores. However, with social media and Xbox Live inundated with gamers talking about playing games that they would not usually play, Valve, the PC game digital distribution service and marketplace, and Sony, the makers of the PlayStation consoles, launched their own gamified UI systems for their online networks in 2007 and 2008 respectively (Jackobsson, 2011). In a two-year study of the Xbox Live gaming community and its uptake of the new UI, Mikeal Jakobsson (2011) identified the system as a form of extrinsic MMOG.

Jacobson's study identified that the system of gamerscores and achievements operated in a social context very similarly to how quests are consumed and completed in MMOGs such as World of Warcraft. Interestingly Jacobson argues that achievements in the UI system and achievements awarded in MMOGs function socially in exactly the same way. They promote motivation to "grind"; that is the achievements, badges, vanity items, scores and any form of reward underpin a socially constructed system that insists extrinsically to the actual purpose of the game. The system, accepted willingly or unwillingly, consciously or otherwise by the community, issues powerful injunctions to partake in tasks that are in essence mundane and boring. Building from a Bartle typology of social identifiers of achievers, killers, socialisers and explorers, Jacobson identifies achievers as an independent substrata comprised of: casual achievers who do not particularly think about achievements or gamerscore until an achievement is awarded. Achievement hunters, who go to great lengths to unlock as many achievements in as many games as possible, and completists, who work at collecting every possible achievement and gamerscore point from each game that they choose to play on its own merit.

Richard Bartle's player typologies is one of the most significant concepts from games design that has been transferred to gamification. Bartle is renowned for his work in MMOG design and one of the founding fathers of the genre, and he comes close to identifying the ideological nature of play in identifying how players function in different ways within gamified systems.

Bartles four principle typologies are:

- Explorers, those who play to enjoy exploring the game world and system
- Achievers, those players who sought to maximize their success within the game by completing tasks
- Socializers, those who played to interact with others within a game
- Killers, those players who sought open competition and conflict with other players of the game

Highly influential in both design and study of games, they have been utilized to design game worlds and mechanics to suit the supposed needs of different styles of play. However, often overlooked is Bartle's critical observation that these modalities are ways of apprehending types of gameplay. They are created within virtual game worlds by the gamified system, and as such, they are dynamic, players fluctuating between play styles based on how they feel at any given moment. These typologies have become considerable but often rigid forces in gamification; correctly understanding them is about ethics in the design of virtual worlds and gamified systems. If designers do not think about ethics, rights and responsibilities then neither will the users of the system (Bartle, 2003, pp 678–706). The analyst Carl Jung considered ideological self-awareness vital to the most difficult and important task that humankind could perform, the creation of good games, an act of civilizing importance only done correctly by people in touch with their instinctual values (Van der Post, 1976).

Jacobson argues that a core property of the gamified system is T.L Taylor's (2006) notional social construct "Coveillance". Taylor identified Coveillance as being a working property of the achievement system inherent in MMO design, quest completion, achievements and MMOs and online virtual worlds generally. Coveillance is the lateral detailed observation of online achievements and detailed in-game behavior between community members. Both Taylor and Jacobson highlight the intrinsic issues within the system relating to the extrinsic social construct of the gamified system in that the fun elements of these systems operate in conjunction with issues of observation and control. Indeed, the socially constructed "game" is comparable to an MMO in another significant element: the game never ends. Therefore, any design must allow for self-direction on behalf of the players as enabling them to progress as they see fit. Typologies are thus highly relevant after the fact of ideological design influences. It is important that a design allows for different belief systems and ideological perspectives—a gamified UI system is a design approach that is constructed to support differing subjective approaches to fulfilling the needs of the intrinsic system. This can only be done by designing gamification with as simple a design method as possible that accounts for ideological subjective approaches of players towards "grinding" for the benefit of an intrinsic system.

Animosity towards the gamified system and intersubjective antagonism in a social context not only detract from the enjoyment of the system and immersion in the community but also detract from what gamers call immersion or flow. In the case of Microsoft's UI, animosities disrupted player immersion in the actual games they were using the system to play, despite the system promoting the sales of games. The message here for gamified business systems is clear. While promoting sales through gamification may initially be successful, it can affect brand image and undermine user loyalty. Again simplicity may hold the answer. Shaun Baron, Microsoft Studios UX researcher, developed a streamlined model for promoting immersion in games through design that has important implications for accounting for subjective ideological perspectives. Baron's model of Cognitive Flow (Baron,

2012) removes the overreliance on player typology to suggest a four-point design model to promote immersion through the successful application of choices and feedback:

- games should have concrete goals with clearly manageable rules
- choices and expected actions fit clearly with users' capabilities
- choices and actions require timely feedback and confirmation
- games need to remove extraneous information and clutter from UIs and visual fields; immersion in a gamified system is not dependent on graphical fidelity and effects.

Johan Huizinga posited that it was play, rather than work, that was the formative element in human culture. For Huizinga, humanity's most important activity belonged to the realm of fantasy; play was the structuring motivational element of all culture, the function by which man created subjectivity (Huizinga, 1949). In Huizinga's understanding, the need for the ludic mind to impose a symbolic order on the chaos of reality resulted in the birth of mythology, ritual, religion, sports, games, drama, philosophy and warfare. At the time of writing, Huizinga's thesis was shocking. Most conventional notions held that it was the development of the stone tool and the culturally specific notion of "work" that rewarded man with the wherewithal to tame nature (Mumford, 1967). In fact, Huizinga's thesis that play was the origin of all human culture was considered so subversive that English translations tempered his thesis to suggest that play was a post-structuring "ratchet"—one that did not create culture but helped shape notions of it, highlighting the societal need for the separate modality of work.

Underpinning the problematic of Huizinga's thesis was his assertion that "playing" is essentially not a serious activity. If anything, and Huizinga is notoriously elusive on this point (Rodriguez, 2006), play was a human function that masked serious human structures and their potential for creating behaviors and structuring thought. Thus, Huizinga is clearly the originator of any thorough understanding of "gamification". Furthermore, in placing a primacy on play, Huizinga was affecting the contemporary shift in philosophic thought and method. The Cartesian *"thinking"* subject of the science of metaphysics, the individual who defined itself as "I" and referred to itself as "me", a subject of self-governing and relative certainty, had been displaced by the irrational and profoundly vulnerable subject of Freud's psychoanalysis (Ruti, 2012). Huizinga's subject could only be certain that it remained undefined by rational thought and reality and was defined only by its relation to what is unthought-of—the modality of play and the unconscious structures of fantasy.

That fantasy and imagination underpin our collective reality is, due to psychoanalysis, no surprise to us. What was new then was the assumption of a position we could assume that would reward us with a unique singular perspective of subjective reality. It was a position that dictated that we are at a point closest to who we really are when we are not insisting in reality, but at the point we can get farthest from it, exactly at the point when we escape into fantasy; we are actually insisting in our real state when we are at play. Cultural theorists such as Zizek have utilized this position adroitly by arguing the structural force of unconscious fantasy captures us all in the unspoken rules and unwritten rituals of institutions and ideology (Žižek, 1989). In short, we should be thinking about what we are thinking about when we profess not to be thinking at all. For Huizinga, who was being deadly serious as his analysis of war demonstrates, this was when play enslaves us in competition. In his essential understanding of human existence, Huizinga was being correctly psychoanalytical. To Freud's list of pathways to the unconscious he was adding play. To Huizinga, human consciousness is a gamified system in and of itself.

The influence of German Idealism on Huizinga's thesis can trace its origins from Schelling and Hegel through Buytendijk, as evident in their use of dialectical reasoning and the relationship between movements, thoughts and play (Walz, 2010). Buytendijk examined play and games as dialectically transcending the biological opposition between player and play-other, which can take the form of another player, a play object or the environmental space and setting of the game (Walz, 2010). In the opening pages of *Homo Ludens* Huizinga criticizes Buytendijk for on overly biological interpretation of play, which, placing its emphasis on player interaction and environments, can only identify the structural nature of play as a secondary vehicle for subjective change, missing the holistic nature of playing and what it means both psychologically and anthropologically (Walz, 2010). Moreover, Huizinga diverges from Buytendijk in that he identifies play and games as the base factor of all culture that find primordial expression in the creation of myths and rituals. Huizinga takes Buytendijk's identification of the play instinct as a biological life drive of man and animal as common knowledge. However, they converge at the point that they both consider "man as player" as a subject always seeking to understand play as a functioning force in the jeopardy of reality and as subject always seeking luck in life (Walz, 2010).

Defined by anxiety, Huizinga's subject is a prisoner of jeopardy, luck and chance within a dialectic of modalities—reality, fantasy, and play. For game scholars this is problematic as Huizinga alludes to the subject at play as entering the "magic circle". Again, this is an elusive abstraction within his work, only mentioned on a handful of occasions. Taking Huizinga's magic circle to the well-used analogy of a football match, we can see dialectical functioning in its registers of the temporal, spatial and social and why its moniker is well deserved. For those outside the magic circle of a football match the scoring of a goal is little more than a human kicking a spherical object into a net. However, for those interpellated within the magic circle, a goal is a complex interaction of ideological and ritualistic behaviors. The "players" on the pitch are playing the game in itself, following a standard set of gamified rules. Of itself, the place of the ceremony of the game is also within the magic circle, the stadium operates to interpellate both players, their teams and their supporters into a reality where certain behaviours become normal, if not mandatory, requirements associated with the injunction to enjoy. Spectators in the crowd "act out" a certain set of behaviours that to the uninitiated would appear as ritualist chants and totemistic greetings and challenges. In and of itself the game of skill, chance and uncertainty that is football interpolates all those into a time, space and social register whose injunctions to enjoy Huizinga sees in the Germanic concept of the *gelp*, a *gelpan* being a ceremony of mutual bragging and execration that connects across time and space previous, present and future games (in this case the games played by the team of footballers) (Huizinga, 1949). However, these injunctions cross time and space in more ways than in the exposition of the *gelpan:* supporters sitting at home or in a bar in front of a televised game are in the magic circle. The fan wearing his colours on the way to work on a Monday morning, or telling an excitable friend about the game and activity within the stadium he witnessed, are again in the magic circle. In its essence, the magic circle is an ideological fantasy space that functions as interpellator across time, space and sociality. It is also an ideological fantasy space that can justify antisocial, violent and illegal behavior, a space in which its own politics and policy function and can transgress those of the larger community.

For Huizinga there is exactly no difference between any form of human ritual and ceremony and the time, space and politico-sociality of a game. Socializing ritualistic behavior requires play, and being in the modality of play is a magical space. Therefore, all symbolizing works originated within a ritual gamified space; the ritual production of play and the gamified production of ritual are the same in and of itself. Thus for Huizinga the human need to repeat agitating notions of reality, coupled with ludic creativity, is an important regulatory force of symbolic reality. Moreover, it is a structuring force that is ideological; it forms the mechanism by which we form an understanding of what we can enjoy, how much we can enjoy *it* and where and when *it* can be enjoyable. Therefore, the ludic realm offers an illusion of control and is an immensely efficient psychic means of controlling the movement of desire, of nudging desire, along a preordained and predetermined track (Ruti, 2012). Huizinga identified deleterious possibilities inherent in this cyclical relation between ideology and the play instinct. It has the ability to bring about an unrivalled rise in aesthetic enjoyment, becoming the substitute for religion, and the play form of myth can be utilized to conceal ideological design. Gamified systems of ideological behavior are as old as the world and of the lowest order of play. They can create their own mythical vocabulary of social control and signifiers that make up a politicized form of " . . . collective voodoo and mumbo-jumbo" (Huizinga, 1949, pp. 197–203).

Contemporary game scholars discredit Huizinga's magic circle and therefore any definition of the modality of play as fundamental rather than notional. Instead, like Buytendijk, placing a primacy on interaction between players of a game, the creation of rules as unique to games and a wider cultural context of studying games as a concrete socio-political reality as divorced from "real" life (Zimmerman, 2012). This neglect of a holistic definition of play as fundamental to understanding games design has concurrently bled into gamification and the "design" of gamified systems. Whilst Huizinga indeed argues games can be understood as separate from "real" life, he never advocates that gamified systems can be understood as uniquely different from everyday life, or that rules and the creation of rules are the sole fundament of playing (Zimmerman, 2012).

Conclusions

As Bartle, Taylor, Baron and Jacobson have demonstrated, gamified systems provide the space for ideological functioning to develop. In parallel, the trajectory of designing for user-centred emotional engagement, from product to branded UX, demonstrates that this ideological function is often designed into the experience. In confirming Huizinga's thesis, Bartle, Taylor, Baron and Jacobson consider that there are ideological, ethical and value judgments made in every stage of the design of gamified systems of all kinds, many of which can be best apprehended as extrinsic MMORPGs. Players/users find ways of behaving. They create ideological markers that identify them socially both within the system and extrinsically in a wider community, demonstrated clearly in the case study of MVP and Xbox Live; they generate a *semantic exoskeleton* from the available cultural capital. Whether these ideological markers and behaviours are wholly extrinsic, brought to the system by individuals, and then further developed intrinsically, or alternatively, they are intrinsic to the system and inherent in its design, or are an inchoate dynamic of both is a moot question here. Gamification need not be overly complicated but simply defined by the value proposition of the business at all stages to produce a holistic experience for all stakeholders. The employees' experience needs uniting with the ideology of the business by the system, not divided in the name of competition. In its most basic sense, successful gamification requires a system to present users with choices that reflect the ideology of the business the gamified system serves.

In keeping with the roots of both Huizinga's work and psychoanalysis in German Idealism, "The Trinity of Gamification" details the subject as held in a dialectical process that informs sociability and identity. The subject in itself is motivated by irrational, often to itself, motivations for pleasure. These are tempered by the reality principle of rewards controlled by governing rules that "pay off" in the form of the unrational gamble and luck that the ludic process of play induces and that the subject seeks as entertaining. However, this dialectic requires movement and repetition, and this requires the realisation that, for the system to survive and coveillence to not create antisocial and/or subversive behavior, the system must be designed for emergent behaviours and evolve through use.

Moreover, the fact that ideological behavioural markers and social typologies become apparent in gamified systems is indicative that our identities are not as stable as our post-ideological notions of freedom would lead us to believe. Gamified systems that unconsciously follow meritocratic ideology favour certain ways of behaving and certain "worldviews" and de facto penalizes others; they are linear, rational and capitalist. Those personality traits that are top of the list for rewards are articulateness and the ability to make others believe in your abilities and success rate of your competitive nature, and the ability to be highly flexible and always searching for the next challenge to surmount. However, these are all top of another list—those of psychopathic behaviour. The important point here for gamification is that self-respect is dependent on the recognition we receive from the others; the big Other of a gamified system needs to account for the fact it can shape sociality and therefore personality. Can bad gamification engineer psychopathic traits? As we have seen, it is theoretically possible.

In short, rather than gamification models being subsumed as an ideology in and of itself, as design voodoo, the most important approach is to design an ideology of openly and consciously a gamified system that is more sophisticated than "first past the post" or "faster/louder" conversion rates. Ideally, a gamified system can work as a system of different choices, enjoyed as part of the open culture of an organization. To Ian Bogost and many others in games studies and in the commercial design sphere, gamified reward systems are essentially loyalty programs. Some, like frequent flyer programs or supermarket reward cards, offer improved social standing and service benefits or/and physical rewards. Others however, like Xbox Live, encourage repeat purchases in return for social status, whilst others, social media for instance, amplify everyday coveillant practices; ordinary everyday behavior itself is gamified, but there is a choice as to how this is both accepted by the players/users and how this is played/used. Many become self-referential loyalty systems, that it would arguably seem from the above evidence breed both ambiguity and animosity. For Bogost games, like loyalty, demand choice. The players of games of any description will ask to which God they are pledging their fealty, and differences in how the system aids a society to develop social value for its members inevitably decides which system generates the most loyal players (Bogost, 2010). Moreover, whilst the old Marxist interpretation of ideology argues that we do not know what we are doing, we do it anyway. In the post-ideological model of cynicism, we know what we are doing but we carry on doing it, through psychoanalysis still carries the weight of a marxisante interpretation. Gamers are perceptive of coveillance and the only option to avoid subversion of system, resentment and dissent and animosity, which would appear to be to a design focus that accounts for ethical choices on behalf of individuals, to play the game how they see fit and rewards be focused to value subjects' ethical and moral viewpoints. Many of the new systems in HR are indeed focused on individual character and talent development in line with the aims of the company.

Figure 10.1 The trinity of Gamification, SJ Webley

Ethics and ethical freedom thus have an important role to play, for as Bartle warns us, ethics become a part of the machine of a gamified system and are far more instrumental to the extrinsic behavior and sociality of the system than many gamification gurus would have us believe. If an ethical culture is not identified and created in an ideological sense, then the system mechanics will create its own, and it will operate in a social sense through coveillence. To reiterate the psychosocial ludic link between ideologies, social status, coveillance and its function in gamification, the design and operational function of the Chinese system of Sesame Credit bears important credence. What is needed is a dialectical construction of motivation, jeopardy and reward within an ideological architecture that is only ethically achieved through the synchronising of ideological values in a multiway feedback loop.

Simultaneously, the relationship between ideology, behaviour and ethics has not gone unnoticed in the UX field. As UX concerns have transformed into CX concerns, much more attention has started to be given to EX—a serious one that cannot just be engineered in terms of chocolate bon bons, badges and leaderboards. At the time of writing, HR professionals are being targeted with a wide variety of technical solutions, from standalone apps and gamified simulations to plug-ins for HRIS systems, all promising insights into different aspects of the EX, ranging from recruitment and selection, performance management and talent management. Octalysis's "Epic meaning and calling" in this context should be the corporate ideology—the brand values, mission statement and value proposition that drives the company overall. It was quite some years ago that the *Harvard Business Review* linked the relationships between profitability, customer loyalty, employee satisfaction, loyalty and productivity (Heskett et al., 2008), so we know that gamification for business growth does not need to be complicated, evangelical, or mystified. Similarly, harnessing the human instinct to play to corporate or social ideology is not necessarily coercive or dubious, but it is also not necessarily a magic bullet for change. Digital transformation design is a digital-first, design-led, user-centred method for engineering transformation of complex human-centred systems and requires designing multi-stakeholder engagement mechanics into complex multi-touchpoint eco-systems, on a micro and macro level simultaneously, and ensuring future proof coevolution of the tool *and its context*. Digital transformation relies on designing for the engagement of end users, so "emotional" affordances must be isolated and incorporated into the user experience (UX) to embed agency into the system. In a corporate context, this means the outwards-facing UX and inwards-facing EX should be commensurate and indeed then also generative of the SX, or shareholder experience, all of which should have been designed for in a holistic and meaningful feedback loop (Plaxton, 2016), one that is with or without of bespoke gamified elements on a case-by-case basis but one that unites the employee experience (EX) with the customer experience (CX) and the shareholder experience (SX).

Employee Experience (EX) × Customer Experience (CX)
= Shareholder Experience (SX)

Figure 10.2 The Plaxton-Cham Stakeholder Experience Feedback Loop

Using these two simple frameworks, ethical and inclusive motivation can be gamified on a micro level, between the users and the system, but also in a coherent macro context, between all the stakeholders. Indeed, the complex nested hierarchy in the Plaxton-Cham Stakeholder Experience Loop can be adapted to frame any multiparty complex ideological system including Sesame Credit. Suffice to say, an ideology is a semantic construct that engenders persuasion, emotion and trust to engineer the ideo-pleasurable construction of the self, through the acquisition of the cultural capital that is associated with it.

As we move into an era where tools are built that exemplify this fact, generating metadata that further illuminates this proposition and its future, it is not difficult to see that all manifest ideologies are gamified systems, offering cultural collateral for the ideo-pleasurable construction of one's identity and attendant socio-cultural experience, through reflective interaction. If we can recognize that these complex, distributed, evolving human-centred networks of people and media through machines, such as multiplatform global marketing campaigns; big organizational infrastructures; markets and economies; and virtual worlds and simulations are indeed extrinsic MMPORGs, then we may have a chance of circumventing the digital disruption of the very socio-cultural fabric of our lives, or else, designed for the play instinct, we will be absolutely lost in gamification, collective voodoo and mumbo jumbo beyond the event horizon.

Notes

1. Register number on the INPI department in Brazil: BR PI 10 2013 026835–6 Register date: 17th of October, 2013
2. SO 9241–210 | API UX
3. Internal presentation under NDA 2010, DigitasLBi http://www.digitaslbi.com/uk/
4. A Framework for the Evaluation of the MultiPlatform Branded UX', MA by Research, Kingston University, (unpublished) http://www.experience-consultancy.com
5. Internal presentation under NDA 2014, Seren http://www.ey-seren.com
6. http://collabcubed.com/2011/11/01/the-tidy-street-project/

Bibliography

Adamson, A. (2008) BrandDigital: Simple Ways Top Brands Succeed in the Digital World. New York: Palgrave Mamillan.

Baron, S., 2012. *Cognitive Flow: The Psychology of Great Game Design*. [Online] Available at: http://gamasutra.com/view/feature/166972/cognitive_flow_the_psychology_of_php [Accessed 04 April 2016].

Bartle, R., 2003. *Designing Virtual Worlds*. 1st edn. London: New Riders.

Bauhaus Weimar, 2016. Available at: http://bauhaus-online.de/en/atlas/das-bauhaus/idee/bauhaus-weimar [Accessed: 30 March 2016].

Bogost, I., 2010. *Gamasutra.com*. [Online] Available at: http://www.gamasutra.com/view/feature/132657/persuasive_games_checkins_check_.php?page=3 [Accessed 10 February 2016].

Borghini, S., Diamond, N., Kozinets, R.V., McGrath, M.A., Muñiz, A.M. and Sherry, J.F., 2009. 'Why are themed brandstores so powerful? Retail brand ideology at American girl place', *Journal of Retailing*, 85(3), pp. 363–375. doi: 10.1016/j.jretai.2009.05.003.

Boyle, L. (2007) The Brand Experience. Available at: http://www.chiefmarketer.com/special-reports-chief- marketer/the-brand-experience-04032007 Chief Marketer.

Cham, Karen, 2006. Aesthetics and Interactive Art. In: *CHArt Twenty-Second Annual Conference: Fast forward—Art History, Curation and Practice after Media*, 9–10 Nov, London, UK.

Chou, Y.K., 2015. *Actionable Gamification: Beyond points, Badges and Leaderboards*. Edited by Jerry Fuqua and Wendy Yuan. Fremont, CA: Createspace Independent Publishing Platform.

Creemers, R., 2015. *China's Chilling Plan to Use Social Credit Ratings to Keep Score on Its Citizens*. [Online] Available at: http://edition.cnn.com/2015/10/27/opinions/china-social-credit-score-creemers/ [Accessed 04 April 2016].

Delle Monache, S. and Rocchesso, D., 2014. Bauhaus legacy in research through design: The case of basic sonic interaction design. http://www.ijdesign.org/ojs/index.php/IJDesign/article/viewFile/1543/645

The Gamification of Business, 2013. Available at: http://www.forbes.com/sites/gartnergroup/2013/01/21/the-gamification-of-business/ [Accessed 30 March 2016].

Grant, C., 2008. *Cheaters Branded on Xbox Live, Gamerscores Reset.* [Online] Available at: http://www.engadget.com/2008/03/25/cheaters-branded-on-xbox-live-gamerscore-reset/ [Accessed 04 April 2016].

Grigg, W.N., 2015. *China Now Assigns Credit Scores to Citizens Based on Govt Loyalty—Here's Why It's Terrifying.* [Online] Available at: http://thefreethoughtproject.com/china-assigns-credit-scores-citizens-based-govt-loyalty-terrifying/ [Accessed 04 April 2016].

Hassenzahl, M., 2013. 'Designing moments of meaning and pleasure', *Experience www.ijdesign.org*, 7(3). http://www.ijdesign.org/ojs/index.php/IJDesign/article/viewFile/1480/585

Hatton, C., 2015. *China 'Social Credit': Beijing Sets Up Huge System.* [Online] Available at: http://www.bbc.co.uk/news/world-asia-china-34592186 [Accessed 04 April 2016].

Heskett, J.L., Jones, T.O., Loveman, G.W., Sasser, E.W. and Schlesinger, L.A. 2008. *Putting the Service-Profit Chain to Work.* Available at: https://hbr.org/2008/07/putting-the-service-profit-chain-to-work/ar/1 [Accessed 5 April 2016].

Huizinga, J., 1949. *Homo Ludens A Study of the Play-Element in Culture.* London: Routledge & Kegan Paul.

Jackobsson, M., 2011. 'The achievement machine: Understanding Xbox 360 achievements in gaming practices', *Game Studies*, 11(1). http://gamestudies.org/1101/articles/jakobsson [Accessed 04 April 2016].

Jordan, P.W., 2000. *Designing Pleasurable Products: An Introduction to the New Human Factors.* New York: Taylor & Francis.

Kandinsky, W., 1980. *Point and Line to Plane.* New York: Dover Publications.

Laurel, B., 1991. *Computers as Theatre.* 2nd edn. Boston, MA: Addison-Wesley Educational Publishers.

Levy, S.J. and Luedicke, M.K., 2012. 'From marketing ideology to branding ideology', *Journal of Macromarketing*, 33(1), pp. 58–66. doi: 10.1177/0276146712459656.

Lindström, M. and Lindstrom, M., 2008. *Buyology: How Everything We Believe About Why We Buy Is Wrong.* London: Random House Business Books.

Löwgren, J., Stolterman, E. and Lowgren, J., 2004. *Thoughtful Interaction Design: A Design Perspective on Information Technology.* Cambridge, MA: The MIT Press.

MacLean, A., Bellotti, V. and Shum, S., 1993. Developing the Design Space with Design Space Analysis. In: P.F. Byerley, P.J. Barnard, & J. May, eds. *Computers, Communication and Usability: Design Issues, Research and Methods for Integrated Services*, pp. 197–219. (North Holland Studies in Telecommunication).

Moran, T.P. and Newell, A., 1983. *Psychology of Human-Computer Interaction—Stuart K. Card—Hardcover.* Edited by Stuart K. Card. Hillsdale, NJ: Lawrence Erlbaum Associates.

Mumford, L., 1967. *The Myth of the Machine, Technics and Human Development.* New York: Harcourt Brace Jovanovich, Inc.

Norman, D.A., 2002. *The Design of Everyday Things.* New York: Basic Books.

Penny, S. 1996. *From A to D and Back Again: The Emerging Aesthetics of Interactive Art.* Leonardo Electronic Almanac Volume 4, No. 4 Available at: http://www.leoalmanac.org/wp-content/uploads/2012/07/LEA-v4-n4.pdf [Accessed 30 March 2016].

Pérez-Quiñones, Manuel A., and Sibert, John L., 1996. A Collaborative Model of Feedback in Human-Computer Interaction. In: *Proceedings of the SIGCHI Conference on Human Factors in Computing Systems*, New York, ACM.

Piller, F.T. and Tseng, M.M., 2010. *Handbook of Research in Mass Customization and Personalization: V. 1: Strategies and Concepts: V. 2: Applications and Cases*. Singapore: World Scientific Publishing Co Pte.

Plaxton, L., 2016. *Mapping the Employee Experience—An HR Perspective—Customer Experience Magazine*. Available at: http://cxm.co.uk/mapping-employee-experience-hr-perspective/ [Accessed 5 April 2016].

Post, L. v. d., 1976. *Jung and the Story of Our Time*. London: Penguin Books.

Preece, J., Rogers, Y. and Sharp, H., 2002. *Interaction Design: Beyond Human-Computer Interaction*. New York, NY: John Wiley & Sons.

Rodriguez, H., 2006. 'The playful and the serious: An approximation to Huizinga's homo ludens', *Games Studies*, 6(1). http://gamestudies.org/0601/articles/rodriges [Accessed 04 April 2016].

Ruti, M., 2012. *The Singularity of Being: Lacan and the Immortal Within*. New York: Fordham University Press.

Schroeder, J.E., 2009. 'The cultural codes of branding', *Marketing Theory*, 9(1), pp. 123–126. doi: 10.1177/1470593108100067.

Shaffer, E., 2009. *Beyond Usability: Designing Web Sites for Persuasion, Emotion, and Trust: UXmatters*. Available at: http://www.uxmatters.com/mt/archives/2009/01/beyond-usability-designing-web-sites-for-persuasion-emotion-and-trust.php#sthash.Q36uk9ZJ.dpuf [Accessed 5 April 2016].

Taylor, T., 2006. 'Does WoW change everything?', *Games and Culture*, 1(4), pp. 1–20.

Taylor, T.L., 2006. *Play between Worlds: Exploring Online Gaming Culture*. Cambridge, MA: MIT Press.

Walz, S.P., 2010. *Towards a Ludic Archetecture: The Space and Play of Games*. Pittsburgh, PA: ECT Press. http://repository.cmu.edu/etcpress/5

Zimmerman, E., 2012. *Gamasutra.com*. [Online] Available at: http://www.gamasutra.com/view/feature/135063/jerked_around_by_the_magic_circle_.php [Accessed 12 February 2016].

Žižek, S., 1989. *The Sublime Object of Ideology*. London: Verso.

Zhu, H., 2005. *Software Design Methodology: From Principles to Architectural Styles*. Oxford: A Butterworth-Heinemann Title.

11 Total Gamification and the Limits of Our Imagination

Per H. Hedberg and Mattias Svahn[1]

> Is post-industrialized society moving toward a decentralized form of totalitarianism? We consider the role of gamification in a radical societal transformation.

When I entered the university as a management student twenty years ago, I observed that many of the students had it all figured out.[2] They prepared for the business life ahead of us and didn't seem interested in exploring other things. At the time I never understood why, but now that I have reached middle age it has become clearer. The students believed they knew already what their main concerns in life were going to be—they didn't need to explore and pursued instead their known concerns, focusing their efforts on the competitions for the prestigious educations, job offers, and eligible romantic candidates. Why waste effort on other things? Devoting oneself to a handful of issues is the obvious, ancient strategy for a high expected payoff. Yet this focused approach is likely to become more common.

My eleven-year-old son—an enthusiastic gamer of FIFA, the online soccer game (Electronic Arts 2016), recently suggested to me that the game could be applied to the personal realm. One feature of FIFA Online is that it scores each soccer player (e.g., Lionel Messi) from 1 to 99 for skills like shooting, dribbling, passing, and defending. My son thought that the same scoring system could be applied to our family relationships. When he heard that I had had a girlfriend before his mom, he suggested that the past girlfriend might have had only 93 in kissing whereas his mother, my wife, probably had 98 in kissing, and similarly high scores for skills like cooking, hugging, being kind, and having sex.

Just like the management students, the eleven-year-old singled out some key dimensions in his outlook on the world. Every person needs to reduce the complexity of the world around them to some extent. What is less obvious is some people's unquestioning confidence in singling out certain dimensions as the only ones worthy of consideration—taking for granted that it is this particular handful of dimensions that are the matter. Yet such confidence is now finding stronger justification.

An observer who looks at the FIFA gamer and the management students could view both of them as taking part in games. Games are always explicitly about something—typically about achieving a specified goal while honoring specified rules—and do involve a focus on some key dimensions. How will the proliferation of games and gamification in society affect us? For starters it should lead people to view more situations in terms of a few key dimensions. Going further, what would it be like to grow up in an artificial ecology where your every situation is defined by a number of games? To investigate the ramifications of a world full of games, let us consider what games have been and what they are becoming.

Games Have Distinctive Qualities

Entering a game means entering a common interpretive frame: a socially shared understanding for how events are to be interpreted. For example, society accepts violence in an ice hockey rink that it wouldn't accept on a city street (Montola, Stenros, and Waern 2009). The game frame is often referred to as a "magic circle" following Dutch historian John Huizinga (1949/2002). How do we bring about a game frame? The magical switch is the mutual agreement among players to observe a set of rules and goals merely because these rules and goals make the game play possible. Such rules and goals are constitutive—they bring the game to life—and they need to be clear. We can probably all call to mind playing a game that came to a halt when a player did not know the rules or the goal of the game.

It is by virtue of the frame that a game is "about" something. The rules and goals single out certain dimensions (issues) rather than others. For example, soccer is about getting the ball into the goal box, although the game could instead have been about cultivating the most beautiful soccer lawn or about making the most accurate personality judgments regarding the spectators.

As games have rules they impose restrictions on the players' choices, but the restrictions have a quality of openness. The rules are decided, not eternal; nothing in a game is sacred (Hedberg 2010). This does not mean that everything is allowed—some moves might be impossible to make in the game or lead to a lower score—but nothing is unthinkable in the sense of taboos. For example, in real life we might not be allowed even to entertain the idea of purchasing sex or removing a particular country from the map, but in a game we could. A game can liberate players (e.g., to step out of one's car in Grand Theft Auto, pick up a golf club, and beat a bystander to death with it).

The Change under Way: The Spread of Gamification

> . . . all kinds of games: paper-based strategy games and first person shooters, classical board games and glitzy gambling games; math puzzles and professional sports; austere text adventures and giggly teenage party games.
>
> (Salen and Zimmerman 2004, p. 1)

Electronically mediated games like FIFA 2016 or a wearable fitness tracker like Run Zombies (Six to Start Inc N. Alderman 2016) are relatively novel, but depending on our definition of games and gamification, there is a long history of game activities in human society and in human lives. The Olympic Games took place as breaks in ongoing wars among city states in Greece more than two thousand years ago. War exercises have been practiced for millennia. Even gamification arguably has a long history. Consider "the piety lottery".

This lottery is said to have been created in 1769 by Gerhard Terstegen, a German-language poet in what was then Prussia. It was a card game with 365 cards, one for every day of the year. Each card contained a prayer or a brief religious aphorism. Every morning the user would choose a random card and read it to himself or herself, pondering the content and then presumably living according to it for the remainder of the day. In this way the user could play a random game with challenges and stakes in his or her own reality while staying within the framework for how a good Christian of the day should behave. "The piety lottery" was a consumer product, like Runkeepers, and similar apps of today, designed to be purchased by individuals as a response to societal values—daily piety in the 1700s, keeping fit in the 2010s.

Are the games and the gamification that we are currently engaged in any different from those in times past? Some of them are, whereas some are traditional game forms finding their way into new domains. In any case the argument is one of degrees. We are becoming increasingly enmeshed in games.

First, games are evolving into new forms. A kind of games that have become known as *pervasive games* (Montola, Stenros, and Waern 2009; Montola 2010; Rosens 2015) are not limited to particular contexts and can extend indefinitely over time. For example, "invisible theater", which sets a political drama in a public space without announcing it as such, may lure unaware passers-by to participate. Similarly, in "dark play", players may expose unwitting individuals to danger—one example being a driver who closes her eyes when she is driving through a crossing, as a form of Russian roulette (Montola, Stenros, and Waern 2009). The common denominator for these games is that no meta-communicative messages are provided that reveal them as nonordinary. No one says, "This is play" or "This is only a game".

In other words, games may lack demarcation lines indicating where the game begins and ends. For such pervasive games, there is no longer a dichotomy between contexts that are ordinary and contexts that are non-ordinary. Just as in the cases of invisible theater and dark play, there is no need for meta-communicative messages when gamifying one's geographical location with the place app Swarm (Foursquare Inc. 2016). Similarly, in the earlier-mentioned ancient version of pervasive games, for the management students at the university there was no need to see the value system they bought into for it to operate. Swarm notifications, wearable fitness trackers, and the value system for the management students are all like water to the fish.

Second, in parallel with the introduction of pervasive games, older forms of games have spread to novel domains. If human life so far mostly took place outside gamification (i.e., the application of game elements to a non-game context[3]), we propose that soon most activities will be subject to gamification and that continued accumulation of gamification features may lead ultimately to all activities in society taking place within a covering web of interconnected games. Thanks to digitalization we have the processing capacity to let cross-referencing game elements accumulate.

As games proliferate, they will blend into zones that were previously game-free. A couple of years ago in *The New Yorker* Ben Mauk (2013) exemplified from a list that is growing:

> Today, you can track your cross-training with Nike+, become mayor of your coffee shop with Foursquare, win badges for energy conservation with Opower, level up in German, Spanish, or Italian on Duolingo, out-clean your spouse in ChoreWars, or try some of the hundreds of other apps and sites that use gaming features to help you lose weight, balance your budget, or just gamify your entire life.

Anyone doubting that gamification-free, anarchistic areas are becoming fewer in post-industrial society may ponder a recent funding effort at Indiegogo for a Runkeeper-style app on people's sex life—now we can track ours as well as others' performances in sexual intercourse [https://www.indiegogo.com/projects/lovely-the-smart-wearable-sex-toy-for-couples#/story].[4]

This gradual shift into a game-ruled society is already having demonstrable impact on societal practices. If gamification is attractive in people's own lives, it is a dream come true for human resource departments (Simpson and Jenkins 2015). Gamification is a way to channel employee motivation towards corporate goals. Whenever we can conceive of a metric, we can provide gamification software for it. Do employees send too many emails? Deduct points for them every time they send one. Do meetings go on for too long? Reward managers with a gold star when they end a meeting early.

Gamification has been criticized on many different grounds (e.g., Bogost 2015). Regardless of moral and esthetic question marks, however, drawing on people's motivation to respond to games is one way to engage people.

This is true even though most games fail at this. We may (and do) take for granted that there will be games that can attract and absorb users successfully. What we want to examine is the kind of world that arises when games are ever-present. Our basic proposition is that sufficiently much gamification in society will provide its members with qualitatively different socialization.

Total Gamification

Some people have already moved far along the gamification process. How is life changed once we spend more of it in this form of designed ecology? Where are we headed?

> . . . games show their dual nature as the ground for human liberation—the "magic circle" of Huizinga (1955), where we are at our least constrained and most ourselves—and as having the potential to engender a peculiar slavery, an enjoyable ensnaring of the soul.
>
> (Pesce 2015, p. 108)

It is true that gamification enables liberation as well as enjoyable slavery. However, we propose there is a more fundamental form of ensnarement by gamification than the regular story of monitoring and oppression (e.g., Kim 2015) would suggest: the ensnarement of people's concepts and imagination. This ensnarement involves game elements that have meaning as signs.

Because games are created through deliberate design, their elements can typically be identified. Some game elements designate specific objects or events; these elements are therein signs (Lindley 2005; Compagno 2015). For example, in the game of rock-paper-scissors, a fist means rock, an open hand means paper and two fingers spread in a V-shape means scissors. In FIFA Online, 22 blobs on the screen represent the soccer players, and another blob on the screen represents the soccer ball. In this way FIFA harnesses our fascination for real soccer players like Zlatan Ibrahimović or Lionel Messi and invites us to play with representations of our idols. As we will see, however, signs in games acquire additional importance as games become sufficiently prevalent. To see this point, consider how game signs can form a system of cross-references that is explicit, growing, and mentally taxing.

People are guided by that which they know. When they go into the unknown or otherwise orient themselves in unfamiliar terrain, they rely on what's familiar (things they know and are familiar with) as their reference points. Well-known game elements (say, the eating character of Pacman) are no exception; they can serve as reference points for us in understanding other things (say, Pacman as a villain in a recent movie, *Pixels*). When game designers want to "ground" a novel game in what is known and relevant to potential users, they can therefore refer to well-known elements from other games

(Svahn and Lange 2009). These elements then acquire the status of signs in the new game, signs that designate familiar game elements from elsewhere. Because such signs are game elements (that refer to other game elements), they are just a special case of intertextuality. A movie parallel would be a Quentin Tarantino movie like *Inglourious Basterds*, which lets references to other movies play on equal footing with references to World War II. The more prevalent games become, the more often they will provide us our reference points. At the extreme end of this trajectory, *all the reference points to which game elements refer will themselves be elements in other games.*

So what? Already the human world consists largely of sign systems. Are there any properties of game elements that would make them special as reference points or guideposts for us—in our lives and in society? Yes, what is special is the explicitness with which the designed rules and goals of games single out certain issues and dimensions, in accordance with the explicitly agreed-upon common interpretive frames. For as long as the players don't take active part in the game design, the explicit design and the explicit agreement in games means that what games are about has been predefined for the players.

The explicit nature of game signs shows in the cumulative effect of a world full of games. Remember that a game is "about" a few key dimensions. Games that reference each other—potentially in parallel—will provide players with a set of "aboutnesses", a set of concerns. FIFA Online gamers already have to take account of both the rules of soccer and the rules of using handheld controls. But this combination doesn't come close to the effect in the future of many parallel game concerns. As games with different goals and different domains begin to refer to each other, the conceptual nesting of simultaneously applicable game concerns will accumulate. Digital records enable accumulation of references at a different scale. The number of dimensions that have been singled out and have been defined for the players will increase, with a growing combinatorial effect.

We can only keep so much in mind (and we apologize to those of you who now feel you have reached your limit). As the number of games that are simultaneously applicable to a person increases, at some point it will be difficult for the person to attend to all the key dimensions, issues, or concerns in the games (Hedberg and Higgins 2011). Theoretically, people should always have the ability to come up with their own conceptions, but as game references accumulate, people should eventually be overloaded cognitively with the cross-referencing set of games. (As the games will be attractive and absorbing, players will usually not be motivated to escape them.) At that point there is little room even for different interpretations of the situation. As every human context becomes dominated by games, the space for improvisation becomes predefined by the game dimensions. All that people are inclined to imagine is channeled by (the dimensions singled out by) the rules and options provided by the combined set of games. At that point we will have chosen (and thanks to digitalization will have accomplished) to make our lives and human existence a total institution.[5]

Really, a Total Institution?

Erving Goffman described more than 50 years ago how a total institution (e.g., a prison, mental asylum, or concentration camp) encompasses work, play, and sleep. According to Goffman, in the total institution, the inmates' autonomy is reduced to the extreme, and might not be perceptible at any time during the 24 hours (Goffman 1961; Davies 1989).

In the case of complete gamification, the total institution is mental, involving the imagination, rather than physical as in a formal prison; and the autonomy of gamification's "inmates" is not reduced but is predefined, such that their exploration takes place within dimensions provided for them. Under these provisos, in total gamification one's day is scheduled in full. In addition, because games are enjoyable, there is no motivation for the players in total gamification (as there is for regular inmates) to develop coping mechanisms to obtain some measure of autonomy. Thus the mechanisms of subordination might be especially effective in games.

Someone might object to the analogy between gamification and total institutions by pointing out that participation and behavior in games is voluntary. But what does it mean for something to be voluntary? Little if anything of what we ordinarily refer to as behavior is involuntary. The oddity of the standard example of involuntariness, the knee-jerk reflex, serves to prove the point. Furthermore, one kind of power is influencing what people want to do (i.e., what they will do voluntarily). In other words, "voluntariness" has debatable value in an interactive ecology where other actors are trying to influence our preferences. Indeed, there are many well-known total institutions (e.g., religious institutions like convents) that people enter voluntarily.

At the present time, only a minority of us are considering entering a convent. But what if society in its entirety is becoming a total institution? We propose this is where we're headed. Gamification ushers in incentives for a totalitarian system, which seems inexorable. It is difficult to think of any substantial obstacles or counterforces that could stop or change this development trajectory. Let us consider two candidate sources of resistance: human dignity and sacred standards.

Happy in a World for Animals?

Gamification is attractive. No nonhuman animal is likely to resist the invitation to a gamified world. Animals (and children) are drawn to it. This is why operant conditioning works so well regardless of whether we deal with bees, rats, or chimpanzees. Notably people, too, play games voluntarily. Will adult human beings be enthusiastic about living in a totally gamified world? Even if it is like the pheromone-driven communities of the ants and the bees?

Humans are probably unique among animals in recognizing that life is finite. This insight seems to give rise to uniquely human existential motivations, regarding not only death but also regarding meaning, identity, and free will (see, e.g., Montgomery, Hedberg, and Montgomery 2011). For a person who knows that he or she will eventually die, it is not self-evident that fun or pleasure is the gold-standard for one's life and choices. Is the good life even possible in a pheromone-ruled ant society? Plus, if free will is cherished, what about the arguably even more basic notion of free imagination? When my every situation is subject to a number of attractive games that absorb my cognitive abilities, I will respond to the world that I register: a combination of game frames. Among the victims of total gamification, then, are authenticity and authorship.

Sacredness: An Obstacle No Longer

"Wollt ihr das totale Spiel? Wollt ihr es, wenn nötig, totaler und radikaler, als wir es uns heute überhaupt erst vorstellen können?" Do you think it is bad taste to make a play of words on a speech in 1943 by Joseph Goebbels? Probably it is, but don't worry—in the future nothing is sacred.

Resistance to a future, human ant-society could derive from people's identity commitments—the conscious or unconscious standards people have for themselves in terms of who they believe they are and ought to be—which tend to make certain issues sacred. Such absolute or inviolable, sacred issues may constitute an obstacle to uninhibited acts in games (e.g., Grand Theft Auto) and gamification. When people find something to be sacred (say the preservation of an animal species or children's right not to be exploited as labor), they typically believe it cannot even be considered as options in their decision-making. Violating what is sacred (e.g., referring frivolously to Nazi-German speeches) is bad taste or worse.

So sacred issues could stop society from moving to total gamification. But what is bad taste today might be acceptable practice tomorrow (Hedberg 2012). And as we have seen, within a game nothing is sacred. Moreover, increased sophistication in game design should make games more, not less, attractive. Therefore, the influence between games and people's values is likely to go from game play to changed values, rather than the other way around. Games and gamification may even turn out to be a Trojan horse for societal value change: games accustom players to interaction that is free from sacred standards.

Toward the Enjoyable Post-Human Society

The 19th-century transition, labeled by Ferdinand Tönnies (1887), from *Gemeinschaft* (the small intimate world most typically exemplified by family life) to *Gesellschaft* (the public world of large-scale society) was so momentous that it might have given birth to the discipline of sociology. Currently, we propose, societies progress beyond Gemeinschaft and Gesellschaft—now we are taking the further step of *gamification* toward a gameful society: gamification is the next step in cultural evolution. Soon we may all be engaged in one big totalitarian set of interconnected games.

A lot of people nowadays might have a hard time distinguishing what it's like in Gesellschaft versus what it's like in Gemeinschaft, because the transition took place so long ago. For the same reason, people's resistance to gamification is going to be correlated with their age. We are becoming different people in a gamified world, but only those of us who have experienced something else will notice the difference. It might be a measure of how far the development has gone that some people might already take for granted the change that gamification is bringing about.

A worry, of course—for those of us who have experienced something else—is that gamification is man-made, pulling us into a humanly designed ecology. This course of action may lead to consequences too complex for human beings to comprehend. As examples of our fatal conceit in believing ourselves to understand the consequences of our creations, there are sometimes poor outcomes from decision-making in situations that we are not equipped to fathom—for example, because we are not evolutionarily equipped to understand the way the problem is presented to us or because we don't take account of the full implications of our individual acts. Gamification is marching into unknown waters.

Are we merely viewing the new as evil? Or are we uncomfortable with a gilded cage, however large and however gilded it might be? Robert Nozick once proposed an experience machine that would provide endless bliss to the individuals who would live in it; but when given the choice, people don't seem to want it (Nozick 1974). If we could see the end of the line, would we want the kind of happiness that games will buy us?

In any case, for the record, my wife is a lot better than Messi. So I guess I won.

Notes

1. Thanks to Pål Ahrén and Lars Frick for improving our writing of this chapter.
2. Throughout the text the first-person accounts are from the first author.
3. For the theoretically inclined reader let us expand briefly on what gamification is. The "ification" that is added to "game" (to achieve "gamification") denotes that game elements that elicit a playful mind frame now do so in a context where there was originally no intention to elicit a playful mind frame; thus game elements are now put to service in a non-game context. To grasp the potential of gamification it is useful to go beyond the surface and recognize that games operate on several levels. Briefly (following Lindley 2005), games may tell a story more or less effectively (narrative layer), they have game-structure that more or less effectively enable play (game-play layer), and they may more or less effectively refer to familiar "realities" such that they unfold as representations (simulation layer). This conception is broad enough to encompass not only FIFA 16 but also chess, soccer, live action role-playing, and many other games. Although an ideal game could be high on all these elements, few are. For example, Myst would be weak on game-play, chess would be weak on narrative, and

Tetris would be weak on narrative and simulation. The application of games in gamification will inherit the uneven set of strengths. Nonetheless serious consideration of all three game dimensions should provide the gamifier with a powerful repertoire of design choices than would relying only on the gameplay layer. Indeed, gamification also offers an interesting theoretical twist on the aforementioned framework in terms of simulation. Because gamification is introduction of a game into some previously ordinary context, the simulation properties of the game could colonize the "reality" as it used to exist outside the game, such that the simulation replaces whatever familiar "real" processes there were. When all has been gamified, reality will then have been absorbed by simulation.
4. In a volume on the business of gamification it could seem mandatory to include a business case in every essay. As we hope to have showed, however, there is no lack of business cases of gamification. Indeed, as we hope to show, we doubt that any aspect of human experience and imagination will escape gamification. Then, to pick a particular case to pursue in depth would distract us from, rather than expose, what gamification will do for us and to us.
5. This is compatible with Jean Baudrillard's vision of dominating simulacra, and provides an explanation for how such an end-state comes about.

Bibliography

Games Cited

Electronic Arts. 2016. "FIFA 2016, Video Game." https://www.easports.com/fifa Accessed 2016–03–10.

Run Zombies. 2016 "Six to Start, Naomi Alderman." https://zombiesrungame.com/. Accessed 2016–03–10.

Swarm Foursquare INC. 2016. https://www.swarmapp.com/. Accessed 2016–03–10.

Literature

Bogost, Ian. 2015. "Why Gamification Is Bullshit 2." In *The Gameful World: Approaches, Issues, Applications*, edited by Steffen P. Walz & Sebastian Deterding, 65–80. Cambridge, MA: MIT Press.

Compagno, Dario. 2015. "Standing on the Shoulders of Giants: A Semiotic Analysis of Assassin's Creed 2." In *International Handbook of Semiotics*, edited by Peter Pericles Trifonas, 1003–1024. Heidelberg: Springer Verlag.

Davies, C. 1989. "Goffman's Concept of the Total Institution: Criticisms and Revisions." *Human Studies* 12 (1): 77–95.

Fetscher, Iring. *Joseph Goebbels im Berliner Sportpalast 1943--" Wollt ihr den totalen Krieg?"*. Europaische Verlaganstalt, 1998.

Goffman, Erving. 1961. "On the Characteristics of Total Institutions." In *Asylums: Essays on the Social Situation of Mental Patients and Other Inmates*, edited by William B. Helmreich, 1–125. New Brunswick: Transaction Publishers.

Hedberg, Per H. 2010. Workshop on advertising at SSE on 19 April 2010.

Hedberg, Per H. 2012. "Interpersonal society." PhD diss. Stockholm: Stockholm School of Economics.

Hedberg, Per H. and E. Tory Higgins. 2011. "What Remains on Your Mind after You Are Done? Flexible Regulation of Knowledge Accessibility." *Journal of Experimental Social Psychology* 47: 882–890.
Huizinga, John. 1949/2002. *Homo Ludens Ils 86*. London: Routledge.
Indiegogo Lovely. "The Smart Wearable Sex Toy for Couples." https://www.indiegogo.com/projects/lovely-the-smart-wearable-sex-toy-for-couples#/story Online, Accessed 2016-03-11.
Kim, Tae Wan. 2015. "Gamification and Exploitation." *Academy of Management Proceedings*, vol. 2015, no. 1, 14502. Academy of Management.
Lindley, Craig. 2005. "The Semiotics of Time Structure in Ludic Space." *Game Studies* July (1). http://www.gamestudies.org/0501/lindley/ Accessed 2016-03-10.
Mauk, Ben, "When work is a game, who wins?" *The New Yorker*, September 17, 2013.
Montgomery, Henry, Per H. Hedberg, and William Montgomery. 2011. "Life and (Partial) Death: How Psychological Connectedness Guides Preferences." In *Perspectives on Thinking, Judging, and Decision Making*, edited by Wibecke Brun, Gideon Keren, Geir Kirkebøen, & Henry Montgomery, 236–49. Oslo: Universitetsforlaget.
Montola, Markus. 2010. "A Ludological View on the Pervasive Mixed-Reality Game Research Paradigm." *Personal and Ubiquitous Computing* 15 (1): 3–12.
Montola, Markus, Jaakko Stenros, and Annika Waern. 2009. *Pervasive Games: Theory and Design*. Amsterdam: Taylor & Francis.
Nozick, Robert. 1974. *Anarchy, State, and Utopia*. New York: Basic Books.
Pesce, Mark. 2015. "Contraludics." In *The Gameful World: Approaches, Issues, Applications*, edited by Steffen P. Walz, Sebastian Deterding, 65–80. Cambridge, MA: MIT Press.
Rosens, Tom. 2015. *How Can You Make a Commercial Pervasive Game?* Baltimore: AmericaStarBooks.
Salen, Katie and Eric Zimmerman. 2004. *Rules of Play: Game Design Fundamentals*. Cambridge, MA: MIT Press.
Simpson, Penny and Jenkins Pete. 2015. *Gamification and Human Resources: An Overview*. Online. https://www.brighton.ac.uk/_pdf/research/crome/gamification-and-hr-overview-january-2015.pdf Accessed 2016-03-10.
Svahn, Mattias and Lange Fredrik. 2009. "Marketing the Category of Pervasive Games." In *Pervasive Games Theory and Design*, edited by Markus Montola, Jaakko Stenros, & Annika Waern. Amsterdam: Morgan Kaufmann Publishers Inc. 219–29.
Terstegen, G. 2014. The Spiritual Lottery, a Selection, Tr. [Into Engl. Verse] from 'Frommen Lotterie', by E.A. Durand . . . —Primary Source Edition Paperback—February 22, http://www.amazon.com/Spiritual-Lottery-Selection-Terstegens-Lotterie/dp/1294676806.
Tönnies, Ferdinand. 1887. *Gesellschaft und Gemeinschaft: Grundbegriffe der reinen Soziologie*. Leipzig: Fues.

12 Old Things—New Names

Peter Zackariasson

> *This book first arose out of a passage in Borges, out of the laughter that shattered, as I read the passage, all the familiar landmarks of thought—our thought, the thought that bears the stamp of our age and our geography—breaking up all the ordered surfaces and all the planes with which we are accustomed to tame the wild profusion of existing things and continuing long afterwards to disturb and threaten with collapse our age-old definitions between the Same and the Other.*
> (Foucault, 1989, p. xvi)

To categorize—animals, objects or other things that make up the structure of our world—seems to have a powerful grip over us—both in our understanding of what these things are perceived as being, and also of what these things do to the structure of our world. Categorization thus seems to be the ungodly resemblance of the godly hammer of Thor, in Norse mythology: an unstoppable force that changes the course of humankind (and gods); categorization is an ontological hammer that changes how we understand and make sense of things. It is this understanding that Foucault (1989) in his introduction to *The Order of Things* exposed through the use of Borges fictitious taxonomy of animals, allegedly found in an ancient Chinese encyclopedia: *Those that belong to the emperor, Embalmed ones, Those that are trained, Sucking pigs, Mermaids (or Sirens), Fabulous ones, Stray dogs, Those that are included in this classification, Those that tremble as if they were mad, Innumerable ones, Those drawn with a very fine camel hair brush, Et cetera, Those that have just broken the flower vase,* and *Those that, at a distance, resemble flies.*

This is how we should understand the craze of gamification—as an ontological hammer that has the ambition to scatter our "old" understandings of the structures of our world and with one stroke display new knowledge in its wake. Indeed it is through this move that Zichermann and Linder (2010, 2013), and their fellow consultants and PR agencies, have managed to turn a concept into an industry practice. Or so it seems at least! Where gamification is now the new buzzword for market communication, brand building, customer retention, human resource, work motivation, education—and so on. What processes cannot be disciplined into gamification! There are today numerous books, just like this one, on the subject—books that both hail gamification as the answer to the ultimate question of life, the universe and everything (e.g., McGonigal, 2012) but also books that are highly critical about gamification (e.g., Fuchs et al., 2014).

The numerous, and vastly diverse, comments on gamification, both in business and in academia, was the starting point for this book. As Dymek writes in the introduction to this edition, there is today a real need to critically define what gamification is and what it is not. In this concluding chapter, I will argue that although gamification has the power to change our perception of things (as words do), there is nothing inherently new about gamification. The different aspects included when describing gamification can be found in abundance in previous practices and literature. So what we are faced with is a new concept for existing practices. The value of this can be discussed, as there are cultural, technical and economical aspects that support the changes constructed by using a new concept.

Being a business scholar, I will further argue that it makes all the sense in applying gamification in practice—to frame practices and construct business possibilities. We all know that words matter. Calling something a game or a simulation can make all the difference—depending on the setting in which this is done, just as calling out a naked king for being nude has the power of exposing what is built through words and categorizations.

For this chapter I draw the line of gamification at the doorstep to academia. It is a buzzword that creates the phenomenon when it is spoken for. It is as much created by the numerous marketers and PR consultants as it is something tangible outside of this vocabulary. Unfortunately gamification seems too powerful, too mesmerizing, for academia and is invited into the rooms of critical thinking. Although we need to remind ourselves that any concept is like a vampire—which cannot enter a house without being invited by the owner—so we need to stop inviting gamification uncritically into academia. Gamification has become a vampire that drains academia of its blood as it disguises itself in to a theory, into a shape that looks like other analytical frameworks we always have known. But gamification is nothing like that. This is the problem with gamification, being a very useful concept for consultants and PR agencies—it makes the worst theory possible.

What Is New?

There is an idea that gamification is new. But we need to reconfigure this idea, because that is only partly true. Gamification is not new, but there is today better technology to create applications that draw of game structures into area that are not perceived as games. Using game mechanics to motivate and reward individuals, for different purposes, both in business and in education, is thus not new. This has always been part of setting of reward structures, and if we are to believe the arguments of Huizinga (1938/1949) quite fundamental to the forming of our society.

When I was young, in the late 1980s, it was quite popular for teenagers to work in Norway during longer school breaks, especially during the summertime when we had several months off from school. The perks were that you could make fairly large amount of money during a short time and you were away from your parents for several weeks on a row. Both of these were much appreciated as a teenager. I worked in the fishing industry, gutting fish forty hours a week. I did not mind the work; it could even be meditative and harmonious when you got into a flow (yes, that kind described by Csikszentmihalyi [2008] can even be applied to gutting fish). The salary was based on how many fishes you gutted, and the result was published on a big scoreboard for everyone to see. Although the correlation between the scoreboard and our motivation was marginal at best, the persons who were up there in the top were ascribed somewhat of an unspoken status. It was a board that you vocally ridiculed, but in practice we all complied to the structure enforced on us.

Now, was this a gamification of gutting fish? Well yes, if we are to believe how gamification today is defined. There was no one in the 1980s talking about gamification. But I must admit that my presence in either academia of business management was at that time somewhat limited. But the point is that the structures that are included into gamification are nothing new. They were well documented and experienced prior to the 21st century, as they also were implemented into different setting—including fish factories in Norway.

Beyond my personal experience of motivational programs, Cochoy and Hagberg (this volume) demonstrated this in their description of the growth of consumer loyalty programs and other marketing tool in grocery stores. This is yet another setting in business where these structures has been widely used. There were still no signs of gamification in these studies, but both game mechanics for promoting consumption and full-blown games to engage consumers. Cochoy and Hagberg's observations strengthen the idea of structures that were developed and used, which leads us to conclude that the processes that gamification are made to include are not new.

There are two connected phenomenon that can explain that the concept of gamification was possible to introduce, and that the idea spread like a wildfire. The first is the technological development that has made it possible for big data to be utilized in social media platforms. With these possibilities it was possible to turn game mechanics up to eleven in order to create content and reach—richness and reach. What previously had been local and manual could now be turned into an automated system engaging thousand of users. The second aspect is video game culture. Prior to around 2005–2010 it was impossible to introduce games into organisations, if they were not packaged as a well-delimited game (for training, etc.) or renamed as simulations of others. But moving into the 21st century, the persons born in the early 1970s—Generation G—were now holding positions in business, just as they still were playing video games. Thus the distance between video games and business structures was fading, as understanding and acceptance of games were established in management structures.

I would like to offer an understanding of gamification as an umbrella concept with the ambition to speak in the name of all cases where game mechanics are introduced into structures that are not games. As such it would wrongfully claim any novelty, only offering an ontological shift in making games into business—or business into games.

Gamification Is Bullshit

In 2011 Ian Bogost made the much-commended proposal that gamification was bullshit, something that he developed further in 2014. Although he credits much of the attention he received to the headline alone, and not the actual content, the message in this is not as blunt as face value would have it. Building on the moral philosopher Frankfurt (2005), bullshit is understood as a concept that is used to conceal, impress or coerce, thus leaving Bogost with the impression that "games becomes a business opportunity for those who might harness the fear to help corporations believe they are benefiting from the power . . . a coercive strategy" (Bogost, 2014: 65). Both games used in business and game mechanics are all made into being part of gamification. In that role they are also made into serving in the interest of business—the morally questionable neo-liberal structures of capitalism.

For Bogost (2011, 2014) this is not about gamification being a concept for use but a concept that is coerced onto consumers and coworkers through business professions and consulting agencies that do their best to make everything that has something about games to be about gamification. In this process all different aspects where games have an impact—on learning or for injecting public debates—are swooped up in the mouth of the gamification monster. "For gamification, games are not a medium capable of producing sophisticated experiences in the service of diverse functions and goals, but merely a conventional rhetorical hook into a state of anxiety in contemporary business" (2014: 76).

In any understanding of our capitalistic business logics, there is much to be wanted. Yes, a reflexive relationship toward processes that are applied. Yes, a humanistic relationship toward the effect of structures. Yes, a democratic means toward the betterment of men and women. Although Bogost's concerns about business ethics are warranted, my grim reading is far more pragmatic: Isn't this exactly what business are supposed to do within the current ideology? What is expected from business managers and marketers within this ideology? Because capitalism is an ideology (Boltanski and

Chiapello, 2005), and ideologies, according to Dumont (1994), share a set of shared beliefs, inscribed in institutions, bound up with actions, and anchored in reality.

In the ideology of capitalism, gamification finds most of its values. It is made into a concept that has the power of offering something that is perceived as new. And new is what business thrives on, the possibilities of selling the new—or of applying the new in hopes for improvements. When Internet in the early 1990s started to make its way forcefully into business, it was perceived as a new tool for improvements, a tool that had the possibility to increase productivity. This was the ideology of capitalism making sense of a new technology according to the values of that ideology. But as we all know, productivity had nothing to do with the Internet. It changed much of the business landscapes but not according to the old logic—but according to the logics of an information society (Castells, 1996). What we were left with was then understood as the productivity paradox (Brynjolfsson, 1993)—remarkable growth in technology and slow growth in productivity. In the same way, gamification is made into the new, in a long line of new concepts—for the capitalistic ideology.

Like Bogost (2011, 2014) I agree that bullshit is a suitable term to be used when it comes to gamification. But unlike Bogost, I see no other way for this concept to gain traction then to be adopted by the capitalistic ideology. It is through this ideology that gamification gains its meaning—using all available tools to maximize output. According to this ideology, the primary ethical pillar of businesses is to maximize shareholder values. Secondarily, there are the concerns of humanity and sustainability. In this setting gamification makes total sense. Where Bogost sees the flaws of delimitation of gamification, this ideology sees possibilities.

Gamification is thus a way to frame processes that include elements of games in a nongaming context. True, although the reason for doing this is to create the impression of improvements in return-on-investment or productivity.

The Failure of Gamification as a Theory

Although gamification seems to be an excellent tool for constructing business and consulting practices, it is not a theory. Let me be even clearer on that: is it not a theory—really!

As more and more academics are commenting on gamification, it is gaining a higher presence in both research and education. Books like this have become quite common. So have courses and university programs that use gamification to package different aspects of games in different settings: for learning, business and other settings. In this adoption of a concept that clearly has its value in practice, it is my fear that gamification will be normalized and the rigor that academia traditionally is obliged to apply when engaging with any phenomenon will be thrown out the door, in our eagerness to engage with the new.

If this happens, it has the danger of transforming gamification—from a phenomenon to a theory, from a descriptive term to an explanatory term. But gamification does not offer any explanation of anything. Putting a sparkling dress on a pig does not make it a princess; it is without a doubt still only a pig. What the term *gamification* does is to categorize a process that uses game mechanics—that is all. But if we explain what happens in this process as game mechanics are introduced, we need theories. We need many different theories, depending on what it is we are trying to explain, or make sense of. In that endeavour, pointing at the process that has now been added with game mechanics and saying that it is gamification does not bring us anywhere. We need theories.

Starting a sentence with, "A theory is", might seem like a perilous undertaking, as any understanding of theory points to it being multiple. It is different, depending on when and how you are using theories having the possibility of being many different things at the same time. Theories are thus both multiple, but is it also what makes social life possible. Life is not dependent on theories, but we are dependent on theories to explain life. All of us have theories. Theories makes it possible for any of us to understand what we perceive, to act on what someone says or on one's beliefs about relationships between actors. Although theories are present in our daily lives, at the base of any understanding we have, these are not "scientific".

The value of explaining desirable knowledge was brought to our attention already by Plato. These were the philosophers who were different from the "spectators" of life. The role of the philosopher, according to Plato, was to make sense of things and construct knowledge on the basis of this. The difference between the laymen theorizing was that "Spectators have beliefs; philosophers have knowledge" (Czarniawska, 2013: 99). Or as Plato (1993: 196) explained it, "Theatre-goers and sightseers are devoted to beautiful sounds and colours and shapes, and to works of art which consist of these elements, but their minds are constitutionally incapable of seeing and devoting themselves to beauty itself."

If we consult an encyclopedia today for guidance on theory, it reads, "THEORIES, SCIENTIFIC: The term 'theory' is used variously in science to refer to un unproven hunch, a scientific field (as in 'electromagnetic theory'), and a conceptual device for systematically characterizing the state-transition behavior of a system. Philosophy of science have tended to view the latter as the most fundamental, and most analyses of theories focus on it" (Suppe, 2000: 885). Theory as a "conceptual device" is thus our main tool in academia, in order to makes sense of "state-transition behavior". In this sense gamification needs to be explained, rather than being used to explain.

We thus need to refuse gamification as in explaining anything; and we need to employ social, psychological and cultural theories in order to explain gamification. This means that our contribution to the whole discussion and craze about gamification is not to be swept away by the bright lights of a new concept. The same requirement for scientific rigour still applies. In this case we must be willing to take this concept apart, challenge what is taken for granted and how it is applied to different structures in society and expose the consequences gamification has.

The Future of Gamification

There is no doubt that gamification has had a fairly huge impact on business and education. As a concept it is very appealing! It speaks right to the heart of Generation G, which has much experience in gaming from childhood onward. Thus gamification would not have been possible before it was introduced. One might argue that the value of gamification is the effect it has on bending of inflexible institutions that previously shunned everything that had to do with games as trivial and nonintellectual. But as we have learned, games are everything but that, a medium that is both meaningful and intelligent. As such it makes sense to use gamification as a vehicle to induce business with game structures.

For me it seems that gamification has enough stamina to start a more conscious incorporation of gaming patterns in business. These powerful structures can be used to continue what already has been incorporated in marketing communication and other areas. As we start working down this road, gamification will diminish in value. We will develop our knowledge in relating gaming patterns to other structures, and how we describe these relationships will be more sophisticated—no one size fits all. Once gamification is eradicated from our terminology, as a distant memory of us trying to understand, we can truly speak of game structures as empowering our lives.

But until that time comes, I expect academia to stand tall in its defense in how we understand the implementation of games in business. There is a pressing need to employ an all-out arsenal of theories to make sense of what is happening and not let the phenomenon explain itself. Gamification cannot explain; it can only be explained.

References

Bogost, Ian. 2014. Why Gamification is Bullshit. In Steffen P. Walz and Sebastian Deterding eds. *The Gameful World: Approaches, Issues, Applications*. Cambridge, MA: The MIT Press. 65–80.

Bogost, Ian. 2011. *Gamification is Bullshit*. Paper presented at: For the Win: Serious Gamification, Philadelphia, PA, August 8–9.

Boltanski, Luc and Chiapello, Eve. 2005. *The New Spirit of Capitalism*. London & New York: Verso.
Brynjolfsson, Erik. 1993. "The productivity paradox of information technology." *Communications of the ACM*, 36(12): 66–77.
Castells, Manuel. 1996. *The Information Age: Economy, Society and Culture*. Volume I: The Rise of the Network Society. Oxford: Blackwell.
Csikszentmihalyi, Mihaly. 2008. *Flow: The Psychology of Optimal Experience*. London: Harper Perennial.
Czarniawska, Barbara. 2013. What Social Science Theory Is and What It Is Not. In Hervé Corvellec ed. *What is Theory: Answers from the Social and Cultural Sciences*. Copenhagen: Liber/Copenhagen Business School Press. 99–118.
Dumont, Louis. 1994. *German Ideology: From France to Germany and Back*. Chicago: University of Chicago Press.
Foucault, Michel. 1989. *The Order of Things: An Archaeology of the Human Sciences*. London and New York: Routledge.
Frankfurt, Harry. 2005. *On Bullshit*. Princeton, NJ: Princeton University Press.
Fuchs, Mathias, Fizek, Sonia and Ruffino, Paolo eds. 2014. *Rethinking Gamification*. Lüneburg: Meson Press by Hybrid.
Huizinga, Johan. 1938/1949. *Homo Ludens: A Study of the Play-Element in Culture*. London: Routledge.
McGonigal, Jane. 2012. *Reality is Broken: Why Games Make Us Better and How They Can Change the World*. New York: Vintage.
Plato. 1993. *Republic*. Translated by Robin Waterfield. Oxford: Oxford University Press.
Suppe, Frederick. 2000. Definition of Theories, Scientific. In *Concise Routledge Encyclopedia of Philosophy*. London and New York: Routledge. 885–886. See https://www.amazon.com/Concise-Routledge-encyclopedia-philosophy/dp/B000H5Z5YO/ref=sr_1_1?ie=UTF8&qid=1467809540&sr=8-1&keywords=concise+routledge
Zichermann, Gabe and Linder, Joselin. 2013. *The Gamification Revolution: How Leaders Leverage Game Mechanics to Crush the Competition*. New York: McGraw-Hill Professional.
Zichermann, Gabe and Linder, Joselin. 2010. *Game-Based Marketing: Inspire Customer Loyalty Through Rewards, Challenges, and Contests*. Hoboken: John Wiley & Sons Ltd.

Index

Aarseth Espen 107
aboutness 213
achievements 32, 45, 61, 110, 132–3, 148–53, 164–6, 195–6
active participation 115
Actor-Network Theory/ANT 146, 152, 154
aesthetical, the (Kierkegaard's concept) 172–4
affects 163, 168, 170–7
agency 26, 31–2, 46–8, 169–70
agile project management 22
algorithm, rhetoric gaming, control 61, 67, 74–7
alignment of company strategic and consumer goals *vs.* interplay between goals 60, 66–7, 74
animals 7, 214, 215
ant-society 215
anxiety 152, 163, 170–6
artificial ecology 209

backlash of gamification 165
Badges, Leaderboards, Achievements, Points (BLAP) gamification 164, 175
Badgeville (company) 128
Bateson, Gregory 7–8
BioShock (game) 165
Bottlebank Arcade (game) 164
bought media 113
brand community 112, 116, 117, 134, 135
branding 105, 116, 191–2
bullshit 222–3
Burke, Kenneth 60, 65–9, 72–6
Burke's rhetoric 64, 67–8
buzzword 219–20

Caillois, Roger 5–8, 112
capitalism 50–2, 222–3

categorization 219–20; of marketing communications media 112–14
co-creation 125, 133
cognitive lock-in 137
community triangle 124
Commute Greener (game) 164
competitions 208–9; marketing (*see* marketing campaigns)
conditioning 214
contest 41, 47, 87–9, 105
co-production 125
corrupting the game 138
Counter Strike: Global Offensive (game) 175
cross-referencing game elements 211, 212, 213
cybertext 107

dark play 210
digital marketing 144
digital text 107–8
Dobscha, Susan 62–3, 76, 153

earn 81–3, 87, 89, 92–5
earned media 113
effectiveness 17–18
Elder Scrolls, The (game) 175
emotion 17–18, 59, 61, 123, 138, 191–3
employee experience (of gamification) 184, 204
endgame 31, 212
engagement 122, 135, 137, 182; consumer 61, 93, 101–2, 144; dysfunction 117; economy of 34; employee 21–2, 46
ethical, the (Kierkegaard's concept) 172–4
ethics 34, 172–4, 197, 203, 222
ethnographic method 145

Everybody's Gone to the Rapture (game) 176–7
existential philosophy 168, 171–4
experience 14, 26, 43–6, 61, 100, 111, 123; environment 125; machine 216

fail conditions 165, 170; *see also* win conditions
fiction 10–11, 15, 16, 74
Foursquare (application) 101, 211
Freud, Sigmund 198–9

Gadamer, Hans-Georg 63
gain 81–3, 87–9, 92–5
game: addiction 82–3, 87, 91–2, 95, 135; dynamics 123; frame 209; mechanics 21, 28, 41, 48, 61, 62, 100, 122, 130, 132, 145, 168, 184, 186, 191, 220; mechanism 15–17; from perspectives in humanities 65; play as culture-producing activity 65; rules as subject of rhetoric play, breaking rules 64–6, 70, 72, 74, 77; theory 5, 168–70
gamefulness 123
gameful prescriptions 147, 152
game studies 31, 65, 110–14, 183, 187
Gemeinschaft and Gesellschaft 215, 216
Glass of Water, A (application) 164
Goebbels, Joseph 215
Goffman, Erving 8, 214
Grand Theft Auto (game) 44, 209, 215
green consumption 145, 147–8, 150–6
Greenify (game) 164

Half-Life (game) 175
hashtag: Instagram 151; rhetoric resource 61, 67–73
hedonism 91, 123, 155
Huizinga, Johan 5, 24–5, 41, 63, 65, 183, 198–202
Human Computer Interaction (HCI) 182–3, 185, 187, 189–90, 192

identification 60, 65–70, 77
ideology 27, 41–2, 62, 102–3, 182–3, 193, 203–4, 222–3
immersion 111, 133, 169
interaction 123; human computer 189–94
involvement 17, 123, 125, 169

Kierkegaard, Søren 163, 168, 170–4, 176, 178
Kotler, Philip 103, 116

liberation and slavery 212
Life is Strange (game) 176–7
loyalty 122, 123, 132, 135; program 61, 89–92, 101; schemes 89–92, 101, 114, 115, 117, 186, 202–3, 221
ludic 122, 128, 168–9; mind 198; psychosocial link 203
ludo: aesthehical 164, 174, 177; ethical 174–5
ludology 111, 168–70, 174–6

magic circle 25, 199–200
marketing 59, 89–92, 99, 102, 144–5, 147, 156, 182; campaigns 66–76, 87–9, 93, 105–10, 126–38, 147–54; communications 99–121, 102–4; communications and gamification 61, 97–111, 101–2, 112–14; cultural perspective on 104; definition of 104; ideology 102–3
Massively Multiplayer Online Role-Playing Games (MMORPG) 175, 194, 201
May, Rollo 171
McDonaldization 41–6, 52
meaningful gamification 164–6, 170, 174–6
modding 48–50
motivation 23, 26, 122, 123, 133, 164–6, 174, 177, 221; extrinsic 164–6, 174; intrinsic 164–6
Multimodal Discourse Analysis (MDA) 107–10
Murray, Janet 112, 114, 163, 167–70

narrative 107, 110–12, 168–70, 174–80, 187
narrato: aesthetical 175–6; ethical 176–7
narratology 111, 168–70; *see also* narrative
netnography 126
non-paid media *see* earned media
novelty 220–2

Octalysis gamification framework 186–7, 192, 203
Opower (application) 164
Oroeco (application) 164

Index

outcomes: cocreated 122; game 81–2, 94–5
overjustification effect 165
owned media 114

paid media *see* bought media
participant observation 6, 104, 126
participation 17–18, 62, 68, 72, 75, 123, 152, 214; active (*see* active participation); coercive 32
people-centered approach 166–8, 176
performative 17, 72, 84, 145, 156–7
phenomenology 171–4
piety lottery 210
playbor 28, 117
player typologies (Richard Bartle's) 196
play frame 6–8, 11, 15, 16, 18
PR *see* public relations
productivity 17, 21, 23, 27, 28, 38, 41, 61, 203, 223; paradox 223
progress 23–4, 26, 64, 65, 70, 129, 150, 153, 167
Propp, Vladimir 112, 169
psychoanalysis 183, 187, 198, 201–2
public relations 113, 114–18, 219–20

RedCritter (application) 28–33
relationship 64, 102, 104, 114, 115, 123, 171, 190, 222; brand-consumer 123; commercial 89; customer relationship management 40; emotional 193; marketing 62, 77, 90, 92, 102, 116–17; work 12
resistance 22, 43, 52, 61, 214; consumer resistance 60–3, 67, 70, 76–7
retailing 81–95
reward: extrinsic 123, 135, 138, 164–5; intrinsic 123, 125, 135, 138
rhetoric 21, 102, 104, 137, 222; digital rhetoric of playing 60, 63–4, 66–7, 77
Ritson, Mark 62–3, 76
Riven (game) 169
role: concept 9–10, 14; playing 8–10, 15–17, 50

sacredness 215
Samsung Nation (application) 122, 126, 127, 135
Schüll, Natasha 82, 83, 87, 91, 95, 98

self-determination theory 23–4
Sesame Credit (rating system) 193–4, 203–4
smartphone 92, 94, 101, 105, 145–6, 153; apps 92–4, 108
smart systems 166–7
social media/networks 71, 75, 100–9, 127, 146, 164, 186
socio-material 145–6, 156
storytelling 111, 112, 169, 175; interactive 111
sustainability 147, 152–4, 163–8, 177, 223

Taylorism 2.0 27, 33
techno-economic approach 166–8, 176; *see also* people-centered approach
technology of gamification 40, 46, 62, 146, 152–4, 166, 221
terministic screens, terminology filtering and framing 60, 66, 74–6
Tetris (game) 44, 169
total gamification 212, 213, 215
total institution 213, 214
transformation 168–70, 174–5
traversal function 108, 109–10

User Centred Design (UCD) 182–3, 187, 189–90
User Experience (UX) 182, 184, 186, 191–3, 197, 201, 203–4
User Experience Design (UXD) 182, 183, 184, 187–8, 190
User Interface Design (UID) 186, 190
utilitarian 123

Vampire Hunter (game) 164
video game culture 221–2
visualization 163, 166–8, 172
voluntariness 214

win 81–3, 85, 87–9, 92–5
win conditions 165, 170
Wittgenstein, Ludwig 72
World of Warcraft (game) 175, 196
World's Deepest Bin (game) 164

Xbox 194–6, 201–2

Žižek, Slavoj 53, 199
Zombies, Run! 3 (game) 165